Playwrights on Playwriting

Other Anthologies edited by Toby Cole

Acting: A Handbook of the Stanislavsky Method
Actors on Acting (with Helen Krich Chinoy)
Directors on Directing (with Helen Krich Chinoy)

Playwrights on Playwriting

THE MEANING AND MAKING OF MODERN
DRAMA FROM IBSEN TO IONESCO

Edited by TOBY COLE
Introduction by JOHN GASSNER

A DRAMABOOK
HILL AND WANG • NEW YORK
A DIVISION OF FARRAR, STRAUS AND GIROUX

For Aron and Johnny
who helped the most

FIRST DRAMABOOK EDITION AUGUST 1961

First published in 1960 by Hill and Wang
a division of Farrar, Straus and Giroux
Twenty-fourth printing, 1991

PREFACE

MODERN DRAMATISTS have freely exercised the privilege of fame to express their views of life on both sides of the theatre's curtain. A book drawn from these comments would be many times the size of this one; but its contribution to our topic would be peripheral. A surprisingly smaller group of playwrights have addressed themselves centrally to the art and craft of playwriting. They are represented here.

Most of the acknowledged masters are present. But great gift in playwriting is not always accompanied by acuity in formulating dramatic theory. In some instances we encounter major statements by playwrights whose plays were not equal to their precepts. Zola's naturalist manifesto reminds us that innovators are sometimes outdistanced by followers who benefit by the formers' extension of dramatic form when, as Strindberg says, "the new wine has burst the old bottles."

Part I, *Credos and Concepts,* with its fervent expressions of artistic conviction, its battle cries and proclamations, reflects the modern dramatist's restless search for form toward and away from realism. The marvelous ways in which these abstractions have been substantiated in many of the finest plays of the period comprise Part 2, *Creations.* It is my hope that this ordering of the materials documents the way in which dramatists have animated this era's ideas of the theatre. It should be noted, with particular reference to Part 2, that dates given after the titles represent the year in which the selection was written, rather than the time of composition or production of the plays discussed.

My task was singularly favored in aim and scope by the personal encouragement and aid of two of our finest scholar-critics: Eric Bentley, Brander Matthews Professor of Dramatic Literature at Columbia University, and John Gassner, Sterling Professor of Playwriting and Dramatic Literature at Yale University. I am deeply grateful to them both.

Robert Corrigan, editor of the *Tulane Drama Review,*

generously gave me first call on the *Review*'s valuable Documents Series. From this source came Strindberg's "On Modern Drama and Modern Theatre," and essays by Toller and Duerrenmatt translated by Børge Gedsø Madsen, Marketa Goetz, and Dr. Gerhard Nellhaus, respectively.

I should like to express my appreciation to Joseph. M. Bernstein for his valuable counsel on editorial matters as well as his translations of Giraudoux, Cocteau, and García Lorca.

Thanks are due to Evert Sprinchorn of Vassar College who brought to my attention and translated the Ibsen Notes on *Hedda Gabler*, and corrected other items from the Danish and Norwegian; to Samuel Draper for a new rendering of Zola's "Naturalism on the Stage"; to John Willett for the first publication rights to his translation of Brecht's "A Short Organum for the Theatre"; to Eric Bentley, once again, for his selection from Hebbel's *Journals* and contributions to Brecht's "Organum."

Kind consent for the use of material was given by Francisco García Lorca, Jean-Pierre Giraudoux, Mrs. Eugene O'Neill, Jean Cocteau, Eugene Ionesco, and various publishers who are acknowledged throughout the volume.

Finally, in a personal vein, I want to thank my sister-in-law, Helen Krich Chinoy of the Smith College Theatre Department.

TOBY COLE

CONTENTS

PART 2 **Creations**

INTRODUCTION

(1)

IT IS no secret to anyone familiar with the theatre that modern playwrights have been a self-conscious breed. Anyone whose wares are so conspicuously on display and make such excellent targets for critical marksmanship is bound to be self-conscious. Modern playwriting, moreover, came into being during the latter half of the nineteenth century when intellectual conflict was making itself felt in the theatre and writers were even becoming oracular. Old dispensations in the arts were being challenged; new dispensations were being explained and defended. The age of literary criticism was moving toward high noon. Critics were becoming playwrights, play producers, or stage directors; and it followed that the playwright could turn critic if the critic could turn playwright. Imbued with new intellectualism and estheticism, showmanship itself—once a simple, if not indeed simpleminded, activity—began to buzz with theories supplied by scenic artists such as Appia and Craig and directors such as Antoine and Stanislavsky. Objectives were constantly affirmed or revised in a theatrical world from which improvisation and intellectual innocence had departed while ideas and ideologies multiplied. The modern theatre, it would seem, was born with a program, and it will probably end with one.

From the abundant literature on the modern drama written by the playwrights themselves Toby Cole has compiled a volume rich in matter and provocative in manner. To read the discourse of intelligent writers on their principles and problems is to observe the modern drama in the making. We merely allow for the fact that there is always a breach between ambition and attainment, and especially so in an art so utterly dependent upon stage production and the intervention of the actor. The danger of succumbing to "the intentional fallacy" need not deter us from attending to the playwrights' objectives once it is understood that we shall judge the play

rather than the authors' intentions. It is not likely, moreover, that their pronouncements will make bigoted converts of us and limit our horizons or so bewilder us
with their variety as to make us incapable of judgment.
We live in an eclectic age, are unlikely to be seduced
into exclusive dramatic theory, and have been inured to
contradictions.

Fortunately, too, the playwrights afford a relatively
simple perspective. We find them engaged to two kinds
of theatre—the *modern* and the *modernistic*. The first
sought realism of content, style, and form; the second
aspired toward poetic and imaginative art. The first began
to expel romantic and pseudorealistic drama from the
theatre by the 1870's, the second to challenge, modify,
and supplant realism by the 1890's. But romantic drama
was never conclusively routed by the realists, and realistic
drama has not been substantially displaced by neoromanti-
cists, symbolists, expressionists, and other proponents of
poetic or imaginative drama. Styles of dramatic composition have jostled each other and contracted marriages
throughout our century.

It is surely true, besides, that realism is as much a
"style" as any nonrealistic fashion of playwriting. Style
in the latter case is merely so conspicuous as to give an
impression of stylization, whereas style in realism is concealed to such a degree as to afford the illusion of naturalness. We are concerned with theatrical reality whether
we erect or banish an imaginary "fourth wall" between
the actor and the audience. The realists endeavored to
make the theatre less theatrical after it had been meretri-
ciously "theatricalized," while their usually younger opponents, the antirealists, wanted to make the theatre
more theatrical after it had been "de-theatricalized." The
culprits in the first instance had been mediocre romanti-
cists *and* show-business operators; the culprits in the
second instance, mediocre realists *and* show-business
operators. Whether distinguished playwrights spoke for
or against realism, then, they were equally aiming for
distinguished theatre.

It does not of course follow that they were invariably
successful, or that they were superior to error in their
respective procedures. Scientism trapped naturalists and
partiality for the commonplace mired realists, while an
overfondness for subjectivity made symbolists turn poetry

into mist and expressionists transform dreams into night-mares. It follows only that we do not have to take ir-reversible sides in an ideological war when different play-wrights offer conflicting opinions or programs. The play-wrights themselves set us an example: Maeterlinck, for instance, acclaims Ibsen as a great symbolist writer while Shaw honors him as the supreme dramatist of ideas. Synge avows himself the enemy of Ibsen and Zola whereas he could have convincingly contended that he was making it possible for creative realism to thrive in Ireland. O'Neill is at one point convinced that naturalism is in-solvent but is not deterred from composing naturalistic tragedy in *Desire Under the Elms* or from bringing his latter-day career to a climax with *The Iceman Cometh* and *Long Day's Journey Into Night*. Most of the im-portant modern playwrights, from Ibsen and Strindberg to O'Neill and O'Casey, did not actually make exclusive commitments to any philosophy or style of theatre, al-though they sometimes wrote as if they were making them.

In reading *Playwrights on Playwriting* it is well to realize that the authors' most fervent generalizations usually proclaim a departure from convention that may no longer seem necessary or urgent. To appreciate the force of their pronouncements we should possess some knowledge of the practices they rejected; or else we should be capable of imaginatively identifying these practices, which current malpractice or the insidious re-turn of discredited practices (humdrum realism, preten-tious symbolism, or morbid expressionism) will make dis-couragingly easy. Thus Shaw had a certain vapid kind of contrived playwriting in mind when he struck at "Sardoodledom," and Strindberg was not tilting at a paper dragon when he fought for multidimensional characterization. In his polemical essays he had in mind the nineteenth-century practice, present alike in Bouci-cault's plays and Dickens' fiction, of reducing the in-dividual to a type and the type to a trait; character-draw-ing became caricature. We must realize the extent of the provocation when Strindberg declares that "a character on the stage came to signify a gentleman who was fixed and finished—nothing was required but some bodily de-fect—a club foot, a wooden leg, a red nose. . . ."
It should be apparent that the playwrights speak to

us most effectively when they have in view the problems and principles with which they were involved as *creators* rather than as theoreticians. We turn to their essays for an introduction to their collective and individual aims and practices. We must agree with Brooks Atkinson when he reminds us that "rules are only a by-product of creation, which is the sole business of art." It is not in search of "rules" that we seek out a playwright's commentary. We still want to read it because it may cast some light on his personal effort and achievement, as well as because it may rouse us from the torpor of standardized expectations and responses. It is not absolute principle, for example, but stimulation (including the stimulation of dissent) that we derive from Bernard Shaw's declaration that "A play with a discussion is a modern play; a play with only an emotional situation is an old-fashioned one."

It is evident, too, that the effectiveness of a prescription depends partly on the patient. Shaw could safely assume that old-fashioned playwrights would not write discussion plays, but he must have known better than any of his readers that a discussion play would be dull if written by a dullard and old-fashioned if written by an old-fashioned thinker, or by no thinker at all but a Philistine—however new-fangled the chatter that constitutes the outer garment of his thought. Conversely, it is also possible to be distinctly "modern" while discoursing not at all skeptically on such "old-fashioned" matters as morality and manners —when the discourse, let us say, is by Lionel Trilling rather than by Bruce Barton or some publicist of "positive living." It may also happen that the prescription does wonders for the patient at one time and very little for him at another; "discussion drama" yielded *Man and Superman* at one time and *Fanny's First Play* at another. We cannot escape the conclusion that playwrights writing on playwriting are worth heeding in so far as they are provocative and suggestive rather than prescriptive.

It is not even certain that they always know exactly what they have accomplished or that they accomplished what they intended—it is even possible for a writer to have deviated into something remarkable by *missing* his predetermined target. But it does not follow either that a playwright's understanding or even misunderstanding of his work is without significance. That Chekhov thought he had written *The Cherry Orchard* as a "comedy" is important to our understanding of the play, particularly in a translation, even if we should be convinced—and grateful (as I am)—that he did not. Shaw's prefaces are gratifying and revealing even when they bear only a faint relation to the play they introduce. They may represent the mental climate in which the play came to life—and the mental climate is a significant quality of Shavian playwriting.

In the case of a specific program, indeed, the direct result may matter less than the indirect. Yeats, for example, dreamed of furthering the cause of poetic drama in establishing the Irish national theatre, but there was only one Yeats in Ireland. He got noteworthy drama from his colleagues of the Abbey Theatre almost exclusively in prose plays of peasant life such as Synge's *Riders to the Sea* and *The Playboy of the Western World.* He wanted, above all, *romantic* drama from the Irish theatre; even Maeterlinck was not romantic enough for him. He did get the somewhat unfinished *Deirdre of the Sorrows* from Synge in 1910, but it was not romanticism drawn from the glorious Celtic past but a clamorous realism wrung out of the inglorious present that saved his declining Abbey Theatre when O'Casey rescued it with *Juno and the Paycock* and *The Plough and the Stars.* Nevertheless, Yeats found and fostered "poetic drama," too, in the very realism of the young O'Casey; the paradoxes of creation never cease. It is a paradox, too, that when, after 1917, Yeats came to the peak of his personal effort to create poetic drama, he wrote not for his Irish national theatre but for private drawing-room performances and took for his model not a native but an exotic, Japanese form of drama.

The case of Maurice Maeterlinck is equally instructive. When the Belgian symbolist wrote his celebrated essay on *The Tragic in Daily Life* in 1896 he proposed plotless, static drama as the ideal form for the modern theatre, and his program won considerable support. Subsequently he revised his eloquently expressed views, revoked them indeed as a youthful extravagance (in a letter to the late Barrett Clark), and wrote "active," more or less melodramatic, plays. Nevertheless Miss Cole exercised exemplary judgment in reprinting the essay in which he advocated "static drama." He was at the height of his powers as a playwright when he wrote this apologia, and it defended his practice in such poetic one-acters as *The Intruder, Interior,* and *The Blind* which won the admiration of the modern theatre's arch-realist, the great Stanislavsky, himself. Synge's related practice in the virtually plotless *Riders to the Sea,* produced in Dublin eight years after Maeterlinck's essay, resulted in the greatest one-act tragedy in the English language. Maeterlinck had his finger on the pulse of modern drama in expressing a widely felt dissatisfaction with plotty playwriting which resulted in attacks on the "well-made play" from such different schools of writing as those represented by Strindberg, Shaw, Yeats (in the very same essay in which he asserts romantic ideals), and Andreyev, who proclaimed—I should say, rather prematurely—that life in the modern world had moved inward. For better or worse, plot and external action did lose status in the modern drama, as they did, more thoroughly, in fiction. The Zolaist naturalistic "slice of life," the Shavian discussion-play, subjective and psychological drama—these and other types of dramatic writing have reflected the same tendency. Well-regarded plays such as *The Glass Menagerie* and Carson McCullers' *Member of the Wedding* (as well as present-day avant-garde works by Beckett, Ionesco, and others) continue to exemplify the vitality of a principle Maeterlinck laid down, too romantically and dogmatically yet by no means absurdly, more than half a century before.

(2)

In one respect or another, then, the effort to create a modern theatre receives support and personal interpretation from every playwright represented in the present collection. The strivings for such a theatre have been manifold, and it is risky to predicate unity in diversity for the main pursuit of modern dramatic theory and practice. One would have to allow too many exceptions to the rule for the rule to have any validity. But paramount in the modern experiments and achievements is the determination to express some aspect of reality, some measure of experience, some vision or conviction. This is the organizing principle of Ibsen's work when he develops modern realism and of Brecht's when the latter promulgates his antinaturalistic "epic realism"; and it

appears alike in the social optimism of Shaw's and
O'Casey's plays and the nihilism of Beckett's and
Ionesco's.

The search for truth of experience comes into view
when Ibsen declares as early as 1874 that "All that I have
written these last ten years I have lived through spiritually"; it reappears when Zola declares: "I am waiting for
someone to rid us of fictitious characters, of these symbols
of virtue and vice which have no worth as human data.
. . . I am waiting for everyone to throw out the tricks
of the trade, the contrived formulas, the tears and superficial laughs." The errors of Zola-sponsored naturalism
have been aired often enough; they need not discredit
the ambition to give dimension to character, a degree
of meaningful determinacy to behavior, and fluidity to
dramatic action. Nor is Strindberg to be ignored when
he makes a necessary distinction between microscopic
or "little" naturalism that sees only the minutiae of
reality and the naturalism that provides the wide prospect of, let us say, Hauptmann's *The Weavers* rather than
the same author's *Lonely Lives* or *Before Sunrise,* with
its doctrinaire genetics and small-souled sociology.

Nothing perhaps corrects false perspectives better than
Strindberg's distinctions, set down in 1889 and still indispensable to theatre, in the great essay "On Modern
Drama and Modern Theatre" Miss Cole has so ably edited
for inclusion in *Playwrights on Playwriting.* On one hand,
we find in the theatre "the little art that does not see the
forest for the trees," the "misunderstood naturalism"
that photographs everything but actually reveals nothing.
On the other hand, we have the possibility of *"the
great naturalism"* (that of *The Power of Darkness* and
The Plough and the Stars, for example) which,
Strindberg says, seeks out "the great battles" and takes
delight in the conflict of powerful human forces. And
Strindberg adds the one requirement least likely to occur
to the "little naturalists"—he expects playwrights to see
reality through a *temperament.* When he rejects a reflection of life devoid of temperament as inadequate
because "soulless" he does something momentous,
whether he does so knowingly or unknowingly; he invites
not only passion but poetry into the modern theatre.
Once these are present in a play, along with what
Strindberg calls "significant motif," the differences be-

tween realistic and imaginative, naturalistic and poetic drama become technical and, in the main, superficial.

Once this is understood, we do not have to feel that we are either pushed back from the modern theatre or thrust out of it whenever the poets and the advocates of "the theatre theatrical" speak their piece. We are moving in the right direction of the expressive dramatist rather than the juggler when Maeterlinck asks the playwright to deal with an essential life "beyond the life of every day" and calls for an "atmosphere of the soul" in the theatre, although we may well prefer Chekhov's "atmosphere" to Maeterlinck's. We can appreciate Maeterlinck's point when, in calling for "sorcery" in the drama, he finds "sorcery" in *The Master Builder*, even if we suspect pinchbeck mysticism when he writes such puerile sentences as "It is this sorcery that imposes action or the power of the beyond. And we have to yield to it. Whether we want to or not." We can also agree with Yeats and Synge when they want the theatre to be rich in language. "On the stage we must have reality, and we must have joy," Synge's famous sentence in the preface to *The Playboy of the Western World*, does not order playwrights to leap out of time and space by means of mystical rocketry. Synge, whose beautiful dialogue comes from the Irish peasantry, is not so far removed as we might expect from John Galsworthy, the confirmed naturalist of the English stage. In "Some Platitudes Concerning Drama" Galsworthy praises *The Playboy of the Western World* for its natural matching of matter and poetic style. He objects only to an "ill-mating of forms" (in plays, I take it, where verbal poetry and the subject matter are at odds) and warns that the poetry in ordinary naturalistic drama "can only be that of perfect rightness of proportion, rhythm, shape—the poetry, in fact, that lies in all vital things."

In this brief introduction it is impossible to dwell upon the various ways in which modern playwrights have tried to make the best of the two possible worlds of "reality" and "poetry," or endeavored to treat them as identical or interchangeable. But it is also true of course that a number of modern playwrights (Yeats, Lorca, Giraudoux, and Ionesco—to mention just a few) have, at one time or another, proposed imaginative flights that would whisk

us out of the orbit of everyday life. I do not believe that
they have usually realized their program without botch-
ing their plays or even at times "realizing" themselves
right out of the theatre. It would appear, too, that the
reality of everyday life often seeped right back into their
more or less successful plays. Giraudoux's characters are
often piquantly mundane in the midst of the fantastic
and supernatural action of such plays as *Amphitryon
38, Intermezzo,* and *Ondine.* Cocteau's return to the
Oedipus legend in *The Infernal Machine* is spiced with
many an intentionally anachronistic detail more native
to the Parisian boulevard theatres than to the classic
theatre of austere tragic vision.

In spite of these qualifications, however, it is gratifying
to observe that the flight of the modernistic playwright
has often been *into the theatre*—where all good playwrights belong—rather than into the blue inane. This has
been evident in the practice of Giraudoux, Anouilh,
Ionesco, Wilder, and other twentieth-century playwrights.
The necessity of landing in the theatre was understood
by them all, as their comments show. Moreover, their
"flight into the theatre"—that is, the "theatricalization"
or distinctly theatrical realization of the subject matter
of the play—could actually result in an intensification
and highlighting of reality, as in Brecht's *Mother Courage*
and Wilder's *The Skin of Our Teeth.* It became certain
in our time that the "theatre theatrical" did not necessarily conflict with the playwright's engagement to
modern life. He could use the theatre as show-window,
pillory, or rostrum as, for instance, Brecht did in different plays. These and other expressive uses of the
theatre have been widely recognized by contemporary
playwrights; and at least in its best practice, the modern-
ists' flight from illusionism into imaginative theatricality
has advanced, rather than retarded, the contemporary
theatre.

How well contemporary reality is presented or projected, how soundly appraised, how conclusively judged
—these questions must, of course, receive answers that
will fit the individual case. Fortunately Miss Cole has
devoted the second part of her compilation to notations
by playwrights on the specific plays they have written—
from *A Doll's House* in 1879 to Ionesco's *The Bald
Soprano* and *The Chairs* in our own time. These essays,

which are concerned with individual creation, are illuminating in themselves, and they are instructive when read in conjunction with the plays to which they pertain. They take us into the creator's workshop. The notes are not offered as a passport to the heart of the mystery of creation, and they cannot of course take the place of the final work, which will probably differ from the author's best-laid original plans. The insights afforded by the notes are, nevertheless, important additions to the *Credos and Concepts* of the first section of the book, exemplifying or confirming them, fixing them in a specific context, and perhaps, when read in conjunction with the play itself, illustrating the difference between the aim and the fulfilment. In all respects, then, *Playwrights on Playwriting* is an important theatrical and literary document; and more than that, it is a collection of opinion and data that should have practical value to playwrights in our time and in the foreseeable future. Looking into this book, we may not be able to tell which grain of an idea or principle will grow, but we have much to choose from in the data Toby Cole and her publishers have so generously made available.

JOHN GASSNER

PART 1 Credos and Concepts

HENRIK IBSEN
(1828-1906)

The Task of the Poet[1] (1874)

. . . AND WHAT does it mean, then, to be a poet? It was a long time before I realized that to be a poet means essentially to see, but mark well, to see in such a way that whatever is seen is perceived by the audience just as the poet saw it. But only what has been lived through can be seen in that way and accepted in that way. And the secret of modern literature lies precisely in this matter of experiences that are lived through. All that I have written these last ten years, I have lived through spiritually. But no poet lives through anything in isolation. What he lives through all of his countrymen live through with him. If that were not so, what would bridge the gap between the producing and the receiving minds?

And what is it, then, that I have lived through and that has inspired me? The range has been large. In part I have been inspired by something which only rarely and only in my best moments has stirred vividly within me as something great and beautiful. I have been inspired by that which, so to speak, has stood higher than my everyday self, and I have been inspired by this because I wanted to confront it and make it part of myself.

But I have also been inspired by the opposite, by what appears on introspection as the dregs and sediment of one's own nature. Writing has in this case been to me like a bath from which I have risen feeling cleaner, healthier, and freer. Yes, gentlemen, nobody can picture poetically anything for which he himself has not to a certain degree and at least at times served as a model. And who is the man among us who has not now and then felt and recog-

[1] Henrik Ibsen: "Speech to the Norwegian Students, September 10, 1874," *Speeches and New Letters,* translated by Arne Kildal (Boston. Richard G. Badger, 1910), pp. 49–52. After an absence of ten years, Ibsen spent a couple of months in Norway during the summer of 1874. On September 10, Norwegian students marched in procession to Ibsen's home. This speech is Ibsen's reply to their greeting.

nized within himself a contradiction between word and deed, between will and duty, between life and theory in general? Or who is there among us who has not, at least at times, been egoistically sufficient unto himself, and half unconsciously, half in good faith, sought to extenuate his conduct both to others and to himself?

I believe that in saying all this to you, to the students, my remarks have found exactly the right audience. You will understand them as they are meant to be understood. For a student has essentially the same task as the poet: to make clear to himself, and thereby to others, the temporal and eternal questions which are astir in the age and in the community to which he belongs.

In this respect I dare to say of myself that I have endeavored to be a good student during my stay abroad. A poet is by nature farsighted. Never have I seen my homeland and the true life of my homeland so fully, so clearly, and at such close range, as I did in my absence when I was far away from it.

And now, my dear countrymen, in conclusion a few words which are also related to something I have lived through. When Emperor Julian stands at the end of his career, and everything collapses around him, there is nothing which makes him so despondent as the thought that all he has gained was this: to be remembered by cool and clear heads with respectful appreciation, while his opponents live on, rich in the love of warm, living hearts. This thought was the result of much that I had lived through; it had its origin in a question that I had sometimes asked myself, down there in my solitude. Now the young people of Norway have come to me here tonight and given me my answer in word and song, have given me my answer more warmly and clearly than I had ever expected to hear it. I shall take this answer with me as the richest reward of my visit with my countrymen at home, and it is my hope and my belief that what I experience tonight will be an experience to "live through" which will sometime be reflected in a work of mine. And if this happens, if sometime I shall send such a book home, then I ask that the students receive it as a handshake and a thanks for this meeting. I ask you to receive it as the ones who had a share in the making of it.

Translation revised by Evert Sprinchorn

ÉMILE ZOLA
(1840-1902)

Naturalism on the Stage[1] (1881)

THE IMPULSE of the century is toward naturalism. Today this force, racing toward us, is being emphasized more and more, and everything must obey it. This force has abducted the novel and the drama. The development of the naturalistic force has progressed more quickly in the novel to the point of triumph; on the stage it is just beginning to appear. This was bound to be. The theatre has always been a stronghold of convention for many reasons which I want to explain later. I would like to come simply to this point: the naturalistic formula, however complete and defined in the novel, is far from being well stated in the theatre, and I conclude that the formula must be realized and that it will take on a strictness of form emanating from its scientific nature, or else the drama will become blunted and more and more inferior.

Some people are very angry with me, and they shout, "But what do you want? What further development do you need? Is this evolution not already an accomplished fact? Have not Émile Augier, Dumas *fils*, and Victorien Sardou pushed as far as possible the observation and the painting of our society? Let us stop at this point—we are already too concerned with the realities of this world." First of all, these people are naïve to want to stop this naturalistic development; nothing is stable in society, everything is carried along by sustained motion. People go, nevertheless, where they ought to go. The naturalistic evolution, I contend, far from being an accomplished fact, has hardly begun. Up to now we have experienced only the first attempts. We should wait until certain ideas have made their mark, and until the public becomes accustomed to these ideas and until their force destroys the obstacles one by one. I have attempted in looking over Sardou, Dumas *fils*, and Augier to explain for what reasons I consider them workmen who are clearing the ground of rubbish,

[1] Émile Zola, "Le Naturalisme au théâtre," *Le Roman expérimental* (Paris: E. Fasquelle, 1902).

and not as creators, not geniuses who are building a monument. Moreover, after them, I am waiting for something else.

This something else which arouses indignation and calls forth so much jesting is, however, very simple. We have only to read Balzac, Flaubert, and the Goncourts again —in a word, the naturalistic novelists—to find out what it is. I am waiting for someone to put a man of flesh and bones on the stage, taken from reality, scientifically analyzed, and described without one lie. I am waiting for someone to rid us of fictitious characters, of these symbols of virtue and vice which have no worth as human data. I am waiting for environment to determine the characters and the characters to act according to the logic of facts combined with logic of their own disposition. I am waiting for the time when there is no prestidigitation of any kind, no more waving of the magic wand, changing persons and things from one minute to the next. I am waiting for the time when no one will tell us any more unbelievable stories, when no one will any longer spoil the effects of true observations by imposing romantic incidents, the result of which destroys even the good parts of a play.

I am waiting for everyone to throw out the tricks of the trade, the contrived formulas, the tears and superficial laughs. I am waiting for a dramatic work void of declamations, majestic speech, and noble sentiments, to have the unimpeachable morality of truth and to teach us the frightening lesson of sincere investigation. I am waiting, finally, until the development of naturalism already achieved in the novel takes over the stage, until the playwrights return to the source of science and modern arts, to the study of nature, to the anatomy of man, to the painting of life in an exact reproduction more original and powerful than anyone has so far dared to risk on the boards.

This is what I am waiting for. Some people shrug their shoulders, laugh, and reply that I shall wait forever. Their decisive argument is that I must not expect these things on the stage. The theatre is not the novel. The theatre has given us what it could give us. We must be content with the result. Now we are at the very center of the quarrel. I am trying to uproot the conditions of existence on the stage. If what I ask is impossible, then lies have a place on the boards: a play must have some romantic places, revolve around certain situations, and end at the proper time. My detractors take a "professional" view of the theatre: first, any analysis is boring, the audience demands facts, always facts; then there is the convention of the stage—an action must be played in three hours no matter what its length in time; then the characters are given a certain value which necessitates a fictional setting. I will not quote all the arguments. Now I come to the audience's intervention, which is considerable; the audience wishes this, the audience does not want that; it prefers four sympathetic puppets to one real character drawn from life. In a word, the stage is the domain of conventionality; everything is conventional from the decorations to the footlights which illuminate the actors who are led by a string. Truth can be shown only in small unnoticed doses. Some people even go so far as to swear that the theatre will die the day that it ceases to be an entertaining lie, destined to console the spectators in the evening for the sad realities of the day.

I am acquainted with all this reasoning, and I shall try to respond to it presently, when I reach my conclusion. Each genre of literature has its own conditions of existence. A novel, read alone in the comfort of one's own room, is not a play which is acted before two thousand spectators. The novelist has time and space before him. All kinds of liberties are permitted him; he can use one hundred pages, if he wishes, to analyze at his leisure a certain character; he can describe his surroundings as much as he pleases; he can cut his story short, can retrace his steps, changing scenes twenty times—in a word, he is absolute master of his medium. The dramatist, on the contrary, is enclosed in a rigid frame; he must obey all kinds of necessities. He moves only in the milieu of obstacles. Finally, there is the question of the isolated reader and the audience as a group; the solitary reader tolerates everything, goes where he is led, even when he is annoyed, whereas the audience as a whole is filled with prudishness, fright, and sensibilities which the author must recognize and unfortunately deal with. Since all this is true, it is precisely for this reason that the stage is the last citadel of conventionality as I stated earlier. If the naturalistic movement had not encountered in the theatre such difficult ground, covered with obstacles, naturalism would have taken root on the stage with the intensity and success it has had in the novel. The theatre, under its conditions of existence, must be the last, most labored and disputed conquest of the spirit of truth. . . .

Let us admit for a moment that the critics are right when they assert that naturalism is impossible in the theatre. Here is what these critics believe. Conventionality is a hard and fast rule on the stage; the lie will always have its place there. We are condemned to a continuance of Sardou's juggling, to the theories and witticisms of Dumas *fils,* and to the nice characters of Émile Augier. We will not create anything greater than the genius of these authors; we must accept them as the glory of our time on the stage. They are what they are because our theatre wishes them to be such. If they have not gone further in the drama, if they have not obeyed more perfectly the important wave of truth which is carrying us forward, it is the theatre which forbids them to be influenced by the truth. So in the theatre there is a barrier which blocks the road even to the strongest. Very well, then! But it is the theatre which you condemn; it is to the stage that you have given the mortal blow. You crush the theatre under the novel, you assign it an inferior place, you make it contemptible and useless in the eyes of generations to come. What do you wish us to do with the stage, we who are followers of the truth, anatomists, analysts, explorers of life, compilers of human data, if you prove to us that in the theatre we cannot use our methods or tools? Really! The theatre lives only on conventionalities; it must lie; it refuses to accept our experimental literature! Oh, well, then, the century will put the theatre aside, abandon it to the hands of the public entertainers, and will perform its great and superb work elsewhere. You pronounce the verdict, and you kill the stage. It is very evident that the naturalistic evolution will extend itself more and more because it is the very intelligence of the century. While the novelists are digging always further toward the truth, producing newer and more exact human documents, the theatre will flounder more every day in the center of its romantic fictions, worn-out plots, and skillfulness of construction. The situation will become more annoying because the public will certainly acquire a taste for reality in reading novels. The naturalistic movement is making itself forcibly felt. There will come a time when the public will shrug its shoulders and demand an innovation in the theatre. Either the stage will be naturalistic, or it will not exist at all; such is the formal conclusion.

I have the strongest faith in the future of our theatre. I no longer admit that the critics are right in saying that naturalism is impossible on the stage, and I am going to explain under what conditions the movement will, without any doubt, be brought about.

No, it is not true that the stage must remain stationary; it is not true that its actual conventionalities are the fundamental conditions of its existence. Everything goes on, I repeat; everything goes forward. The authors of today will be overruled; they cannot have the presumption to decide dramatic literature forever. What these authors have stammered about the opposition will clearly affirm; but the stage will not be shaken up because of the disagreement; it will enter, on the contrary, into a wider and straighter path. People have always resisted the march forward; they have denied to the newcomers the power and the right to accomplish what has not been performed by their elders. But the older generation will remain angry and blind in vain. The social and literary evolutions have an irresistible force; they can cross with one leap enormous obstacles which were said to be impassable. The theatre has been in vain what it is today; it will be tomorrow what it should be. And when the event takes place, everybody will think it perfectly natural.

Here I enter into mere probabilities, and I am no longer pretending to have the same scientific exactitude. As long as I have reasoned on facts, I have proved the truth of my position. Now I am content to foretell the future. The evolution will take place; that is certain. But will it pass to the left? Will it pass to the right? I do not really know. One can reason about it, nothing more.

Moreover, it is certain that the conditions existing on the stage will always be different. The novel, thanks to its free form, will remain perhaps the perfect tool of the century, while the stage will follow it and complete its action. The marvelous powers of the theatre must not be forgotten nor must its immediate effect upon the audience. No better instrument for propaganda exists. If the novel, then, is read by the fireside, in several instances, with a patience tolerating the longest details, the naturalistic drama should proclaim above all that it has no relation to this isolated

reader, but to a crowd who demand clearness and conciseness. I do not see that the naturalistic formula is antagonis-
tic to this conciseness and clearness. The novel analyzes
at length with a minuteness of detail which overlooks
nothing; the stage can analyze as briefly as it wishes by
actions and words. In Balzac's work a word or a cry is often
sufficient to describe the entire character. This cry belongs
essentially to the theatre. As to the acts, they are consistent with analysis in action, the most striking form of
action one can make. When we have gotten rid of the
child's play of a plot, the infantile game of tying up complicated threads in order to have the pleasure of untying
them again; when a play shall be only a real and logical
story, we shall have perfect analysis; we shall analyze forcibly the double influence of characters over facts, of facts
over characters. This idea is what has led me to say so
often that the naturalistic formula carries us back to the
source itself of our national stage with its classical formula.
In Corneille's tragedies and Molière's comedies, we find
this continuous analysis of character which I find necessary; plot takes a secondary place, and the work is a long
dissertation in dialogue on man. Only instead of an abstract man, I would substitute a natural man, put him in
his proper surroundings, and analyze all the physical and
social causes which make him what he is. To me, in a
word, the classical formula is a good one, on condition
that the scientific method is employed in the study of society itself, in the same way that the science of chemistry
is the study of compounds and their properties.

As to the long descriptions used in the novel, they cannot be used on the stage; that is evident. The naturalistic
novelists describe at length, not for the pleasure of
describing as they have been reproached for doing, but
because description is part of their formula to put down
full details about the character, and to make him complete by means of his environment. Such a novelist no
longer looks on man as an intellectual abstraction as he
was looked upon in the seventeenth century; he is a thinking animal, who forms part of nature, and who is subject to
the multiple influences of the soil in which he grows and
where he lives. That is why a climate, a country, a horizon,
are often decisively important. The novelist no longer separates his character from the air he breathes; he does not
describe him because of any rhetorical need, as the

didactic poets did, as Delille does, for example; he simply makes a note of the material conditions in which he finds his characters at every hour, and in which the facts are produced, in order to be absolutely thorough, and so that his inquiry may belong to the world's comprehensive view and reproduce reality in its entirety. Descriptions need not be transplanted to the stage; they are found there naturally. Is not the stage set a continual description more exact and startling than the descriptions in a novel? A set is only painted cardboard, some people say; indeed, but in a novel it is still less than painted cardboard— it is blackened paper despite which the illusion is created. After the scenery, set off so strikingly, and so surprisingly true, that we have recently seen in our theatres, no one can any longer deny the possibility of producing the reality of environment on the stage. It is up to dramatic authors now to utilize this reality; they will furnish the characters and the facts; the set designers, under the author's direction, will furnish the descriptions, as exact as shall be necessary. It is up to the dramatic author to make use of environments as novelists do, since the novelists know how to introduce and make such environments real.

I will add that, since the theatre is a material reproduction of life, external surroundings have always been a necessity there. In the seventeenth century, however, nature was not considered important, and, as man was looked upon only as a purely intellectual being, the scenery was vague—a peristyle of a temple, any kind of a room or public place would do. Today the naturalistic movement has brought about a more and more perfect exactness in stage scenery. Such fidelity was produced inevitably, little by little. I even find in this exactness proof of the unheralded task that naturalism has accomplished in the theatre since the beginning of the century. I cannot study thoroughly this question of scenery and accessories; I must content myself by stating that description is not only possible on the stage, but it is, moreover, a necessity which is imposed on the theatre as an essential condition of its existence.

I do not have to talk about the change of place. The unity of place has not been observed for a long time. The playwrights do not hesitate to depict an entire existence, to take the audience to both ends of the earth. Here con-

ventionality remains mistress as she is also in the novel. The
same idea applies to the question of time—but one must
cheat a little here. A plot which calls for fifteen days, for
example, must be played in the three hours which we set
apart for reading a novel or seeing it played at the
theatre. We are not the creative force which governs the
world; we are only second-rate creators who analyze, sum-
marize by trial and error, who are happy and acclaimed as
geniuses when we can disengage one ray of the truth.

I come now to the language. My detractors say that
there is a special style for the stage. They want it to be a
style completely different from that of daily conversation,
more sonorous, more sensitive, written in a higher key,
cut in facets, no doubt to make the theatre's chandeliers
sparkle. In our time, for example, Dumas *fils* has the
reputation of being a great playwright. His witticisms are
celebrated. They are shot off like skyrockets, falling in
showers to the audience's applause. Besides, all his characters speak the same language, the language of witty
Paris, spinning with paradoxes, always aiming for a good
hit, sharp and hard. I do not deny the sparkle of this
language—but it is a superficial sparkle which contains no
truth. Nothing is more fatiguing than these continual
mocking sentences. I would prefer greater flexibility and
naturalness. These sentences are at once too well and not
well enough written. The true stylists of our age are the
novelists—you must look to Gustave Flaubert and to the
Goncourts to find impeccable, living, and original style.
When you compare Dumas' style to that of these great
prose authors you find it does not stand up in correctness,
color, or emotion. What I want to hear in the theatre is
spoken language. If we are not able to reproduce on
the stage a conversation with its repetitions, its length,
and its useful words, the emotion and tone of the conversation could be kept; the individual turn of mind of
each speaker, the reality, in a word, reproduced to the
necessary extent. The Goncourts have made a curious
attempt at this style in *Henriette Maréchal,* that play
which no one wanted to listen to and which no one knows
anything about. The Greek actors spoke through a brass
tube; during the time of Louis XIV the comedians sang
their roles in a singsong tone to give them more pomp;
today we are content to say there is a language of the
theatre which is more sonorous and explosive. You can see

from these examples what progress we have made. One day the public will perceive that the best style in the theatre is that which best sets forth the spoken conversation, which puts the exact word in its proper place, giving it its just value. The naturalistic novelists have already written excellent models of dialogue, reduced to strictly useful words. The question of sentimental characters now remains. I do not disguise the fact that such a question is of capital importance. The public remains cold when its passion for an ideal character of loyalty and honor is not satisfied. A play which presents the audience with living characters taken from real life looks black and austere to it, when the play does not completely exasperate the public. It is on this point especially that the battle of naturalism is fought. We must learn to be patient. At the present time a secret change is taking place in the public's feeling; people are coming little by little, encouraged by the spirit of the century, to agree to a bold interpretation of real life and are even beginning to acquire a taste for it. When audiences can no longer stand certain lies, we shall have very nearly gained our point. Already the novelists' work is preparing the ground for our audiences. A time will come when a master playwright can reveal his ideas on the stage, finding there a public enthusiastically in favor of the truth. It will be a question of tact and strength. Such audiences will see then that the greatest and most useful lessons will be taught by depicting life as it is, and not by repeated generalities nor by speeches of bravado which are spoken merely to please our ears.

The two formulas are before us: the naturalistic formula which makes the stage a study and picture of real life; and the conventional formula which makes the stage an amusement for the mind, an intellectual guessing game, an art of adjustment and symmetry regulated after a certain code. In fact, everything depends on the idea one has of literature and of the drama in particular. If we admit that literature is an inquiry about things and human beings made by original minds, we are naturalists. If we pretend that literature is a framework superimposed upon the truth, that a writer must make use of observation merely in order to exhibit his power of invention and arrangement, we are idealists and proclaim the necessity of conventionality. . . .

And I add that we shall have life on the stage as we already have it in the novel. This would-be logic of actual plays, this equality and symmetry obtained by processes of reasoning, which come from ancient metaphysics, will collapse before the natural logic of facts and human beings such as reality gives us. In place of a theatre of fabrication, we shall have a stage of observation. How will the evolution be brought about? Tomorrow will give us the answer. I have tried to forecast the future, but leave to genius its realization. I have already stated my conclusion: our stage will be naturalistic, or it will cease to be.

Now that I have attempted to put my ideas together, may I hope people will no longer put words into my mouth which I have never spoken? Will they continue to see, in my critical judgment, I do not know what ludicrous inflations of vanity or repulsive retaliations? I am only the most sincere soldier of truth. If I am mistaken, my opinions are here in print; and fifty years from now I shall be judged, in my turn; I may be accused of injustice, blindness, and useless violence. I accept the verdict of the future.

Translated by Samuel Draper

AUGUST STRINDBERG
(1849-1912)

On Modern Drama and Modern Theatre[1] (1889)

... THERE ARE some who wish to date the new drama from the Goncourt brothers' *Henriette Maréchal*, performed at the Théâtre Français as early as 1865 and booed. But the reasons for this dating are not well founded, since the Goncourts represent a Christian physiological movement of older times and in the structure of their play simply used a few bold devices which every realistic movement before them has known how to utilize.

Rather the naturalistic drama will probably continue to regard *Thérèse Raquin* from 1873 as its first milestone. ... When Zola approaches the theatre to make a serious attempt to apply new methods, he is attracted immediately by a great and powerful motif, in this case a murder of one spouse in order that the other may gain the freedom to make another choice. But he does not proceed like Dumas or Augier, excusing the murder partly because of the prevailing legal system, which did not permit divorce; he neither excuses nor accuses, for he has canceled these concepts, but limits himself to a description of the development, indicating the motive of the act and showing its consequences. And in the pangs of conscience of the

[1] August Strindberg, "Om modernt drama och modern teater," *Samlade Skrifter* (Stockholm: Albert Bonnicrs Forlag, 1913), XVII, 281–303. In the incisive and thoroughly informative essay written in March, 1889, from which this selection is excerpted, Strindberg traces briefly the historical development of the French drama from the classical plays of Corneille, Racine, and Molière to the naturalistic innovations of André Antoine at the Théâtre Libre in Paris. During the course of the essay, Strindberg not only analyzes and evaluates the different schools of thought and movements in the French drama, but gives at the same time an illuminating account of the development of his own dramatic principles during the 1880's. After reading the essay, the reader has a clear picture of the nature of Strindberg's dramatic preferences by the year 1889, which he embodied in his own creative work of the late 1880's, beginning with *The Father* in 1887 and ending with his last *quart d'heure* play *Samum* in the spring of 1889 (Translator's note). Translation © 1960 by Borge Gedso Madsen.

criminals he sees merely an expression of disrupted social harmony, the results of habit and inherited ideas.

Thérèse Raquin is a new departure, but since it is adapted from a novel it is still not perfect in form. The author has had the feeling, however, that through greater unity of place his audience would receive a more complete illusion, by which the action would impress its main feature more forcefully on the spectators. At every curtain rise, the spectator had to be haunted by the memories of the preceding act and thus through the impact of the recurring milieu be captivated by the action. But because of the difficulty in having a before and after the crime sequence, Zola commits the error of letting a year elapse between the first and second acts. Presumably he did not dare offend against the prevailing law about a year's widowhood, otherwise a day between the acts would have been enough, and the play would have made a more unified impression. I therefore once suggested to a director of a theatre, whom I wanted to persuade to produce *Thérèse Raquin*, that he remove the first act. This can be done without any harm to the play, and recently I have seen a deceased French Zolaist make the same suggestion in a work on naturalism.[2]

With *Renée*, Zola seems to have returned to the form of the traditional Parisian comedy, with greater leaps in time and space than are compatible with the difficulty which a modern skeptical mind feels in allowing itself to be tricked into a belief in the conventions of the theatre. At the same time psychology is neglected in this play; the portrayal of character is superficial, and the whole thing is sketchy and melodramatic, which may be the usual result of adapting novels to the stage.

With *Thérèse Raquin* the great style, the deep probing of the human soul had attracted attention for a while, but no successors seem to venture forth. Still, the attempt has been made, since 1882, of regarding Henry Becque's *Les Corbeaux* as an epoch-making work. To me this seems to be a misunderstanding. If art is to be, as it has been said, a piece of nature seen through a temperament, then there really is a piece of nature in Becque's *Crows*, but the temperament is lacking.

A factory owner dies in the first act after, among many other incidents, his son has appeared in the first scene comically got up in his father's dressing gown. This com-

[2] Louis Desprez, *L'Évolution naturaliste* (Strindberg's note).

pletely superfluous little prank, the significance of which I
fail to grasp, was probably included by the dramatist because it happened in real life from which this boring and
rather unimportant episode has been taken. After the death
of the factory owner, his partner, lawyers, paid and unpaid
creditors appear on the scene and seize the inheritance,
so that the family becomes insolvent. That is all!

Here we have the ordinary case which is so much in
demand these days, the *rule*, the human norm, which is so
banal, so insignificant, so dull that after four hours of
suffering you ask yourself the old question: how does this
concern me? This is the objective which is so beloved by
those devoid of temperament, the soulless as they shall be
called!

This is photography which includes everything, even the
grain of dust on the lens of the camera. This is realism,
a working method elevated to art, or the little art which
does not see the forest for the trees. This is the misunderstood naturalism which holds that art merely consists of
drawing a piece of nature in a natural way; it is not the
great naturalism which seeks out the points where the great
battles are fought, which loves to see what you do not
see every day, which delights in the struggle between natural
forces, whether these forces are called love and hate,
rebellious or social instincts, which finds the beautiful or
ugly unimportant if only it is great. It is this grandiose
art which we found in *Germinal* and *La Terre*, and which
we expected to see reappear in the theatre, but which did
not come with Becque's *Corbeaux* or Zola's *Renée*, but
which gradually was to come into existence through the
opening of a new stage, which, under the name of the
Théâtre Libre, is active in the heart of Paris.

. . . There are few theatres at which dramatic works are
produced in all their natural freshness, their innate direct-
ness, in their original form, in other words. First of all they
have to pass through the sieve of censorships and then be
subjected to the collaboration of a systematic, experienced,
and, what is worse, perhaps ignorant director. At the
Théâtre Libre they appear in all their pleasing naïveté
and completeness, without embellishments and puerile abbreviations. If the success is but small, the result is a severe
but useful lesson to the writer; if on the other hand it is
great, the author gets all the credit. Double gain!

And both the credit and the lesson are so much more

valuable because they do not owe anything to a charming staging of the play.

Here one does not find those superb settings which dazzle the eye and make the spectators overlook the emptiness of the action; none of those widely famous virtuosities which, like a scarlet cloak, hide the poverty of the form.

Here the staging of plays is very simple, and the performers consist of a handful of young devotees who combine all the naïveté of inexperience with the conviction and enthusiasm of youth.

Shakespeare was not interpreted better than this when he wrote his masterpieces.

Rapidly a repertoire[3] had arisen so that about twenty plays were performed in a year, *and naturalism which had been declared impossible on the stage by critics and other timid persons, now asserted itself triumphantly there.* Already one sees indications of a search for a form which seems to take the new drama in a direction somewhat different from the first attempts in *Thérèse Raquin* and which breaks away completely from Zola's adaptations of both *L'Assommoir* and *Germinal* with their crowd effects and elaborate theatrical apparatus.

Hardly a full-length play is seen, and Zola himself makes his debut with a one-act play; and when three-act plays were performed, a strong predilection for the unities of time and place was noticeable. Besides, intrigue seems to have been abandoned and the main interest focused on the psychological description of character.

In old Greek the word *drama* seems to have meant event, not action or what we call conscious intrigue. For life does not move as regularly as a constructed drama, and conscious spinners of intrigue very seldom get a chance to carry out their plans in detail. Thus we no longer believe in these cunning plotters who, unhindered, are permitted to control people's destinies, so that the villain in his conscious falseness merely arouses our ridicule as not being true to life.

In the new naturalistic drama a striving for the signifi-

[3] The complete repertoire of the Théâtre Libre will be found in Samuel M. Waxman, *Antoine and the Théâtre Libre* (Cambridge: Harvard University Press, 1926), Appendix A, pp. 221–29.

cant motif was felt at once. Therefore, the action was usually centered around life's two poles, life and death, the act
of birth and the act of death, the fight for the spouse, for
the means of subsistence, for honor, all these struggles—
with their battlefields, cries of woe, wounded and dead—
during which one heard the new philosophy of life conceived as a struggle, blow its fertile winds from the south.

These were tragedies such as had not been seen before.
The young authors of a generation whose school had so far
been a school of suffering—the most terrible, perhaps,
which exists: severe intellectual oppression, even in such
cruel forms as persecution with imprisonment and starva-
tion—these young authors themselves seemed reluctant to
impose their suffering on others more than was absolutely
necessary. Therefore, they made the suffering as brief as
possible, let the pain pour forth in one act, sometimes in a
single scene. Such a little masterpiece was, for example,
Entre Frères by Guiches and Lavedan. The play is so
brief that it is performed in fifteen minutes, and the
genre immediately was called *quart d'heure.*

The action, if it can be called action, is as follows: In a
bed lies an old woman dying, and beside her stand her
three sons. The dying person makes a sign that she wants
to speak, and then she reveals the secret of her life: one of
the sons was conceived in adultery. She falls back unconscious, apparently dead, before she has had time to
tell which of the sons is the illegitimate one.

The sons deliberate and on certain grounds decide that
the youngest one is legitimate. The marquis, the head of
the family, suggests that they keep the secret, but that the
illegitimate heir leave.

At that moment the mother comes to and is able to utter
only these words: "It is the marquis!" The end!

This is the drama reduced to one scene, and why not?
One who has had the job of reading plays which are sub-
mitted to a theatrical director soon observes that every
play seems to have been written for the sake of a single
scene, and that all the author's creative joy centered
around this scene which sustained him during the terrible
pains which exposition, presentation, entanglement, dis-
entanglement, *peripeteia,* and catastrophe caused him.

For the satisfaction of having written a full-length play,
he bores his audience by arousing its curiosity about matters it already knows, harasses the director by making him

maintain a large personnel, makes life miserable for those unfortunate actors who play the secondary parts, as well as the critics, the confidants, the *raisonneurs*, without whom no intrigue or full-length play can materialize, and to whom he must go to the trouble of giving a character.

Therefore carefully constructed five-act plays are very rare; and one has to put up with a lot of superfluous nonsense to get to the gist of the matter. Since I have recently read about twenty-five plays, among them one of four hundred pages with seventeen characters, I have been confirmed in certain suspicions about the reason for the lack of good drama. Every beginner seems to me to be able to write one good act; in that one he is true to life, every word is straightforward, and the action is honest. As soon as he embarks on the writing of long plays, everything becomes labored, contrived, affected, and false. The two-act plays form a genre by themselves, but not a very happy one. It is the head and the tail, with the body missing; it is before and after the catastrophe, usually with a year between. Ordinarily the second act contains the moral lesson: this is how it goes if you do this and that in the first act. Most beautiful in construction are the three-act plays observing the unities of time and place, when the subject is a big one. For example, Ibsen's *Ghosts* should be compared with *Rosmersholm* which was found to be far too long. The taste of the period, this headlong, hectic period, seems to move toward the brief and expressive. Tolstoy's painful *Power of Darkness* at the Théâtre Libre proved incapable of keeping interest alive and even had to fall back on Franco-Russian politics for effect.

A scene, a *quart d'heure*, seems to be the type of play preferred by modern theatregoers, and it has an old history. For it can name as its origin (yes, why not?) the Greek tragedy which contains a concentrated event in a single act, if we regard the trilogy as three separate plays. But if we do not want to go way back to Paradise, we have in the eighteenth century a gentleman called Carmontelle, who was the first to cultivate on a large scale the genre he named *Proverbes Dramatiques,* of which he published ten volumes and is supposed to have left a hundred more in manuscript. The genre was later developed by Leclerq, attained its highest perfection in Musset's and Feuillet's well-known masterpieces—and more recently in Henry Becque's *La Navette* to form the transition to the fully executed one-act play,[4] which may become the formula for the drama to come.

In the proverb one got the gist of the matter, the whole dénouement, the battle of the souls, sometimes approaching tragedy in Musset, without having to be bothered by the clanging of arms or processions of supernumeraries. By means of a table and two chairs one could present the most powerful conflicts life has to offer; and in this type of art all the discoveries of modern psychology could, for the first time, be applied in popularized form.

As is well known, in our day the proverb developed rapidly, was used and misused; it became easily available, and the result was a surfeit of it. The proverb proved, however, to be the seed of a prospective form—when the author and the public favored the same thing—but it declined, was buried and ridiculed, because no one dared use it for greater efforts, as Musset had done, although not always successfully.

By this I do not mean to say that *this is the only possible approach*. The Théâtre Libre did not start its activity by proclaiming any program; it has never developed an aesthetic, never wanted to form a school. Writers have therefore taken advantage of this freedom, and the theatre's poster has shown the most varied forms, new and old together, even as old as the tragic parade, the mystery, and the pantomime. And from the laws of modern aesthetics has also been eliminated the decree that it is not permissible to place an action in the historical past. All prohibitive laws have been canceled, and only the demands of taste and of the modern spirit are allowed to determine the artistic form.

Is this not possibly an emancipation of art, a renaissance, a liberation from a terrible aesthetics which was beginning to make people unhappy, which wanted to change the theatre into a political arena, into a Sunday school, a chapel? Perhaps!

May we too get such a theatre where one can shudder at the most horrible, laugh at the ridiculous, play with toys; where one can get to see everything and not be offended if one gets to see what has so far been hidden behind theological and aesthetic veils, even though the old laws

---

[4] *Den utförda enaktaren.* By this expression Strindberg probably means a one-act play slightly longer than the *quart d'heure* and with regular division into scenes (Translator's note).

of convention be broken; may we get a free theatre where one has freedom for everything, except the freedom to lack talent and be a hypocrite or a fool!

And if we should not get any such theatre, we shall probably manage to survive anyway!

Translated by Børge Gedsø Madsen

ANTON CHEKHOV
(1860-1904)

Advice to Playwrights[1]

TO A. P. CHEKHOV, APRIL 11, 1889

TRY TO be original in your play and as clever as possible; but don't be afraid to show yourself foolish; we must have freedom of thinking, and only he is an emancipated thinker who is not afraid to write foolish things. Don't round things out, don't polish—but be awkward and impudent. Brevity is the sister of talent. Remember, by the way, that declarations of love, the infidelity of husbands and wives; widows', orphans', and all other tears, have long since been written up. The subject ought to be new, but there need be no "fable." And the main thing is—father and mother must eat. Write. Flies purify the air, and plays —the morals.

TO A. P. CHEKHOV, MAY 8, 1889

Now about your play. You undertook to depict a man who has not a grief in the world, and then you took fright. The problem seems to me to be clear. Only he has no grief who is indifferent; and people who are indifferent and aloof are either philosophers or petty, egotistic natures. The latter should be treated negatively, the former—positively. Of course, those unmoved dullards who will suffer no pain even when you burn them with red-hot irons cannot be discussed at all. Even if by a man without grief you understand one who is not indifferent to the life about him, and who bravely and patiently bears the blows of fate, and looks hopefully to the future—there, too, the problem is comparatively simple and clear.

The large number of revisions need not trouble you,

[1] Anton Chekhov, *Letters on the Short Story, the Drama and other Literary Topics,* selected and edited by Louis S. Friedland (New York: Minton, Balch & Co., 1924), pp. 170–80.

for the more of a mosaic the work is, the better. The characters stand to gain by this. The play will be worthless if all the characters resemble you. In this respect your *Money-Box* is monotonous and arouses a feeling of boredom. What are Natasha, Kolya, Tosya for? Is there no life outside of you? And who is interested in knowing my life or yours, my thoughts and your thoughts? Give people people, and not yourself.

Avoid "choice" diction. The language should be simple and forceful. The lackeys should speak simply, without elegance. Retired captains in the reserve, with huge, red noses, newspaper reporters who drink, starving authors, consumptive women toilers, honest young people without a flaw in their make-up, ideal maidens, good-natured nurses —all these have been described again and again, and should be avoided as a pitfall. Still another suggestion: go to the theatre now and then and watch the stage. Compare—that is important. The first act may last as long as a whole hour, but the rest should not be more than twenty minutes each. The crux of the play is the third act, but it must not be so strong a climax as to kill the last act.

TO A. S. SOUVORIN, MAY 30, 1888

As to your play,[2] I try in vain to see why you speak so ill of it. Its defects do not spring from your not being sufficiently talented, or from your not having great enough powers of observation, but from the nature of your creative ability. You are more inclined to austere creation, which was developed in you by extensive reading of classic models, and by your love for these models. Imagine your *Tatyana* written in verse, and you will see that its defects will take on a different aspect. If it were written in verse, nobody would notice that all its characters speak one and the same language, nobody would reproach your characters for uttering nothing but philosophy, and for "feuilletonizing" in the classic form—all this would blend with the classic tone as smoke blends with the air—and one would not observe in your *Tatyana* the absence of the commonplace language and the everyday, petty actions that the modern drama must provide in plenty. . . . Give your characters Latin names, attire them in togas, and you will get the same thing—the defects of your play are

2 *Tatyana Repina.*

irremediable because they are organic. Console yourself
with the fact that they are the product of your actual
qualities, and that if you gave these qualities to other
playwrights, their plays would become more interesting and
clever.

TO A. S. SOUVORIN, DECEMBER 19, 1888

The first act of your *Repina* is put together so
strangely that I am altogether at a loss. In rehearsal this
act seemed to me dreary and unskillfully done, but now I
understand that one cannot make plays otherwise, and I
comprehend the success of this act. After *Tatyana* I consider my own play[3] as so much sweetmeats, although I have
not as yet made clear to myself whether your play is good
or not. In its architectonics there is something that I do
not quite grasp.

TO A. S. SOUVORIN, JANUARY 6, 1889

I like the "vaudeville." It begins in a very original way.
Very hackneyed are: the cousin, the glove, the card falling
out of the pocket, the eavesdropping. . . . In one-act
things you must write *nonsense,*—there lies their strength.
Manage it so that the wife wants seriously to run away,—
she has become bored, and desires new experiences. She
threatens seriously to cuckold her second husband. . . .
The talk about the cuckolding is good. The eavesdropping
is unnecessary; let the husband arrive just after the wife
has finished writing her letter, and has gone out for a
minute to her friends to ask forgiveness, then to return
home for her baggage. The dialogue is suitable and pat.

TO A. S. SOUVORIN, JANUARY 23, 1900

The new play,[4] Acts I and II, I liked, and I find that it
is even better than *Tatyana Repina*. The other is closer to
the theatre, this to life. The third act was not definite, because there is no action; there is not even clarity of idea.
It may be that to make it more certain and clearer, a
fourth act will be required. In the third act the explanation
between the husband and the wife is modeled after Sumba-
tov's *Chains*; and I would prefer that the wife remain be-

[3] *Ivanov.*
[4] *The Question.*

hind the curtain all the time, and that Varya, as happens in life in similar circumstances, should believe more in the father than in the mother.

I have few comments to make. A cultured nobleman entering the priesthood, that has become stale, and no longer arouses curiosity. Those who entered the priesthood just fell into the water; some, remaining ordinary abbots, waxed fat and have long since forgotten every idea; others gave up all and are living in peace. Nothing definite was expected of them, and they gave nothing; and on the stage a young man preparing for the priesthood will simply be received without sympathy by the public, and in his activities and chastity they will see something of the Skoptsi.[5] And, indeed, the actor will not play the part well. You would do better to take a young, learned, mysterious Jesuit dreaming of a united church; or someone else, but someone who will appear greater than a nobleman entering the priesthood.

Varya is well done. At first sight there is an excessive hysteria in the language. She must not use witticisms; but you make all of them fall into this habit; they keep playing on words, and that tires the attention a little; it is too flashy; the language of your charcters is like a white silk dress on which the sun is always shining in full force and which it hurts the eyes to look at. The words "vulgarity" and "vulgar" are hackneyed.

Natasha is very good. You make her a different person in the third act.

The families "Ratishchev" and "Muratov" are too theatrical, not simple. Give Ratishchev to a Little Russian family, for variety.

The father is without a weakness, without a distinct appearance; he does not drink, or smoke, or gamble, or fall ill. You must stitch onto him some attribute or other, so that the actor can have something to grasp.

The father knows of Varya's sin or does not know,—I think it makes no difference, and is of no importance. The sexual sphere, of course, plays an important part in this world, but not everything depends on it,—far from everything; and not everywhere, by far, does it have decisive significance.

When you send the fourth act I shall write more if I think of anything to say. I am glad that you have almost

[5] A fanatic, ascetic religious sect in Russia.

completed the play, and again repeat that you ought to write both plays and novels, first because it is necessary, and second, because for you it is healthful, as it is pleasant to vary your life.

TO MAXIM GORKY, FEBRUARY 15, 1900

I am very sorry that apparently you have given up the idea of coming to Yalta. The Art Theatre from Moscow will be here in May. It will give five performances and then remain for rehearsals. So you come, study the stage at the rehearsals, and then in five to eight days write a play, which I should welcome joyfully with my whole heart.

TO MAXIM GORKY, SEPTEMBER 8, 1900

I have just been reading in the papers that you are writing a play. Write, write, write! It is necessary. Even should the play fail, don't let that discourage you. A failure will be soon forgotten, but a success, however slight, may be of vast service to the theatre.

TO MAXIM GORKY, SEPTEMBER 24, 1900

By all means, *golubchik,* finish the play. You feel that it is not turning out as you should like, but don't trust your feeling, as it may deceive you. One usually dislikes a play while writing it, but afterward it grows on one. Let others judge and make decisions.

TO MAXIM GORKY, OCTOBER 22, 1901

Five days have passed since I read your play *The Petty Bourgeois.* I have not written to you till now because I could not get hold of the fourth act; I have kept waiting for it, and—I still have not got it. And so I have read only three acts, but that I think is enough to judge of the play. It is, as I expected, very good, written à la Gorky, original, very interesting; and, to begin by talking of the defects, I have noticed only one, a defect incorrigible as red hair in a red-haired man—the conservatism of the form. You make new and original people sing new songs to an accompaniment that looks secondhand; you have four acts, the characters deliver edifying discourses, there is a feeling of alarm before long speeches, and so on, and so on. But all that is not important, and it is all, so to speak,

drowned in the good points of the play. Perchikhin—how
live! His daughter is enchanting, Tatyana and Piotr also,
and their mother is a spendid old woman. The central figure of the play, Nil, is vigorously drawn and extremely interesting! In fact, the play takes hold of one from the first
act. Only, God preserve you from letting anyone act
Perchikhin except Artyom, while Alexeyev-Stanislavsky
must certainly play Nil. Those two figures will do just what's
needed; Piotr—Meyerhold. Only, Nil's part, a wonderful
part, must be made two or three times as long. You ought
to end the play with it, to make it the leading part. Only,
do not contrast him with Piotr and Tatyana, let him be
by himself and them by themselves, all wonderful, splendid
people independent of one another. When Nil tries to seem
superior to Piotr and Tatyana, and says of himself that he
is a fine fellow—the element so characteristic of our decent
workingman, the element of modesty, is lost. He boasts, he
argues, but you know one can see what sort of man he is
without that. Let him be merry, let him play pranks through
the whole four acts, let him eat a great deal after his
work—and that will be enough for him to conquer the audience with. Piotr, I repeat, is good. Most likely you don't
even suspect how good he is. Tatyana, too, is a finished
figure, only—(a) she ought really to be a schoolmistress,
ought to be teaching children, ought to come home from
school, ought to be taken up with her pupils and exercise
books, and—(b) it ought to be mentioned in the first or
second act that she has attempted to poison herself; then,
after that hint, the poisoning in the third act will not seem
so startling and will be more in place. Teterev talks too
much: such characters ought to be shown bit by bit among
others, for in any case such people are everywhere merely
incidental—both in life and on the stage. Make Elena dine
with all the rest in the first act, let her sit and make jokes,
or else there is very little of her, and she is not clear.
Her avowal to Piotr is too abrupt; on the stage it would
come out in too high relief. Make her a passionate woman,
if not loving, at least apt to fall in love. . . .

TO MAXIM GORKY, JULY 29, 1902

I have read your play.[6] It is new and unmistakably fine.
The second act is very good; it is the best, the strongest,

6 *The Lower Depths.*

and when I was reading it, especially the end, I almost danced with joy. The tone is gloomy, oppressive; the audience, unaccustomed to such subjects, will walk out of the theatre, and you may well say good-by to your reputation as an optimist, in any case. My wife will play Vassilisa, the immoral and spiteful woman; Vishnevsky walks about the house and imagines himself the Tartar—he is convinced that it is the part for him. Luka, alas! you must not give to Artyom. He will repeat himself in that part and be exhausted; but he would do the policeman wonderfully; it is his part. The part of the actor, in which you have been very successful (it is a magnificent part), should be given to an experienced actor, Stanislavsky perhaps. Kachalov will play the baron.

You left out of the fourth act all the most interesting characters (except the actor), and you must mind, now, that there is no ill effect from it. The act may seem boring and unnecessary, especially if, with the exit of the strongest and most interesting actors, there are left only the mediocrities. The death of the actor is awful; it is as though you gave the spectator a sudden box on the ear apropos of nothing without preparing him in any way. How the baron got into the doss house and why he is a baron is also not quite clear.

TO V. NEMIROVICH-DANCHENKO, NOVEMBER 2, 1903

Apropos of the popular theatres and popular literature— all that is foolishness, sugar candy for the people. You must not lower Gogol to the people, but raise the people to the level of Gogol.

MAURICE MAETERLINCK
(1862-1949)

The Tragic in Daily Life¹ (1896)

... WHEN I go to the theatre, I feel as though I were
spending a few hours with my ancestors, who conceived
life as something that was primitive, arid, and brutal; but
this conception of theirs scarcely even lingers in my memory, and surely it is not one that I can share. I am shown
a deceived husband killing his wife, a woman poisoning her
lover, a son avenging his father, a father slaughtering his
children, children putting their father to death, murdered
kings, ravished virgins, imprisoned citizens—in a word, all
the sublimity of tradition, but alas, how superficial and
material! Blood, surface tears, and death! What can I learn
from creatures who have but one fixed idea, and who have
no time to live, for there is a rival, or a mistress, whom
it behooves them to put to death?

I had hoped to be shown some act of life, traced back
to its sources and to its mystery by connecting links, that
my daily occupations afford me neither power nor occasion
to study. I had gone there hoping that the beauty, the
grandeur, and the earnestness of my humble day-by-day
existence would, for one instant, be revealed to me, that I
would be shown the I know not what presence, power, or
God that is ever with me in my room. I was yearning for
one of the strange moments of a higher life that flit unper-
ceived through my dreariest hours; whereas, almost invariably, all that I beheld was but a man who would tell me,
at wearisome length, why he was jealous, why he poisoned,
or why he killed.

I admire Othello, but he does not appear to me to live
the august daily life of a Hamlet, who has the time to live,
inasmuch as he does not act. Othello is admirably jealous.

---

¹ Maurice Maeterlinck, "The Tragical in Daily Life," *The
Treasure of the Humble,* translated by Alfred Sutro (New
York: Dodd, Mead and Co., 1916), pp. 103–19.

But is it not perhaps an ancient error to imagine that it is at the moments when this passion, or others of equal violence, possesses us, that we live our truest lives? I have grown to believe that an old man, seated in his armchair, waiting patiently, with his lamp beside him; giving unconscious ear to all the eternal laws that reign about his house, interpreting, without comprehending, the silence of doors and windows and the quivering voice of the light, submitting with bent head to the presence of his soul and his destiny—an old man, who conceives not that all the powers of this world, like so many heedful servants, are mingling and keeping vigil in his room, who suspects not that the very sun itself is supporting in space the little table against which he leans, or that every star in heaven and every fiber of the soul are directly concerned in the movement of an eyelid that closes, or a thought that springs to birth—I have grown to believe that he, motionless as he is, does yet live in reality a deeper, more human, and more universal life than the lover who strangles his mistress, the captain who conquers in battle, or "the husband who avenges his honor."

I shall be told, perhaps, that a motionless life would be invisible, that therefore animation must be conferred upon it, and movement, and that such varied movement as would be acceptable is to be found only in the few passions of which use has hitherto been made. I do not know whether it be true that a static theatre is impossible. Indeed, to me it seems to exist already. Most of the tragedies of Aeschylus are tragedies without movement. In both the *Prometheus* and the *Suppliants,* events are lacking; and the entire tragedy of the *Choephori*— surely the most terrible drama of antiquity—does but cling, nightmare-like, around the tomb of Agamemnon, till murder darts forth, as a lightning flash, from the accumulation of prayers, ever falling back upon themselves. Consider, from this point of view, a few more of the finest tragedies of the ancients: *The Eumenides, Antigone, Electra, Oedipus at Colonus.* "They have admired," said Racine in his preface to *Berenice*, "they have admired the *Ajax* of Sophocles, wherein there is nothing but Ajax killing himself with regret for the fury into which he fell after the arms of Achilles were denied him. They have admired *Philoctetes,* whose entire subject is but the coming of Ulysses with intent to seize the arrows of Hercules. Even the *Oedipus,* though full of recognitions, contains less subject matter than the simplest tragedy of our days."

What have we here but life that is almost motionless? In most cases, indeed, you will find that psychological action—infinitely loftier in itself than mere material action, and truly, one might think, well-nigh indispensable—that psychological action even has been suppressed, or at least vastly diminished, in a truly marvelous fashion, with the result that the interest centers solely and entirely in the individual, face to face with the universe. Here we are no longer with the barbarians, nor is man now fretting himself in the midst of elementary passions, as though, forsooth, these were the only things worthy of note: he is at rest, and we have time to observe him. It is no longer a violent, exceptional moment of life that passes before our eyes —it is life itself. Thousands and thousands of laws there are, mightier and more venerable than those of passion; but these laws are silent, and discreet, and slow-moving; and hence it is only in the twilight that they can be seen and heard, in the meditation that comes to us at the tranquil moments of life.

When Ulysses and Neoptolemus come to Philoctetes and demand of him the arms of Hercules, their action is in itself as simple and ordinary as that of a man of our day who goes into a house to visit an invalid, of a traveler who knocks at the door of an inn, or of a mother who, by the fireside, awaits the return of her child. Sophocles indicates the character of his heroes by means of the lightest and quickest of touches. But it may safely be said that the chief interest of the tragedy does not lie in the struggle we witness between cunning and loyalty, between love of country, rancor, and headstrong pride. There is more beyond: for it is man's loftier existence that is laid bare to us. The poet adds to ordinary life something, I know not what, which is the poet's secret: and there comes to us a sudden revelation of life in its stupendous grandeur, in its submissiveness to the unknown powers, in its endless affinities, in its awe-inspiring mystery. Let but the chemist pour a few mysterious drops into a vessel that seems to contain the purest water, and at once masses of crystals will rise to the surface, thus revealing to us all that lay in abeyance there where nothing was visible before to our incomplete eyes. And even thus is it in *Philoctetes*; the primitive psychology of the three leading characters would seem to be merely the sides of the vessel containing the clear water; and this itself is our ordinary life, into which the poet is about to let fall the revelation-bearing drops of his genius. . . .

Indeed, it is not in the actions but in the words that are found the beauty and greatness of tragedies that are truly beautiful and great; and this not solely in the words that accompany and explain the action, for there must perforce be another dialogue besides the one which is superficially necessary. And indeed the only words that count in the play are those that at first seemed useless, for it is therein that the essence lies. Side by side with the necessary dialogue will you almost always find another dialogue that seems superfluous; but examine it carefully, and it will be borne home to you that this is the only one that the soul can listen to profoundly, for here alone is it the soul that is being addressed. You will see, too, that it is the quality and the scope of this unnecessary dialogue that determine the quality and the immeasurable range of the work. Certain it is that, in the ordinary drama, the indispensable dialogue by no means corresponds to reality; and it is just those words that are spoken by the side of the rigid, apparent truth, that constitute the mysterious beauty of the most beautiful tragedies, inasmuch as these are words that conform to a deeper truth, and one that lies incomparably nearer to the invisible soul by which the poem is upheld. One may even affirm that a poem draws the nearer to beauty and loftier truth in the measure that it eliminates words that merely explain the action, and substitutes for them others that reveal, not the so-called "soul-state," but I know not what intangible and unceasing striving of the soul toward its own beauty and truth. And so much the nearer, also, does it draw to the true life. To every man does it happen, in his workaday existence, that some situation of deep seriousness has to be unraveled by means of words. Reflect for an instant. At moments such as those—nay, at the most commonplace of times—is it the thing you say or the reply you receive that has the most value? Are not other forces, other words one cannot hear, brought into being, and do not these determine the event? What I say often counts for so little; but my presence, the attitude of my soul, my future and my past, that which will take birth in me and that which is dead, a secret thought, the stars that approve, my destiny, the thousands of mysteries which surround me and float about yourself—all this it is that speaks to you at that tragic moment, all this it is that brings to me your answer. There is all this beneath every one of my words, and each one of yours; it is this, above all, that we see, it is this above all, that we hear, ourselves notwithstanding. If you have come, you, the "outraged husband," the "deceived lover," the "forsaken wife," intending to kill me, your arm will not be stayed by my most moving entreaty; but it may be that there will come toward you, at that moment, one of these unexpected forces; and my soul, knowing of their vigil near to me, may whisper a secret word whereby, haply, you shall be disarmed. These are the spheres wherein adventures come to issue, this is the dialogue whose echo should be heard. And it is this echo that one does hear—extremely attenuated and variable, it is true—in some of the great works mentioned above. But might we not try to draw nearer to the spheres where it is "in reality" that everything comes to pass?

It would seem as though the endeavor were being made. Some time ago, when dealing with *The Master Builder*, which is the one of Ibsen's dramas wherein this dialogue of the "second degree" attains the deepest tragedy, I endeavored, unskillfully enough, to fix its secrets. For indeed they are kindred handmarks traced on the same wall by the same sightless being, groping for the same light. "What is it," I asked, "what is it that, in *The Master Builder*, the poet has added to life, thereby making it appear so strange, so profound, and so disquieting beneath its trivial surface?" The discovery is not easy, and the old master hides from us more than one secret. It would even seem as though what he has wished to say were but little by the side of what he has been compelled to say. He has freed certain powers of the soul that have never yet been free, and it may well be that these have held him in thrall. "Look you, Hilda," exclaims Solness, "look you! There is sorcery in you, too, as there is in me. It is this sorcery that imposes action on the powers of the beyond. And we *have* to yield to it. Whether we want to or not, we *must*."

There is sorcery in them, as in us all. Hilda and Solness are, I believe, the first characters in drama who feel, for an instant, that they are living in the atmosphere of the soul; and the discovery of this essential life that exists in

them, beyond the life of every day, comes fraught with
terror. Hilda and Solness are two souls to whom a flash
has revealed their situation in the true life. Diverse ways
there are by which knowledge of our fellows may come to
us. Two or three men, perhaps, are seen by me almost daily.
For a long time it is merely by their gestures that I
distinguish them, by their habits, be these of mind or
body, by the manner in which they feel, act, or think. But,
in the course of every friendship of some duration, there
comes to us a mysterious moment when we seem to perceive
the exact relationship of our friend to the unknown that
surrounds him, when we discover the attitude destiny
has assumed toward him. And it is from this moment that
he truly belongs to us. We have seen, once and for all, the
treatment held in store for him by events. We know that
however such a one may seclude himself in the recesses
of his dwelling, in dread lest his slightest movement stir
up that which lies in the great reservoirs of the future, his
forethought will avail him nothing, and the innumerable
events that destiny holds in reserve will discover him wherever he hides, and will knock one after another at his door.
And even so do we know that this other will sally forth in
vain in pursuit of adventure. He will ever return empty-
handed. No sooner are our eyes thus opened than unerring
knowledge would seem to spring to life, self-created, within
our soul; and we know with absolute conviction that the
event that seems to be impending over the head of a certain
man will nevertheless most assuredly not reach him.

From this moment a special part of the soul reigns over
the friendship of even the most unintelligent, the obscurest
of men. Life has become, as it were, transposed. And when
it happens that we meet one of the men who are thus known
to us, though we do but speak of the snow that is falling or
the women that pass by, something there is in each of us
which nods to the other, which examines and asks its
questions without our knowledge, which interests itself in
contingencies and hints at events that it is impossible for
us to understand. . . .

Thus do I conceive it to be with Hilda and Solness; it is
thus surely that they regard each other. Their conversation
resembles nothing that we have ever heard, inasmuch as
the poet has endeavored to blend in one expression both
the inner and the outer dialogue. A new, indescribable
power dominates this somnambulistic drama. All that is

said therein at once hides and reveals the sources of an unknown life. And if we are bewildered at times, let us not forget that our soul often appears to our feeble eyes to be but the maddest of forces, and that there are in man many regions more fertile, more profound, and more interesting than those of his reason or his intelligence. . . .

WILLIAM BUTLER YEATS
(1865-1939)

Language, Character, and Construction[1] (1904)

WHAT ATTRACTS me to drama is that it is, in the most obvious way, what all the arts are upon a last analysis. A farce and a tragedy are alike in this, that they are a moment of intense life. An action is taken out of all other actions; it is reduced to its simplest form, or at any rate to as simple a form as it can be brought to without our losing the sense of its place in the world. The characters that are involved in it are freed from everything that is not a part of that action; and whether it is, as in the less important kinds of drama, a mere bodily activity, a hairbreadth escape or the like, or as it is in the more important kinds, an activity of the souls of the characters, it is an energy, an eddy of life purified from everything but itself. The dramatist must picture life in action, with an unpreoccupied mind, as the musician pictures her in sound and the sculptor in form.

Our plays[2] must be literature or written in the spirit of literature. The modern theatre has died away to what it is because the writers have thought of their audiences instead of their subject. An old writer saw his hero, if it was a play of character, or some dominant passion, if it was a play of passion, like *Phèdre* or *Andromaque,* moving before him, living with a life he did not endeavor to control. The persons acted upon one another as they were

[1] W. B. Yeats, *Plays and Controversies* (London: Macmillan & Co., Ltd. 1923), pp. 91–93, 103, 117–24. Copyright 1924 by The Macmillan Co., 1952 by Bertha Georgie Yeats. Reprinted by permission of The Macmillan Co.

[2] In a letter offering the Abbey Theatre to the Irish National Theatre Company, Miss Horniman asked Yeats to state his plans for the theatre. "The Play, the Player and the Scene," from which this excerpt on the play is drawn, constitutes Yeats's program for the theatre.

bound by their natures to act, and the play was dramatic, not because he had sought out dramatic situations for their own sake, but because will broke itself upon will and passion upon passion. Then the imagination began to cool, the writer began to be less alive, to seek external aids, remembered situations, tricks of the theatre, that had proved themselves again and again. His persons no longer will have a particular character, but he knows that he can rely upon the incidents, and he feels himself fortunate when there is nothing in his play that has not succeeded a thousand times before the curtain has risen. Perhaps he has even read a certain guidebook to the stage published in France, and called *The Thirty-six Situations of Drama*. The costumes will be magnificent, the actresses will be beautiful, the Castle in Spain will be painted by an artist upon the spot. We will come from his play excited if we are foolish, or can condescend to the folly of others, but knowing nothing new about ourselves, and seeing life with no new eyes and hearing it with no new ears. The whole movement of theatrical reform in our day has been a struggle to get rid of this kind of play, and the sincere play, the logical play, that we would have in its place, will always seem, when we hear it for the first time, undramatic, unexciting. It has to stir the heart in a long-disused way, it has to awaken the intellect to a pleasure that ennobles and wearies. I was at the first performance of an Ibsen play given in England. It was *The Doll's House*, and at the fall of the curtain I heard an old dramatic critic say, "It is but a series of conversations terminated by an accident." So far, we here in Dublin mean the same thing as do Mr. Max Beerbohm, Mr. Walkley, and Mr. Archer, who are seeking to restore sincerity to the English stage, but I am not certain that we mean the same thing all through. The utmost sincerity, the most unbroken logic, give me, at any rate, but an imperfect pleasure if there is not a vivid and beautiful language. Ibsen has sincerity and logic beyond any writer of our time, and we are all seeking to learn them at his hands; but is he not a good deal less than the greatest of all times, because he lacks beautiful and vivid language? "Well, well, give me time and you shall hear all about it. If only I had Peter here now," is very like life, is entirely in its place where it comes, and when it is united to other sentences exactly like itself, one is moved, one knows not how, to pity and terror, and yet not moved as if the words themselves could sing and shine. Mr. Max Beerbohm wrote once that a play cannot have style because the people must talk as they talk in daily life. He was thinking, it is obvious, of a play made out of that typically modern life where there is no longer vivid speech. Blake says that a work of art must be minutely articulated by God or man, and man has too little help from that occasional collaborateur when he writes of people whose language has become abstract and dead. Falstaff gives one the sensation of reality, and when one remembers the abundant vocabulary of a time when all but everything present to the mind was present to the senses, one imagines that his words were but little magnified from the words of such a man in real life. Language was still alive then, alive as it is in Gaelic today, as it is in English-speaking Ireland where the Schoolmaster or the newspaper has not corrupted it. I know that we are at the mere beginning, laboriously learning our craft, trying our hands in little plays for the most part, that we may not venture too boldly in our ignorance; but I never hear the vivid, picturesque, ever-varied language of Mr. Synge's persons without feeling that the great collaborateur has his finger in our business. May it not be that the only realistic play that will live as Shakespeare has lived, as Calderon has lived, as the Greeks have lived, will arise out of the common life, where language is as much alive as if it were new come out of Eden? After all, is not the greatest play, not the play that gives the sensation of an external reality, but the play in which there is the greatest abundance of life itself, of the reality that is in our minds? Is it possible to make a work of art, which needs every subtlety of expression if it is to reveal what hides itself continually, out of a dying, or at any rate a very ailing, language? and all language but that of the poets and of the poor is already bedridden. We have, indeed, persiflage, the only speech of educated men that expresses a deliberate enjoyment of words; but persiflage is not a true language. It is impersonal; it is not in the midst but on the edge of life; it covers more character than it discovers: and yet, such as it is, all our comedies are made out of it.

What the ever-moving, delicately molded flesh is to human beauty, vivid musical words are to passion. Somebody has said that every nation begins with poetry and ends with algebra, and passion has always refused to express itself in algebraical terms.

Have we not been in error in demanding from our playwrights personages who do not transcend our common actions any more than our common speech? If we are in the right, all antiquity has been in error. The scholars of a few generations ago were fond of deciding that certain persons were unworthy of the dignity of art. They had, it may be, an overabounding preference for kings and queens, but we are, it may be, very stupid in thinking that the average man is a fit subject at all for the finest art. Art delights in the exception, for it delights in the soul expressing itself according to its own laws and arranging the world about it in its own pattern, as sand strewn upon a drum will change itself into different patterns, according to the notes of music that are sung or played to it. But the average man is average because he has not attained to freedom. Habit, routine, fear of public opinion, fear of punishment here or hereafter, a myriad of things that are "something other than human life," something less than flame, work their will upon his soul and trundle his body here and there. At the first performance of *Ghosts* I could not escape from an illusion unaccountable to me at the time. All the characters seemed to be less than life-size; the stage, though it was but the little Royalty stage, seemed larger than I had ever seen it. Little whimpering puppets moved here and there in the middle of that great abyss. Why did they not speak out with louder voices or move with freer gestures? What was it that weighed upon their souls perpetually? Certainly they were all in prison, and yet there was no prison. In India there are villages so obedient that all the jailer has to do is to draw a circle upon the ground with his staff, and to tell his thief to stand there so many hours; but what law had these people broken that they had to wander round that narrow circle all their lives? May not such art, terrible, satirical, inhuman, be the medicine of great cities, where nobody is ever alone with his own strength? Nor is Maeterlinck very different, for his persons "inquire after Jerusalem in the regions of the grave with weak voices almost inarticulate, wearying repose." Is it the mob that has robbed those angelic persons of the energy of their souls? Will not our next art be rather of the country, of great open spaces, of the soul rejoicing in

itself? Will not the generations to come begin again
to have an overabounding faith in kings and queens,
in masterful spirits, whatever names we call them by? I had
Molière with me on my way to America, and as I read I
seemed to be at home in Ireland listening to that conversation of the people which is so full of riches because
so full of leisure, or to those old stories of the folk which
were made by men who believed so much in the soul, and so
little in anything else, that they were never entirely certain
that the earth was solid under the foot-sole. What is there
left for us, that have seen the newly discovered stability of
things changed from an enthusiasm to a weariness, but to
labor with a high heart, though it may be with weak hands,
to rediscover an art of the theatre that shall be joyful,
fantastic, extravagant, whimsical, beautiful, resonant, and
altogether reckless? The arts are at their greatest when
they seek for a life growing always more scornful of everything that is not itself and passing into its own fullness,
as it were, ever more completely as all that is created out
of the passing mode of society slips from it; and attaining
that fullness, perfectly it may be—and from this is tragic
joy and the perfectness of tragedy—when the world itself
has slipped away in death. We, who are believers, cannot
see reality anywhere but in the soul itself, and seeing it
there we cannot do other than rejoice in every energy,
whether of gesture, or of action, or of speech, coming out
of the personality, the soul's image, even though the very
laws of nature seem as unimportant in comparison as did
the laws of Rome to Coriolanus when his pride was upon
him. Has not the long decline of the arts been but the
shadow of declining faith in an unseen reality?

> If the sun and moon would doubt,
> They'd immediately go out.

Men of letters have sometimes said that the characters
of a romance or of a play must be typical. They mean that
the character must be typical of something which exists in
all men because the writer has found it in his own mind. It
is one of the most inexplicable things about human nature
that a writer, with a strange temperament, an Edgar Allan
Poe, let us say, made what he is by conditions that never
existed before, can create personages and lyric emotions,

which startle us by being at once bizarre and an image of
our own secret thoughts. Are we not face to face with the
microcosm, mirroring everything in universal nature? It
is no more necessary for the characters created by a
romance writer, or a dramatist, to have existed before,
than for his own personality to have done so; characters
and personality alike, as is perhaps true in the instance
of Poe, may draw half their life not from the solid earth but
from some dreamy drug. This is true even of historical
drama, for it was Goethe, the founder of the historical
drama of Germany, who said: "We do the people of
history the honor of naming after them the creations of our
own minds." All that a dramatic writer need do is to
persuade us, during the two hours' traffic of the stage,
that the events of his play did really happen. He must
know enough of the life of his country, or of history, to
create this illusion, but no matter how much he knows he
will fail if his audience is not ready to give up something
of the dead letter. If his mind is full of energy he will
not be satisfied with little knowledge, but he will be far more
likely to alter incidents and characters, willfully even as it
may seem, than to become a literal historian. It was one of
the complaints against Shakespeare, in his own day, that
he made Sir John Falstaff out of a praiseworthy old Lollard
preacher. One day, as he sat over Holinshed's *History of
England*, he persuaded himself that Richard the Second,
with his French culture, "his too great friendliness to his
friends," his beauty of mind, and his fall before dry,
repelling Bolingbroke, would be a good image for an
accustomed mood of fanciful, impracticable lyricism in
his own mind. The historical Richard has passed away forever and the Richard of the play lives more intensely, it
seems, than did ever living man. Yet Richard the Second,
as Shakespeare made him, could never have been born before the Renaissance, before the Italian influence, or even
one hour before the innumerable streams that flowed in
upon Shakespeare's mind; the innumerable experiences we
can never know, brought Shakespeare to the making of
him. He is typical not because he ever existed, but because
he has made us know of something in our minds we had
never known of had he never been imagined.

Emotion of Multitude[3]

I have been thinking a good deal about plays lately, and I have been wondering why I dislike the clear and logical construction which seems necessary if one is to succeed on the Modern Stage. It came into my head the other day that this construction, which all the world has learned from France, has everything of high literature except the emotion of multitude. The Greek drama has got the emotion of multitude from its chorus, which called up famous sorrows, long-leaguered Troy, much-enduring Odysseus, and all the gods and heroes to witness, as it were, some well-ordered fable, some action separated but for this from all but itself. The French play delights in the well-ordered fable, but by leaving out the chorus it has created an art where poetry and imagination, always the children of far-off multitudinous things, must of necessity grow less important than the mere will. This is why, I said to myself, French dramatic poetry is so often a little rhetorical, for rhetoric is the will trying to do the work of the imagination. The Shakespearean Drama gets the emotion of multitude out of the subplot which copies the main plot, much as a shadow upon the wall copies one's body in the firelight. We think of *King Lear* less as the history of one man and his sorrows than as the history of a whole evil time. Lear's shadow is in Gloster, who also has ungrateful children, and the mind goes on imagining other shadows, shadow beyond shadow till it has pictured the world. In *Hamlet*, one hardly notices, so subtly is the web woven, that the murder of Hamlet's father and the sorrow of Hamlet are shadowed in the lives of Fortinbras and Ophelia and Laertes, whose fathers, too, have been killed. It is so in all the plays, or in all but all, and very commonly the subplot is the main plot working itself out in more ordinary men and women, and so doubly calling up before us the image of multitude. Ibsen and Maeterlinck have on the other hand created a new form, for they get multitude from the Wild Duck in the Attic, or from the Crown at the bottom of the Fountain, vague symbols that set the mind wandering from idea to idea, emotion to

[3] W. B. Yeats, "Emotion of Multitude," *Ideas of Good and Evil* (London: A. H. Bullen, 1913), pp. 339–41.

emotion. Indeed all the great Masters have understood, that there cannot be great art without the little limited life of the fable, which is always the better the simpler it is, and the rich, far-wandering, many-imaged life of the half-seen world beyond it. There are some who understand that the simple unmysterious things living as in a clear noonlight are of the nature of the sun, and that vague many-imaged things have in them the strength of the moon. Did not the Egyptian carve it on emerald that all living things have the sun for father and the moon for mother, and has it not been said that a man of genius takes the most after his mother?

JOHN GALSWORTHY
(1867-1933)

Some Platitudes Concerning Drama[1] (1909)

A DRAMA must be shaped so as to have a spire of meaning. Every grouping of life and character has its inherent moral; and the business of the dramatist is so to pose the group as to bring that moral poignantly to the light of day. Such is the moral that exhales from plays like *Lear, Hamlet,* and *Macbeth.* But such is not the moral to be found in the great bulk of contemporary Drama. The moral of the average play is now, and probably has always been, the triumph at all costs of a supposed immediate ethical good over a supposed immediate ethical evil.

The vice of drawing these distorted morals has permeated the Drama to its spine; discolored its art, humanity, and significance; infected its creators, actors, audience, critics; too often turned it from a picture into a caricature. A Drama which lives under the shadow of the distorted moral forgets how to be free, fair, and fine—forgets so completely that it often prides itself on having forgotten.

Now, in writing plays, there are, in this matter of the moral, three courses open to the serious dramatist. The first is: To definitely set before the public that which it wishes to have set before it, the views and codes of life by which the public lives and in which it believes. This way is the most common, successful, and popular. It makes the dramatist's position sure, and not too obviously authoritative.

The second course is: To definitely set before the public those views and codes of life by which the dramatist himself lives, those theories in which he himself believes, the more effectively if they are the opposite of what the public wishes to have placed before it, presenting them so

[1] John Galsworthy, "Some Platitudes Concerning Drama," *The Inn of Tranquility: Studies and Essays* (New York: Charles Scribner's Sons, 1919), pp. 189–202.

that the audience may swallow them like powder in a spoonful of jam.

There is a third course: To set before the public no cut-and-dried codes, but the phenomena of life and character, selected and combined, *but not distorted,* by the dramatist's outlook, set down without fear, favor, or prejudice, leaving the public to draw such poor moral as nature may afford. This third method requires a certain detachment; it requires a sympathy with, a love of, and a curiosity as to, things for their own sake; it requires a far view, together with patient industry, for no immediately practical result.

It was once said of Shakespeare that he had never done any good to anyone, and never would. This, unfortunately, could not, in the sense in which the word "good" was then meant, be said of most modern dramatists. In truth, the good that Shakespeare did to humanity was of a remote, and, shall we say, eternal nature; something of the good that men get from having the sky and the sea to look at. And this partly because he was, in his greater plays at all events, free from the habit of drawing a distorted moral. Now, the playwright who supplies to the public the facts of life distorted by the moral which it expects, does so that he may do the public what he considers an immediate good, by fortifying its prejudices; and the dramatist who supplies to the public facts distorted by his own advanced morality, does so because he considers that he will at once benefit the public by substituting for its worn-out ethics, his own. In both cases the advantage the dramatist hopes to confer on the public is immediate and practical.

But matters change, and morals change; men remain —and to set men, and the facts about them, down faithfully, so that they draw for us the moral of their natural actions, may also possibly be of benefit to the community. It is, at all events, harder then to set men and facts down, as they ought, or ought not to be. This, however, is not to say that a dramatist should, or indeed can, keep himself and his temperamental philosophy out of his work. As a man lives and thinks, so will he write. But it is certain, that to the making of good drama, as to the practice of every other art, there must be brought an almost passionate love of discipline, a white heat of self-respect, a desire to make the truest, fairest, best thing in one's power; and that to these must be added an eye that does not flinch. Such qualities alone will bring to a drama the selfless character which soaks it with inevitability.

The word "pessimist" is frequently applied to the few dramatists who have been content to work in this way. It has been applied, among others, to Euripides, to Shakespeare, to Ibsen; it will be applied to many in the future. Nothing, however, is more dubious than the way in which these two words "pessimist" and "optimist" are used; for the optimist appears to be he who cannot bear the world as it is, and is forced by his nature to picture it as it ought to be, and the pessimist one who cannot only bear the world as it is, but loves it well enough to draw it faithfully. The true lover of the human race is surely he who can put up with it in all its forms, in vice as well as in virtue, in defeat no less than in victory; the true seer he who sees not only joy but sorrow, the true painter of human life one who blinks at nothing. It may be that he is also, incidentally, its true benefactor.

In the whole range of the social fabric there are only two impartial persons, the scientist and the artist, and under the latter heading such dramatists as desire to write not only for today, but for tomorrow, must strive to come.

But dramatists being as they are made—past remedy— it is perhaps more profitable to examine the various points at which their qualities and defects are shown.

The plot! A good plot is that sure edifice which slowly rises out of the interplay of circumstance on temperament, and temperament on circumstance, within the enclosing atmosphere of an idea. A human being is the best plot there is; it may be impossible to see why he is a good plot, because the idea within which he was brought forth cannot be fully grasped; but it is plain that *he is a good plot*. He is organic. And so it must be with a good play. Reason alone produces no good plots; they come by original sin, sure conception, and instinctive after-power of selecting what benefits the germ. A bad plot, on the other hand, is simply a row of stakes, with a character impaled on each— characters who would have liked to live, but came to untimely grief; who started bravely, but fell on these stakes, placed beforehand in a row, and were transfixed one by one, while their ghosts stride on, squeaking and gibbering, through the play. Whether these stakes are made of facts or of ideas, according to the nature of the dramatist who planted them, their effect on the unfortunate characters

is the same; the creatures were begotten to be staked, and
staked they are! The demand for a good plot, not un-
frequently heard, commonly signifies: "Tickle my sensations by stuffing the play with arbitrary adventures, so
that I need not be troubled to take the characters
seriously. Set the persons of the play to action, regardless
of time, sequence, atmosphere, and probability!"

Now, true dramatic action is what characters do, at
once contrary, as it were, to expectation, and yet because
they have already done other things. No dramatist should
let his audience know what is coming; but neither should
he suffer his characters to act without making his audience
feel that those actions are in harmony with temperament,
and arise from previous known actions, together with the
temperaments and previous known actions of the other
characters in the play. The dramatist who hangs his characters to his plot, instead of hanging his plot to his characters, is guilty of cardinal sin.

The dialogue! Good dialogue again is character, mar-
shaled so as continually to stimulate interest or excitement. The reason good dialogue is seldom found in plays
is merely that it is hard to write, for it requires not only a
knowledge of what interests or excites, but such a feeling for
character as brings misery to the dramatist's heart when his
creations speak as they should not speak—ashes to his
mouth when they say things for the sake of saying them—
disgust when they are "smart."

The art of writing true dramatic dialogue is an austere
art, denying itself all license, grudging every sentence
devoted to the mere machinery of the play, suppressing
all jokes and epigrams severed from character, relying for
fun and pathos on the fun and tears of life. From start
to finish good dialogue is handmade, like good lace; clear,
of fine texture, furthering with each thread the harmony
and strength of a design to which all must be subordinated.

But good dialogue is also spiritual action. In so far as
the dramatist divorces his dialogue from spiritual action
—that is to say, from progress of events, or toward events
which are significant of character—he is stultifying τὸ
δρᾶμα the thing done; he may make pleasing disquisitions,
he is not making drama. And in so far as he twists character to suit his moral or his plot, he is neglecting a first principle, that truth to Nature which alone invests art with
handmade quality.

The dramatist's license, in fact, ends with his design. In conception alone he is free. He may take what character or group of characters he chooses, see them with what eyes, knit them with what idea, within the limits of his temperament; but once taken, seen, and knitted, he is bound to treat them like a gentleman, with the tenderest consideration of their mainsprings. Take care of character; action and dialogue will take care of themselves! The true dramatist gives full rein to his temperament in the scope and nature of his subject; having once selected subject and characters, he is just, gentle, restrained, neither gratifying his lust for praise at the expense of his offspring, nor using them as puppets to flout his audience. Being himself the nature that brought them forth, he guides them in the course predestined at their conception. So only have they a chance of defying Time, which is always lying in wait to destroy the false, topical, or fashionable, all—in a word—that is not based on the permanent elements of human nature. The perfect dramatist rounds up his characters and facts within the ring-fence of a dominant idea which fulfills the craving of his spirit; having got them there, he suffers them to live their own lives.

Plot, action, character, dialogue! But there is yet another subject for a platitude. Flavor! An impalpable quality, less easily captured than the scent of a flower, the peculiar and most essential attribute of any work of art! It is the thin, poignant spirit which hovers up out of a play, and is as much its differentiating essence as is caffeine of coffee. Flavor, in fine, is the spirit of the dramatist projected into his work in a state of volatility, so that no one can exactly lay hands on it, here, there, or anywhere. This distinctive essence of a play, marking its brand, is the one thing at which the dramatist cannot work, for it is outside his consciousness. A man may have many moods, he has but one spirit; and this spirit he communicates in some subtle, unconscious way to all his work. It waxes and wanes with the currents of his vitality, but no more alters than a chestnut changes into an oak.

For, in truth, dramas are very like unto trees, springing from seedlings, shaping themselves inevitably in accordance with the laws fast hidden within themselves, drinking sustenance from the earth and air, and in conflict with the natural forces round them. So they slowly come to full growth, until warped, stunted, or risen to fair and gracious height, they stand open to all the winds. And the trees that spring from each dramatist are of different race; he is the spirit of his own sacred grove, into which no stray tree can by any chance enter.

One more platitude. It is not unfashionable to pit one form of drama against another—holding up the naturalistic to the disadvantage of the epic; the epic to the belittlement of the fantastic; the fantastic to the detriment of the naturalistic. Little purpose is thus served. The essential meaning, truth, beauty, and irony of things may be revealed under all these forms. Vision over life and human nature can be as keen and just, the revelation as true, inspiring, delight-giving, and thought-provoking, whatever fashion be employed—it is simply a question of doing it well enough to uncover the kernel of the nut. Whether the violet come from Russia, from Parma, or from England, matters little. Close by the Greek temples at Paestum there are violets that seem redder, and sweeter, than any ever seen—as though they have sprung up out of the footprints of some old pagan goddess; but under the April sun, in a Devonshire lane, the little blue scentless violets capture every bit as much of the spring. And so it is with drama—no matter what its form—it need only be the "real thing," need only have caught some of the precious fluids, revelation, or delight, and imprisoned them within a chalice to which we may put our lips and continually drink.

And yet, starting from this last platitude, one may perhaps be suffered to speculate as to the particular forms that our renascent drama is likely to assume. For our drama is renascent, and nothing will stop its growth. It is not renascent because this or that man is writing, but because of a new spirit. A spirit that is no doubt in part the gradual outcome of the impact on our home-grown art, of Russian, French, and Scandinavian influences, but which in the main rises from an awakened humanity in the conscience of our time.

What, then, are to be the main channels down which the renascent English drama will float in the coming years? It is more than possible that these main channels will come to be two in number and situate far apart.

The one will be the broad and clear-cut channel of naturalism, down which will course a drama poignantly shaped, and inspired with high intention, but faithful to the seething and multiple life around us, drama such as

some are inclined to term photographic, deceived by a
seeming simplicity into forgetfulness of the old proverb,
"*Ars est celare artem*," and oblivious of the fact that, to be
vital, to grip, such drama is in every respect as dependent
on imagination, construction, selection, and elimination—
the main laws of artistry—as ever was the romantic or
rhapsodic play. The question of naturalistic technique
will bear, indeed, much more study than has yet been given
to it. The aim of the dramatist employing it is obviously to
create such an illusion of actual life passing on the stage as
to compel the spectator to pass through an experience of
his own, to think, and talk, and move with the people he
sees thinking, talking, and moving in front of him. A false
phrase, a single word out of tune or time, will destroy that
illusion and spoil the surface as surely as a stone heaved
into a still pool shatters the image seen there. But this
is only the beginning of the reason why the naturalistic is
the most exacting and difficult of all techniques. It is easy
enough to *reproduce* the exact conversation and movements of persons in a room; it is desperately hard to
produce the perfectly natural conversation and movements
of those persons, when each natural phrase spoken and
each natural movement made has not only to contribute
toward the growth and perfection of a drama's soul, but
also to be a revelation, phrase by phrase, movement by
movement, of essential traits of character. To put it
another way, naturalistic art, when alive, indeed to be alive
at all, is simply the art of manipulating a procession of
most delicate symbols. Its service is the swaying and
focusing of men's feelings and thought in the various
departments of human life. It will be like a steady lamp,
held up from time to time, in whose light things will be
seen for a space clearly and in due proportion, freed from
the mists of prejudice and partisanship.

And the other of these two main channels will, I think,
be a twisting and delicious stream, which will bear on its
breast new barques of poetry, shaped, it may be, like prose,
but a prose incarnating through its fantasy and symbolism
all the deeper aspirations, yearning, doubts, and mysterious
stirrings of the human spirit; a poetic prose drama,
emotionalizing us by its diversity and purity of form and
invention, and whose province will be to disclose the elemental soul of man and the forces of Nature, not perhaps
as the old tragedies disclosed them, not necessarily in the

epic mood, but always with beauty and in the spirit of discovery.

Such will, I think be the two vital forms of our drama in the coming generation. And between these two forms there must be no crude unions; they are too far apart, the cross is too violent. For, where there is a seeming blend of lyricism and naturalism, it will on examination be found, I think, to exist only in plays whose subjects or settings—as in Synge's *Playboy of the Western World,* or in Mr. Masefield's *Nan*—are so removed from our ken that we cannot really tell, and therefore do not care, whether an absolute illusion is maintained. The poetry which may and should exist in naturalistic drama, can only be that of perfect rightness of proportion, rhythm, shape—the poetry, in fact, that lies in all vital things. It is the ill-mating of forms that has killed a thousand plays. We want no more bastard drama; no more attempts to dress out the simple dignity of everyday life in the peacock's feathers of false lyricism; no more straw-stuffed heroes or heroines; no more rabbits and goldfish from the conjurer's pockets, nor any limelight. Let us have starlight, moonlight, sunlight, and the light of our own self-respects.

BERNARD SHAW
(1856-1950)

How to Write a Popular Play[1] (1909)

. . . The FORMULA for the well made play is so easy that I give it for the benefit of any reader who feels tempted to try his hand at making the fortune that awaits all successful manufacturers in this line. First, you "have an idea" for a dramatic situation. If it strikes you as a splendidly original idea, whilst it is in fact as old as the hills, so much the better. For instance, the situation of an innocent person convicted by circumstances of a crime may always be depended on. If the person is a woman, she must be convicted of adultery. If a young officer, he must be convicted of selling information to the enemy, though it is really a fascinating female spy who has ensnared him and stolen the incriminating document. If the innocent wife, banished from her home, suffers agonies through her separation from her children, and, when one of them is dying (of any disease the dramatist chooses to inflict), disguises herself as a nurse and attends it through its dying convulsion until the doctor, who should be a serio-comic character, and if possible a faithful old admirer of the lady's, simultaneously announces the recovery of the child and the discovery of the wife's innocence, the success of the play may be regarded as assured if the writer has any sort of knack for his work. Comedy is more difficult, because it requires a sense of humor and a good deal of vivacity; but the process is essentially the same: it is the manufacture of a misunderstanding. Having manufactured it, you place its culmination at the end of the last act but one, which is the point at which the manufacture of the play begins. Then you make your first act out of the necessary introduction of the characters to the audience, after

[1] George Bernard Shaw, Preface, *Three Plays by Brieux* (New York: Brentano's, 1911), pp. xxii–xxvii. Reprinted by permission of The Public Trustee and The Society of Authors.

elaborate explanations, mostly conducted by servants, so-
licitors, and other low life personages (the principals must
all be dukes and colonels and millionaires), of how the
misunderstanding is going to come about. Your last act
consists, of course, of clearing up the misunderstanding,
and generally getting the audience out of the theatre as
best you can.

Now please do not misunderstand me as pretending
that this process is so mechanical that it offers no opportunity for the exercise of talent. On the contrary, it is
so mechanical that without very conspicuous talent nobody
can make much reputation by doing it, though some can
and do make a living at it. And this often leads the
cultivated classes to suppose that all plays are written by
authors of talent. As a matter of fact the majority of
those who in France and England make a living by writing
plays are unknown and, as to education, all but illiterate.
Their names are not worth putting on the playbill, because
their audiences neither know nor care who the author is, and
often believe that the actors improvise the whole piece, just
as they in fact do sometimes improvise the dialogue. To
rise out of this obscurity you must be a Scribe or a Sardou,
doing essentially the same thing, it is true, but doing it
wittily and ingeniously, at moments almost poetically,
and giving the persons of the drama some touches of real
observed character.

WHY THE CRITICS ARE ALWAYS WRONG

Now it is these strokes of talent that set the critics
wrong. For the talent, being all expended on the formula,
at least consecrates the formula in the eyes of the critics.
Nay, they become so accustomed to the formula that at
last they cannot relish or understand a play that has
grown naturally, just as they cannot admire the Venus
of Milo because she has neither a corset nor high heeled
shoes. They are like the peasants who are so accustomed to
food reeking with garlic that when food is served to them
without it they declare that it has no taste and is not food
at all.

This is the explanation of the refusal of the critics of
all nations to accept great original dramatists like Ibsen
and Brieux as real dramatists, or their plays as real
plays. No writer of the first order needs the formula any

more than a sound man needs a crutch. In his simplest
mood, when he is only seeking to amuse, he does not
manufacture a plot: he tells a story. He finds no difficulty
in setting people on the stage to talk and act in an
amusing, exciting or touching way. His characters have
adventures and ideas which are interesting in themselves,
and need not be fitted into the Chinese puzzle of a plot.

THE INTERPRETER OF LIFE

But the great dramatist has something better to do than
to amuse either himself or his audience. He has to interpret
life. This sounds a mere pious phrase of literary criticism;
but a moment's consideration will discover its meaning
and its exactitude. Life as it appears to us in our daily
experience is an unintelligible chaos of happenings. You
pass Othello in the bazaar in Aleppo, Iago on the jetty
in Cyprus, and Desdemona in the nave of St. Mark's
in Venice without the slightest clue to their relations to one
another. The man you see stepping into a chemist's shop
to buy the means of committing murder or suicide, may,
for all you know, want nothing but a liver pill or a tooth-
brush. The statesman who has no other object than to make
you vote for his party at the next election, may be starting
you on an incline at the foot of which lies war, or revolution, or a smallpox epidemic or five years off your lifetime.
The horrible murder of a whole family by the father who
finishes by killing himself, or the driving of a young girl
on to the streets, may be the result of your discharging an
employee in a fit of temper a month before. To attempt to
understand life from merely looking on at it as it happens
in the streets is as hopeless as trying to understand public
questions by studying snapshots of public demonstrations.
If we possessed a series of cinematographs of all the
executions during the Reign of Terror, they might be
exhibited a thousand times without enlightening the audiences in the least as to the meaning of the Revolution:
Robespierre would perish as "un monsieur" and Marie
Antoinette as "une femme." Life as it occurs is senseless:
a policeman may watch it and work in it for thirty years
in the streets and courts of Paris without learning as
much of it or from it as a child or a nun may learn from a
single play by Brieux. For it is the business of Brieux to
pick out the significant incidents from the chaos of daily

happenings, and arrange them so that their relation to one
another becomes significant, thus changing us from bewildered spectators of a monstrous confusion to men
intelligently conscious of the world and its destinies. This
is the highest function that man can perform—the greatest
work he can set his hand to; and this is why the great
dramatists of the world, from Euripides and Aristophanes
to Shakespear and Molière, and from them to Ibsen and
Brieux, take that majestic and pontifical rank which seems
so strangely above all the reasonable pretensions of mere
strolling actors and theatrical authors.

HOW THE GREAT DRAMATISTS TORTURE THE PUBLIC

Now if the critics are wrong in supposing that the formula of the well made play is not only an indispensable factor
in playwriting, but is actually the essence of the play itself
—if their delusion is rebuked and confuted by the practice
of every great dramatist, even when he is only amusing
himself by story telling, what must happen to their poor
formula when it impertinently offers its services to a playwright who has taken on his supreme function as the Interpreter of Life? Not only has he no use for it, but he must
attack and destroy it; for one of the very first lessons he has
to teach to a play-ridden public is that the romantic conventions on which the formula proceeds are all false, and
are doing incalculable harm in these days when everybody reads romances and goes to the theatre. Just as the
historian can teach no real history until he has cured his
readers of the romantic delusion that the greatness of a
queen consists in her being a pretty woman and having her
head cut off, so the playwright of the first order can do
nothing with his audiences until he has cured them of
looking at the stage through the keyhole, and sniffing round
the theatre as prurient people sniff round the divorce
court. The cure is not a popular one. The public suffers
from it exactly as a drunkard or a snuff taker suffers
from an attempt to conquer the habit. The critics especially,
who are forced by their profession to indulge immoderately
in plays adulterated with falsehood and vice, suffer so
acutely when deprived of them for a whole evening that
they hurl disparagements and even abuse and insult at
the merciless dramatist who is torturing them. To a bad
play of the kind they are accustomed to they can be cruel

through superciliousness, irony, impatience, contempt, or even a Rochefoucauldian pleasure in a friend's misfortune. But the hatred provoked by deliberately inflicted pain, the frantic denials as of a prisoner at the bar accused of a disgraceful crime, the clamor for vengeance thinly disguised as artistic justice, the suspicion that the dramatist is using private information and making a personal attack: all these are to be found only when the playwright is no mere *marchand de plaisir*, but, like Brieux, a ruthless revealer of hidden truth and a mighty destroyer of idols.

FEDERICO GARCÍA LORCA
(1899-1936)

The Authority of the Theatre[1] (1934)

MY DEAR FRIENDS: Some time ago I made a solemn promise to refuse every kind of tribute, banquet, or celebration which might be made in my honor, first, because I know that each of them drives another nail into our literary coffin, and second, because I have found that there is nothing more depressing than a formal speech made in our honor, and nothing sadder than organized applause, however sincere.

Besides, between ourselves, I hold that banquets and scrolls bring bad luck upon the one who receives them, bad luck springing from the relief of his friends who think: "Now we have done our duty by him."

A banquet is a gathering of professional people who eat with us, and where we find thrown together every kind of person who likes us least.

Rather than do honor to poets and dramatists, I should prepare challenges and attacks, in which we should be told roundly and passionately: "Are you afraid of doing this?" "Are you incapable of expressing a person's anguish at the sea?" "Daren't you show the despair of soldiers who hate war?"

Necessity and struggle, grounded on a critical love, temper the artist's soul, which easy flattery makes effeminate and destroys. The theatres are full of deceiving sirens, garlanded with hothouse roses, and the public is content, and applauds dummy hearts and superficial dialogue; but the dramatic poet who wishes to save himself from oblivion must not forget the open fields with their wild roses, fields moistened by the dawn where peasants toil,

---

[1] Federico García Lorca, "The Prophecy of Lorca," translated by Albert E. Sloman, *Theatre Arts*, October, 1950, pp. 38–39. Reprinted by courtesy of Francisco García Lorca and Albert E. Sloman. This address was delivered after the opening of *Yerma*.

and the pigeon, wounded by a mysterious hunter, which is dying amongst the rushes with no one to hear its grief.

Shunning sirens, flattery, and congratulations, I have accepted nothing in my honor, on the occasion of the first night of *Yerma*; but it has been the greatest pleasure of my short life as a writer to learn that the theatre world of Madrid was asking the great Margarita Xirgu, an actress with an impeccable artistic career, luminary of the Spanish theatre, and admirable interpreter of the part of Yerma, together with the company which so brilliantly supports her, for a special production.

For the interest and attention in a notable theatrical endeavor which this implies, I wish, now that we are all together, to give to you my deepest and sincerest thanks. I am not speaking tonight as an author, nor as a poet, nor as a simple student of the rich panorama of man's life, but as an ardent lover of the theatre of social action. The theatre is one of the most useful and expressive instruments for a country's edification, the barometer which registers its greatness or its decline. A theatre which in every branch, from tragedy to vaudeville, is sensitive and well oriented, can in a few years change the sensibility of a people, and a broken-down theatre, where wings have given way to cloven hoofs, can coarsen and benumb a whole nation.

The theatre is a school of weeping and of laughter, a rostrum where men are free to expose old and equivocal standards of conduct, and explain with living examples the eternal norms of the heart and feelings of man.

A nation which does not help and does not encourage its theatre is, if not dead, dying; just as the theatre which does not feel the social pulse, the historical pulse, the drama of its people, and catch the genuine color of its landscape and of its spirit, with laughter or with tears, has no right to call itself a theatre, but an amusement hall, or a place for doing that dreadful thing known as "killing time." I am referring to no one, and I want to offend no one; I am not speaking of actual fact, but of a problem that has yet to be solved.

Every day, my friends, I hear about the crisis in the theatre, and I feel always that the defect is not one before our eyes, but deep down in its very nature; it is not a defect of the flower we have before us, of a play, that is, but deeply rooted; in short, a defect of organization. Whilst actors and authors are in the hands of managements that are completely commercial, free, without either literary or state control of any kind, managements devoid of all judgment and offering no kind of safeguard, actors, authors, and the whole theatre will sink lower every day, beyond all hope of salvation.

The delightful light theatre of revue, vaudeville, and farce, forms of which I am a keen spectator, could maintain and even save itself; but plays in verse, the historical play, and the so-called Spanish *zarzuela*, will suffer more and more setbacks, because they are forms which make great demands and which admit of real innovations, and there is neither the authority nor the spirit of sacrifice to impose them on a public which has to be overruled from above, and often contradicted and attacked. The theatre must impose itself on the public, not the public on the theatre. To do this, authors and actors must, whatever the cost, again assume great authority, because the theatregoing public is like a school child; it reveres the stern, severe teacher who demands justice and sees justice done; and puts pins on the chairs of the timid and flattering ones who neither teach themselves nor allow anyone else to teach.

The public can be taught—I say public, of course, not people—it can be taught; for, some years ago, I saw Debussy and Ravel howled down, and I have been present since at loud ovations given by a public of ordinary people to the very works which were earlier rejected. These authors were imposed by the high judgment of authority, superior to that of the ordinary public, just as were Wedekind in Germany and Pirandello in Italy, and so many others.

This has to be done for the good of the theatre and for the glory and status of its interpreters. Dignity must be maintained, in the conviction that such dignity will be amply repaid. To do otherwise is to tremble behind the flies, and kill the fantasies, imagination, and charm of the theatre, which is always, always an art, and will always be a lofty art, even though there may have been a time when everything which pleased was labeled art, so that the tone was lowered, poetry destroyed, and the stage itself a refuge for thieves.

Art above all else. A most noble art, and you, my actor friends, artists above all else. Artists from head to foot, since through love and vocation you have risen to the make-believe and pitiful world of the boards. Artists by occupation and by preoccupation. From the smallest theatre to the most eminent, the word "Art" should be written in auditoriums and dressing rooms, for if not we shall have to write the word "Commerce" or some other that I dare not say. And distinction, discipline, and sacrifice and love.

I don't want to lecture you, because I should be the one receiving a lecture. My words are dictated by enthusiasm and conviction. I labor under no delusion. As a good Andalusian I can think coolly, because I come of an ancient stock. I know that truth does not lie with him who says, "Today, today, today," eating his bread close to the hearth, but with him who watches calmly at a distance the first light of dawn in the country.

I know that those people who say, "Now, now, now," with their eyes fixed on the small jaws of the box office are not right, but those who say, "Tomorrow, tomorrow, tomorrow," and feel the approach of the new life which is hovering over the world.

JEAN GIRAUDOUX
(1882-1944)

Two Laws[1]

TWO LAWS govern—if I may thus express myself—the
eternal status of the playwright.

The first law defines the sad and slightly ridiculous
position of the playwright toward those of his characters he
has created and given to the theatre. Just as a character,
before being played by an actor, is docile toward the
author, familiar, and a part of him—as you may judge
from my own creations—so once he appears before the
audience he becomes a stranger and indifferent. The first
actor who plays him represents the first in a series of
reincarnations by which the character draws further and
further away from his creator and escapes him forever.

In fact, this is true of the play in its entirety. From the
first performance on, it belongs to the actors. The author
wandering in the wings is a kind of ghost whom the
stagehands detest if he listens in or is indiscreet. After the
hundredth performance, particularly if it is a good play,
it belongs to the public. In reality the only thing the playwright can call his own is his bad plays. The independence
of those of his characters who have succeeded is complete:
the life they lead on road tours or in America is a constant
denial of their filial obligations. So while the hero of your
novels follows you everywhere, calling you "father" or "pa-
pa," those of your stage characters you chance to meet—
as I have—in Carcassonne or Los Angeles, have become
total strangers to you.

It was largely to punish them for this independence that
Goethe, Claudel, and so many other writers wrote a new
version for their favorite heroines—but in vain. The new
Marguerite, the new Hélène, or the new Violaine left

1 Jean Giraudoux, *Visitations* (Neuchâtel and Paris: Ides et
Calendes) pp. 121–28. Reprinted by courtesy of Jean-Pierre
Giraudoux.

their creators just as quickly. Once I was at a performance
of Claudel's *Tidings Brought to Mary*. That day, at least,
this law operated in my favor: I noted that the play be-
longed more to me than to Claudel.

How many playwrights are forced to seek in an actor or
actress the memory or reflection of their sons and daughters
who have escaped; just as, in daily life, other parents look
for the same thing in a son-in-law or daughter-in-law. . . .
On the terrace of the Café Weber, in the lobby during
a dress rehearsal, on the lawn of the country house of a
noted actress, how often we have met such couples: Fey-
deau and Mme. Cassive, Jules Renard and Suzanne
Desprez, Maurice Donnay and Réjane. The woman slightly
inattentive, the man alert, reminiscing, chatty, full of
questions, was talking of his absent "child."

The second law, a corollary and inverse of the first,
defines the wonderful position of the playwright toward his
era and its events, and indicates his role therein. Here,
if I wish to be sincere, I must strip myself and my colleagues of all false modesty. The figure who in the play is
merely a voice, without personality, without responsibility,
implacable, but a historian and an avenger, exists in a given
era in flesh and blood: the playwright himself. Of all writers
in the theatre worthy of the name, one should be able to
say, when they appear: Add the archangel! It is futile to
believe that a year or a century can find the resonance
and elevation ultimately befitting the emotional debate
and effort represented by each period of our passage on
earth, if it does not have a spokesman of its tragedy or
drama in order to reach its heights or plumb its depths.
Tragedy and drama are the confession which humanity—
this army of salvation and ruin—must also make in
public, without reticence and in loudest tones, for the
echo of its voice is clearer and more real than its voice
itself. Make no mistake about it. The relationship between
the theatre and religious ceremonial is obvious; it is no
accident that in former times plays were given on all
occasions in front of our cathedrals. The theatre is most at
home on the open space in front of a church. That is what
the audience goes to, on gala evenings in the theatre:
toward the illuminated confession of its petty and giant
destinies.

Calderon is humanity confessing its thirst for eternity,
Corneille its dignity, Racine its weakness, Shakespeare

its appetite for life, Claudel its state of sin and salvation, Goethe its humanity, Kleist its vividness. Epochs have not come to terms with themselves unless crowds, dressed in their most striking costumes of confession, so as, to increase the solemnity of the occasion, come to these radiant confessionals called theatres and arenas, to listen to their own avowals of cowardice and sacrifice, hatred and passion. And unless they also cry: Add the prophet!

For there is no theatre save that of divination. Not that false divination which gives names and dates, but the real thing: the one which reveals to men these amazing truths—that the living must live, that the living must die, that autumn follows summer, spring follows winter, that there are four elements, happiness, millions of catastrophes, that life is a reality, that it is a dream, that man lives by peace, that man lives by blood; in short, what they will never know.

That is theatre: the public recall of those incredible splendors whose visions disturb and overwhelm audiences by night. But—and this it is which heartens me—already by dawn the lesson and the memory are diluted, no doubt in order to make the writer's mission a daily one. Of such is the performance of a play: the sudden awareness in the spectator of the permanent state of this living and indifferent humanity—passion and death.

Translated by Joseph M. Bernstein

EUGENE O'NEILL
(1888-1953)

Memoranda on Masks[1] (1932)

NOT MASKS for all plays, naturally. Obviously not for plays conceived in purely realistic terms. But masks for certain types of plays, especially for the new modern play, as yet only dimly foreshadowed in a few groping specimens, but which must inevitably be written in the future. For I hold more and more surely to the conviction that the use of masks will be discovered eventually to be the freest solution of the modern dramatist's problem as to how—with the greatest possible dramatic clarity and economy of means —he can express those profound hidden conflicts of the mind which the probings of psychology continue to disclose to us. He must find some method to present this inner drama in his work, or confess himself incapable of portraying one of the most characteristic preoccupations and uniquely significant, spiritual impulses of his time. With his old—and more than a bit senile!—standby of realistic technique, he can do no more than, at best, obscurely hint at it through a realistically disguised surface symbolism, superficial and misleading. But that, while sufficiently beguiling to the sentimentally mystical, is hardly enough. A comprehensive expression is demanded here, a chance for eloquent presentation, a new form of drama projected from a fresh insight into the inner forces motivating the actions and reactions of men and women (a new and truer characterization, in other words)—a drama of souls, and the adventures of "free wills," with the masks that govern them and constitute their fates.

For what, at bottom, is the new psychological insight into human cause and effect but a study in masks, an exercise in unmasking? Whether we think the attempted

[1] Eugene O'Neill, "Memoranda on Masks," *The American Spectator,* November, 1932, p. 3. The *American Spectator* articles reprinted by courtesy of Mrs. Carlotta Monterey O'Neill.

unmasking has been successful, or has only created for itself new masks, is of no importance here. What is valid, what is unquestionable, is that this insight has uncovered the mask, has impressed the idea of mask as a symbol of inner reality upon all intelligent people of today; and I know they would welcome the use of masks in the theatre as a necessary, dramatically revealing new convention, and not regard them as any "stunty" resurrection of archaic props.

This was strikingly demonstrated for me in practical experience by *The Great God Brown*, which ran in New York for eight months, nearly all of that time in Broadway theatres—a play in which the use of masks was an integral part of the theme. There was some misunderstanding, of course. But so is there always misunderstanding in the case of every realistic play that attempts to express anything beyond what is contained in a human-interest newspaper story. In the main, however, *The Great God Brown* was accepted and appreciated by both critics and public— a fairly extensive public, as its run gives evidence.

I emphasize this play's success because the fact that a mask drama, the main values of which are psychological, mystical, and abstract, could be played in New York for eight months, has always seemed to me a more significant proof of the deeply responsive possibilities in our public than anything that has happened in our modern theatre before or since.

(2)

Looked at from even the most practical standpoint of the practicing playwright, the mask *is* dramatic in itself, *has always* been dramatic in itself, *is* a proven weapon of attack. At its best, it is more subtly, imaginatively, suggestively dramatic than any actor's face can ever be. Let anyone who doubts this study the Japanese Noh masks, or Chinese theatre masks, or African primitive masks—or right here in America the faces of the big marionettes Robert Edmond Jones made for the production of Stravinsky's *Oedipus*, or Benda's famous masks, or even photographs of them.

(3)

Dogma for the new masked drama. One's outer life passes in a solitude haunted by the masks of others; one's inner life passes in a solitude hounded by the masks of oneself.

(4)

With masked mob a new type of play may be written in which the Mob as King, Hero, Villain, or Fool will be the main character—The Great Democratic Play!

(5)

Why not give all future Classical revivals entirely in masks? *Hamlet,* for example. Masks would liberate this play from its present confining status as exclusively a "star vehicle." We would be able to see the great drama we are now only privileged to read, to identify ourselves with the figure of Hamlet as a symbolic projection of a fate that is in each of us, instead of merely watching a star giving us his version of a great acting role. We would even be able to hear the sublime poetry as the innate expression of the spirit of the drama itself, instead of listening to it as realistic recitation—or ranting—by familiar actors.

(6)

Consider Goethe's *Faust,* which, psychologically speaking, should be the closest to us of all the Classics. In producing this play, I would have Mephistopheles wearing the Mephistophelean mask of the face of Faust. For is not the whole of Goethe's truth *for our time* just that Mephistopheles and Faust are one and the same—*are* Faust?

Second Thoughts[2] (1932)

What would I change in past productions of my plays if I could live through them again? Many things. In some plays, considerable revision of the writing of some of the

[2] Eugene O'Neill, "Second Thoughts," *The American Spectator,* December, 1932, p. 2.

scenes would strike me as imperative. Other plays—*The First Man, Gold, Welded, The Fountain*—I would dismiss as being too painfully bungled in their present form to be worth producing at all.

But one thing I most certainly would not change: the use of masks in *The Hairy Ape,* in my arrangement of Coleridge's "Ancient Mariner," in *All God's Chillun Got Wings* (the symbol of the African primitive mask in the last part of the play, which, in the production in Russian by the Moscow Kamerny Theatre I saw in Paris, is dramatically intensified and emphasized), in *The Great God Brown* and, finally, in *Lazarus Laughed,* in which all the characters except Lazarus remain masked throughout the play. I regard this use of masks as having been uniformly successful.

The change I would make would be to call for more masks in some of these productions and to use them in other productions where they were not used before. In *The Emperor Jones,* for example. All the figures in Jones's flight through the forest should be masked. Masks would dramatically stress their phantasmal quality, as contrasted with the unmasked Jones, intensify the supernatural menace of the tomtom, give the play a more complete and vivid expression. In *The Hairy Ape* a much more extensive use of masks would be of the greatest value in emphasizing the theme of the play. From the opening of the fourth scene, where Yank begins to think, he enters into a masked world; even the familiar faces of his mates in the forecastle have become strange and alien. They should be masked, and the faces of everyone he encounters thereafter, including the symbolic gorilla's.

In *All God's Chillun Got Wings,* all save the seven leading characters should be masked; for all the secondary figures are part and parcel of the Expressionistic background of the play, a world at first indifferent, then cruelly hostile, against which the tragedy of Jim Harris is outlined. In *The Great God Brown* I would now make the masks symbolize more definitely the abstract theme of the play instead of, as in the old production, stressing the more superficial meaning that people wear masks before other people and are mistaken by them for their masks.

In *Marco Millions* all the people of the East should be masked—Kublai, the Princess Kokachin, all of them! For anyone who has been in the East, or who has read

Eastern philosophy, the reason for this is obvious. It is an exact dramatic expression of West confronted by East. Morever, it is the only possible way to project this contrast truthfully in the theatre, for Western actors cannot convey Eastern character realistically, and their only chance to suggest it convincingly is with the help of masks.

As for *Strange Interlude,* that is an attempt at the new masked psychological drama which I have discussed before, without masks—a successful attempt, perhaps, in so far as it concerns only surfaces and their immediate subsurfaces, but not where, occasionally, it tries to probe deeper.

With *Mourning Becomes Electra,* masks were called for in one draft of the three plays. But the Classical connotation was too insistent. Masks in that connection demand great language to speak—which let me out of it with a sickening bump! So I had to discard them. There was a realistic New England insistence in my mind, too, which would have barred great language even in a dramatist capable of writing it, an insistence on the clotted and clogged and inarticulate. So it evolved ultimately into the "masklike faces," which expressed my intention tempered by the circumstances. However, I should like to see *Mourning Becomes Electra* done entirely with masks, now that I can view it solely as a psychological play, quite removed from the confusing preoccupations the Classical derivation of its plot once caused me. Masks would emphasize the drama of the life and death impulses that drive the characters on to their fates and put more in its proper secondary place, as a frame, the story of the New England family.

A Dramatist's Notebook[3] (1933)

I advocate masks for stage crowds, mobs—wherever a sense of impersonal, collective mob psychology is wanted. This was one reason for such an extensive use of them in *Lazarus Laughed.* In masking the crowds in that play, I was visualizing an effect that, intensified by dramatic lighting, would give an audience visually the sense of the Crowd, not as a random collection of individuals, but as a collective whole, an entity. When the Crowd speaks, I

[3] Eugene O'Neill, "A Dramatist's Notebook," *The American Spectator,* January, 1933, p. 2.

wanted an audience to hear the voice of Crowd mind,
Crowd emotion, as one voice of a body composed of, but
quite distinct from, its parts.

And, for more practical reasons, I wanted to preserve
the different crowds of another time and country from the
blighting illusion-shattering recognitions by an audience
of the supers on the stage. Have you ever seen a production of *Julius Caesar?* Did the Roman mob ever suggest to
you anything more Roman than a gum-chewing Coney
Island Mardi Gras or, in the case of a special all-star
revival, a gathering of familiar-faced modern actors
masquerading uncomfortably in togas? But with masks—
and the proper intensive lighting—you would have been
freed from these recognitions; you would have been able
to imagine a Roman mob; you would not even have recognized the Third Avenue and Brooklyn accents among the
supers, so effectively does a mask change the quality of a
voice.

It was interesting to watch, in the final rehearsals of
The Great God Brown, how after using their masks for
a time the actors and actresses reacted to the demand
made by the masks that their bodies become alive and
expressive and participate in the drama. Usually it is only
the actors' faces that participate. Their bodies remain bored
spectators that have been dragged off to the theatre when
they would have much preferred a quiet evening in the
upholstered chair at home.

Meaning no carping disrespect to our actors. I have
been exceedingly lucky in having had some exceptionally
fine acting in the principal roles in my plays, for which I am
exceedingly grateful. Also some damned poor acting. But
let that pass. Most of the poor acting occurred in the
poor plays, and there I hold only myself responsible. In
the main, wherever a part challenged the actors' or actresses' greatest possibilities, they have reacted to the challenge with a splendid creative energy and skill. Especially,
and this is the point I want to make now, where the play
took them away from the strictly realistic parts they were
accustomed to playing. They always welcomed any opportunity that gave them new scope for their talents. So
when I argue here for a non-realistic imaginative theatre
I am hoping, not only for added scope for playwright
and director and scenic designer, but also for a chance for
the actor to develop his art beyond the narrow range to

which our present theatre condemns it. Most important of
all, from the standpoint of future American culture, I am
hoping for added imaginative scope for the audience,
a chance for a public I know is growing yearly more
numerous and more hungry in its spiritual need to participate in imaginative interpretations of life rather than
merely identify itself with faithful surface resemblances of
living.

I harp on the word "imaginative" — and with intention!
But what do I mean by an "imaginative" theatre —
(where I hope for it, for example, in the subtitle of
Lazarus Laughed: A Play for an Imaginative Theatre)?
I mean the one true theatre, the age-old theatre, the
theatre of the Greeks and Elizabethans, a theatre that
could dare to boast — without committing a farcical
sacrilege — that it is a legitimate descendant of the
first theatre that sprang, by virtue of man's imaginative
interpretation of life, out of his worship of Dionysus. I
mean a theatre returned to its highest and sole significant
function as a Temple where the religion of a poetical
interpretation and symbolical celebration of life is communicated to human beings, starved in spirit by their
soul-stifling daily struggle to exist as masks among the
masks of living!

But I anticipate the actors' objection to masks: that
they would extinguish their personalities and deprive them
of their greatest asset in conveying emotion by facial
expression. I claim, however, that masks would give them
the opportunity for a totally new kind of acting, that they
would learn many undeveloped possibilities of their art
if they appeared, even if only for a season or two, in
masked roles. After all, masks did not extinguish the
Greek actor, nor have they kept the acting of the East
from being an art.

BERTOLT BRECHT
(1898-1956)

A Short Organum for the Theatre[1] (1948)

PROLOGUE

THE FOLLOWING sets out to define an aesthetic drawn
from a particular kind of theatrical performance which
has been worked out in practice over the past few decades.
In the theoretical statements, excursions, technical indications occasionally published in the form of notes to the
writer's plays, aesthetics have only been touched on
casually and with comparative lack of interest. There you
saw a particular species of theatre extending or contracting
its social function, perfecting or sifting its artistic methods.
and establishing or maintaining its aesthetics—if the question arose—by rejecting or converting to its own use the
dominant conventions of morality or taste according to its
tactical needs. This theatre justified its tendency to draw
social conclusions by pointing to the social conclusions in
universally accepted works of art, which only fail to
strike the eye because they were the accepted conclusions.
As for the products of our own time, it held that their
lack of any worthwhile content was a sign of decadence; it
accused these entertainment emporiums of having degen-
erated into a branch of the bourgeois narcotics traffic.
The stage's inaccurate representations of our social life,
including those classed as so-called Naturalism, led it
to call for scientifically exact representations; the taste-
less rehashing of empty visual or spiritual palliatives
for the noble logic of the multiplication table. The cult
of beauty, conducted with hostility toward learning
and contempt for the useful, was dismissed by it as
itself contemptible, especially as nothing beautiful re-

[1] Bertolt Brecht, "Kleines Organon für das Theater," *Ver-
suche, 12* (Frankfurt-am-Main: Suhrkamp Verlag). Copyright
1953 by Suhrkamp Verlag, Berlin. Translated by John Willett,
and edited by Eric Bentley. Reprinted by permission of Suhrkamp Verlag and John Willett.

sulted. The battle was for a theatre fit for the scientific age, and where its planners found it too hard to borrow or steal from the armory of aesthetic concepts enough weapons to defend themselves against the aesthetes of the press, they simply threatened "to transform the means of enjoyment into an instrument of instruction, and to convert certain amusement establishments into organs of mass communication" (Notes to the opera *Mahagonny*[2]); i.e., to emigrate from the realm of the merely enjoyable. Aesthetics, that heirloom of a now depraved and parasitic class, was in such a lamentable state that a *Theater* would certainly have gained in reputation and in elbow room if it had rechristened itself *Thaeter* [sic]. And yet what we achieved in the way of theatre for a scientific age was not science but theatre, and the accumulated innovations worked out during the Nazi period and the war—when practical demonstration was impossible—compel some attempt to set this species of theatre in its aesthetic background, or anyhow to sketch for it the outlines of a conceivable aesthetic. It would be an impossibly laborious business to explain the theory of theatrical Alienation[3] except within an aesthetic framework.

Today one could go so far as to compile an aesthetics of the exact sciences. Galileo spoke of the elegance of certain formulae and the point of an experiment; Einstein suggests that the sense of beauty has a part to play in the making of scientific discoveries; while the atomic physicist Robert Oppenheimer praises the scientific attitude, which

[2] A translation of *Mahagonny* is to be found in the *Mahagonny* record album, Columbia Records, New York, 1958. A translation of the Notes by John Willett is published in *The Score* (London: July, 1958). Excerpts appear in the Columbia album and in *The Playwright as Thinker* (New York: 1946) (E. B.).

[3] "Alienation" has become, in America at least, the standard translation of *Verfremdung*. It is not a perfect solution of the problem, as the English word has other meanings in translations of, for example, both Marx and Freud. "Estrangement," however, is probably even more confusing and would be translated into German as *Entfremdung*—even though the latter word has often been translated into English as Alienation! There *is* no perfect solution. The word Effect (in Alienation Effect) also gives trouble. As Mr. Willett says (*The Theatre of Bertolt Brecht*, p. 179): ". . . *Effekt* corresponded to our own stage use of the word *effects:* a *means* by which an effect of estrangement could be got" (E. B.).

"has its own kind of beauty and seems to suit mankind's
position on earth."[4]

So let us cause general dismay by revoking our decision to emigrate from the realm of the merely enjoyable, and even more general dismay by announcing
our decision to take up lodging there. Let us treat the
theatre as a place of entertainment, as is proper in an
aesthetic discussion, and try to discover what kind of
entertainment suits us best.

(1)

"Theatre" consists in this: in making live representations
of reported or invented happenings between human beings,
and doing so with a view to entertainment. At any rate that
is what we shall mean when we speak of theatre, whether
old or new.

(2)

To extend this definition we might add happenings
between humans and gods, but as we are only seeking to
establish bare essentials we can set such matters aside.
Even if we did accept such an extension we should still
have to say that the "theatre" setup's broadest function
was to give pleasure. Here is the noblest function that
we have found for "theatre."

(3)

From the first it has been the theatre's business to
entertain people, as it also has of all the other arts. It is
this business which always gives it its particular dignity;
it needs no other passport than fun, but this it has got
to have. We should not in any way be giving it a higher
status if we were to turn it, e.g., into a purveyor of morality; it would on the contrary run the risk of becoming
debased, and this would occur just as soon as it failed to
make its moral lesson enjoyable, and enjoyable to the
senses at that—a principle, admittedly, by which morality can only gain. Not even instruction can be demanded
of it; at any rate, no more utilitarian lesson than how to

---

[4] Dr. Oppenheimer's secretary reported to me her inability
to locate the source of this remark, here translated from the
German (E. B.).

move pleasurably, whether in the physical or in the spiritual sphere. The theatre must in short remain something entirely superfluous, though this also means that it is the superfluous for which we live. Nothing needs less justification than pleasures.

(4)

Thus what the ancients, following Aristotle, demanded of tragedy is nothing higher or lower than that it should entertain people. Theatre may be said to be derived from ritual, but that is only to say that it becomes theatre once the two have separated; what it brought over from the mysteries was not its former ritual function, but purely and simply the pleasure which accompanied this. And the catharsis of which Aristotle writes—cleansing by fear and pity, or from fear and pity—is a purification which is performed not only in a pleasurable way, but precisely for the purpose of pleasure. To ask or to accept more of the theatre is to set one's own mark too low.

(5)

Even when people speak of higher and lower degrees of pleasure, art stares impassively back at them; for it wishes to fly high and low and to be left in peace, so long as it can give pleasure to people.

(6)

Yet there are weaker (simple) and stronger (complex) pleasures which the theatre can create. The last-named, which are what we are dealing with in great drama, attain their climaxes rather like cohabitation does in love; they are more intricate, richer in communication, more contradictory and more productive of results.

(7)

And different periods' pleasures varied naturally according to the system under which people lived in society at the time. The Greek demos[5] ruled by tyrants had to be enter-

[5] Literally "the demos of the Greek circus" (J. W.).

tained differently from the feudal court of Louis XIV.
The theatre was required to deliver different representations of human social life: not just representations of a
different life, but also representations of a different sort.

(8)

According to the sort of entertainment which was
possible and necessary under the given conditions of
human social life the characters had to be given varying proportions, the situations to be constructed according to varying points of view. One has to tell a story in
quite different ways if these particular Greeks are to be
able to amuse themselves with the inevitability of divine
laws, where ignorance never mitigates the punishment; these
French with the graceful self-discipline demanded of the
great ones of this earth by a courtly code of duty; the
Englishmen of the Elizabethan age with the self-awareness
of the new individual personality, which was then uncontrollably bursting out.

(9)

And we have always to remember that the pleasure
given by representations of such different sorts hardly
ever depended on the representation's likeness to the thing
portrayed. Incorrectness, or considerable improbability
even, was hardly or not at all disturbing, so long as the
incorrectness had a certain consistency and the improbability remained of a constant kind. All that mattered was
the illusion of compelling momentum in the story told, and
this was created by all sorts of poetic and theatrical
means. Even today we are happy to overlook such in-
accuracies if we can get something out of the spiritual
purifications of Sophocles or the sacrificial acts of Racine
or the unbridled frenzies of Shakespeare, by trying to
grasp the immense or splendid emotions of the principal
characters concerned.

(10)

For of all the many sorts of representation of happenings between humans which the theatre has made since
ancient times, and which have given entertainment despite
their incorrectness and improbability, there are even

today an astonishing number that also give entertainment to us.

(11)

In establishing the extent to which we can be satisfied by representations from so many different periods —something that must have been impossible to the children of those vigorous periods themselves—are we not at the same time creating the suspicion that we have failed to discover the special pleasures, the proper entertainment of our own time?

(12)

Again, our enjoyment of the theatre must have become weaker than that of the ancients, even if our way of living in society is still sufficiently like theirs for it to be felt at all. We grasp the old works by a comparatively new method—empathy—on which they rely little. Thus the greater part of our enjoyment is drawn from other sources than those which our predecessors were able to exploit so fully. We are left safely dependent on beauty of language, on elegance of structure, on passages which stimulate our own private imaginations; in short, on the incidentals of the old works. These are precisely the poetical and theatrical means which hide the imprecisions of the story. Our theatres no longer have either the capacity or the wish to tell these stories, even the relatively recent ones of the great Shakespeare, at all clearly; i.e., to make the connection of events credible. And according to Aristotle—and we agree there—narrative is the soul of drama. We are more and more disturbed to see how crudely and carelessly human social life is represented, and that not only in old works but also in contemporary ones constructed according to the old recipes. Our whole way of appreciation is tending to get out of date.

(13)

It is the inaccurate way in which happenings between human beings are represented that restricts our pleasure in the theatre. The reason: we and our forebears have a different relationship to what is being shown.

(14)

For when we look about us for an entertainment whose impact is immediate, for a comprehensive and penetrating pleasure such as our theatre could give us by representations of human social life, we have to think of ourselves as children of a scientific age. Our life as human beings in society—i.e., our life—is determined by the sciences to a quite new extent.

(15)

A few hundred years ago a handful of people, working in different countries but in correspondence with one another, performed certain experiments by which they hoped to wring from Nature her secrets. Members of a class of craftsmen in the already powerful cities, they transmitted their discoveries to people who made practical use of them, without expecting more from the new sciences than personal profit for themselves. Crafts which had progressed by methods virtually unchanged during a thousand years now developed hugely; in many places, which became linked by competition, they gathered from all directions great masses of men, and these, adopting new forms of organization, started producing on a giant scale. Soon mankind was showing powers whose extent it would till that time scarcely have dared to dream of.

(16)

It was as if mankind now for the first time began a conscious and co-ordinated effort to make the planet that was its home fit to live on. Many of the earth's components, such as coal, water, oil, now became treasures. Steam was made to shift vehicles; a few small sparks and the twitching of frogs' legs revealed a natural force which produced light, carried sounds across continents, etc. In all directions man looked about himself with a new vision, to see how he could adapt to his convenience familiar but as yet unexploited objects. His surroundings changed increasingly from decade to decade, then from year to year, then almost from day to day. I who am writing this write it on a machine which at the time of my birth was unknown. I travel in the new vehicles with a rapidity that my grandfather could not imagine;

in those days nothing moved so fast. And I rise in the air, a thing that my father was unable to do. With my father I already spoke across the width of a continent, but it was together with my son that I first saw the motion pictures of the explosion at Hiroshima.

(17)

The new sciences may have made possible this vast alteration and all-important alterability of our surroundings, yet it cannot be said that their spirit determines everything that we do. The reason why the new way of thinking and feeling has not yet penetrated the great mass of men is that the sciences, for all their success in exploiting and dominating nature, have been stopped by the class which they brought to power—the bourgeoisie —from operating in another field where darkness still reigns, namely that of the relations which people have to one another during the exploiting and dominating process. This business, on which all alike depended, was performed without the new intellectual methods that made it possible, ever illuminating the mutual relationships of the people who carried it out. The new approach to nature was not applied to society.

(18)

In the event people's mutual relations have become harder to disentangle than ever before. The gigantic joint undertaking on which they are engaged seems more and more to split them into two groups; increases in production lead to increases in misery; only a minority gain from the exploitation of nature, and they do so only because they also exploit men. What might be progress for all then becomes advancement for a few, and an ever-increasing part of the productive process gets applied to creating means of destruction for mighty wars. During these wars the mothers of every nation, with their children pressed to them, scan the skies in horror for the deadly inventions of science.

(19)

The same attitude as men once showed in face of unpredictable natural catastrophes they now adopt toward

their own undertakings. The bourgeois class, which owes
to science an advancement that it was able, by insuring
that it alone enjoyed the fruits, to convert into domi-
nation, knows very well that its rule would come to an
end if the scientific eye were turned on its own undertakings. And so that new science which was founded about
a hundred years ago and deals with the character of
human society was born in the struggle between rulers
and ruled. Since then a certain scientific spirit has developed at the bottom, among the new class of workers
whose natural element is large-scale production; from
down there the great catastrophes are seen to be undertakings by the rulers.

(20)

But science and art meet on this ground, that both
are there to make men's life easier, the one setting out
to maintain, the other to entertain us. In the age to come
art will create entertainment from that new productivity
which can so greatly improve our maintenance and in itself,
if only it is left unshackled, may prove to be the greatest
pleasure of them all.

(21)

If we want now to surrender ourselves to this great
passion for producing, what ought our representations of
human social life to look like? Which is that productive
attitude in face of nature and of society which we children
of a scientific age would like to take up pleasurably in
our theatre?

(22)

The attitude is a critical one. Faced with a river, it
consists in regulating the river; faced with a fruit tree, in
spraying the fruit tree; faced with movement, in constructing vehicles and airplanes; faced with society, in turning
society upside down. Our representations of human social
life are designed for river dwellers, fruit farmers, build-
ers of vehicles, and upturners of society, whom we invite
into our theatres and beg not to forget their cheerful
occupations while we hand the world over to their minds
and hearts, for them to change as they think fit.

(23)

The theatre can only adopt such a free attitude if it lets itself be carried along by the strongest currents in its society, and associates itself with those who are necessarily most impatient to carry out great alterations there. The bare wish, if nothing else, to evolve an art fit for the times must drive our theatre of the scientific age straight out into the suburbs, where it can stand as it were wide open, at the disposal of those who live hard and produce much, so that they may be fruitfully entertained there with their great problems. They may find it hard to pay for our art, and immediately to grasp the new method of entertainment, and we shall have to learn in many respects what they need and how they need it; but we can be sure of their interest. For these men who seem so far apart from natural science are only apart from it because they are being forcibly kept apart; before they can get their hands on it they have first to develop and put into effect a new science of society; so that these are the true children of the scientific age, who alone can get the theatre moving if it is to move at all. A theatre which makes productivity its main source of entertainment has also to take it for its theme, with greater keenness than ever now that man is everywhere hampered by men from self-production; i.e., from maintaining himself, from entertaining and being entertained. The theatre has to become geared into reality if it is to be in a position to turn out effective representations of reality, and to be allowed to do so.

(24)

But this makes it simpler for the theatre to edge as close as possible to the apparatus of education and mass communication. For although we cannot bother it with the raw material of knowledge in all its variety, which would stop it from being enjoyable, it is still free to find enjoyment in teaching and inquiring. It constructs its workable representations of society, which are then in a position to influence society, wholly and entirely as a game. For those who are building society it sets out society's experiences, past and present alike, in such a manner that the audience can "appreciate" the feelings, insights,

and impulses which are distilled by the wisest, most active,
and most passionate among us from the events of the
day or the century. They must be entertained with the
wisdom that comes from the solution of problems, with
the anger that is a practical expression of sympathy
with the underdog, with the respect due to those who
respect humanity, or rather whatever is kind to humanity;
in short, with whatever delights those who are producing
something.

(25)

This also means that the theatre can let its spectators enjoy the particular ethic of their age, which springs
from productivity. A theatre which converts the critical
approach—i.e., our great productive method—into pleasure finds nothing in the ethical field which it must
do and a great deal that it can. Even the wholly anti-
social can be a source of enjoyment to society so long as
it is presented forcefully and on the grand scale. It then
often proves to have considerable powers of understanding and other unusually valuable capacities, applied admittedly to a destructive end. Even the bursting flood of
a vast catastrophe can be appreciated in all its majesty
by society, if society knows how to master it. Then we
make it our own.

(26)

For such an operation as this we can hardly accept
the theatre as we see it before us. Let us go into one
of these houses and observe the effect which it has on
the spectators. Looking about us, we see somewhat motionless figures in a peculiar condition: they seem strenuously to be tensing all their muscles, except where these
are flabby and exhausted. They scarcely communicate
with each other; their relations are those of a lot of
sleepers, though of such as dream restlessly because, as
is popularly said of those who have nightmares, they are
lying on their backs. True, their eyes are open, but they
stare rather than see, just as they listen rather than hear.
They look at the stage as if in a trance, an expression
which comes from the Middle Ages, the days of witches
and priests. Seeing and hearing are activities, and can
be pleasant ones, but these people seem relieved of ac-

tivity and like men to whom something is being done. This detached state, where they seem to be given over to vague but profound sensations, grows deeper the better the work of the actors, and so we, as we do not approve of this situation, should like them to be as bad as possible.

(27)

As for the world portrayed there, the world from which slices are cut in order to produce these moods and movements of the emotions, its appearance is such, produced from such slight and wretched stuff as a few pieces of cardboard, a little miming, a bit of text, that one has to admire the theatre folk who, with so feeble a reflection of the real world, can move the feelings of their audience so much more strongly than does the world itself.

(28)

In any case we should excuse these theatre folk, for the pleasures which they sell for money and fame could not be induced by an exacter representation of the world, nor could their inexact renderings be presented in a less magical way. Their capacity to represent people can be seen at work in various instances; it is especially the rogues and the minor figures who reveal their knowledge of humanity and differ one from the other, but the central figures have to be kept general, so that it is easier for the onlooker to identify himself with them, and at all costs each trait of character must be drawn from the narrow field within which everyone can say at once: that is how it is. For the spectator wants to be put in possession of quite definite sensations, just as a child does when it climbs onto one of the horses on a roundabout: the sensation of pride that it can ride, and has a horse; the pleasure of being carried, and whirled past other children; the adventurous daydreams in which it pursues others or is pursued, etc. In leading the child to experience all this the degree to which its wooden seat resembles a horse counts little, nor does it matter that the ride is confined to a small circle. The one important point for the spectators in these houses is that they should be able to swap a contradictory world for a consistent one,

one that they scarcely know for one of which they can dream.

(29)

This is the sort of theatre which we face in our operations, and so far it has been fully able to transmute our optimistic friends, whom we have called the children of the scientific era, into a cowed, credulous, hypnotized mass.

(30)

True, for about half a century they have been able to see rather more faithful representations of human social life, as well as individual figures who were in revolt against certain social evils or even against the structure of society as a whole. They felt interested enough to put up with a temporary and exceptional restriction of language, plot, and spiritual scope, for the fresh wind of the scientific spirit nearly withered the charms to which they had grown used. The sacrifice was not especially worthwhile. The greater subtlety of the representations subtracted from one pleasure without satisfying another. The field of human relationships came within our view, but not within our grasp. Our feelings, having been aroused in the old (magic) way, were bound themselves to remain unaltered.

(31)

For always and everywhere theatres were the amusement centers of a class which restricted the scientific spirit to the natural field, not daring to let it loose on the field of human relationships. The tiny proletarian section of the public, reinforced to a negligible and uncertain extent by renegade intellectuals, likewise still needed the old kind of entertainment as a relief from its predetermined way of life.

(32)

So let us march ahead! Away with all obstacles! Since we seem to have landed in a battle, let us fight! Have we not seen how disbelief can move mountains? Is it not enough that we should have found that something is being

kept from us? Before one thing and another there hangs
a curtain; let us draw it up!

(33)

The theatre as we know it shows the structure of society
(represented on the stage) as incapable of being influenced by society (in the auditorium). Oedipus, who offended against certain principles underlying the society of
his time, is executed: the gods see to that; they are beyond criticism. Shakespeare's great solitary figures, bearing on their breast the star of their fate, carry through
with irresistible force their futile and deadly outbursts;
they prepare their own downfall; life, not death, becomes
obscene as they collapse; the catastrophe is beyond criticism. Human sacrifices all round! Barbaric delights! We
know that the barbarians have their art. Let us create
another.

(34)

How much longer are our souls, leaving our "mere"
bodies under cover of the darkness, to plunge into those
dreamlike figures up on the stage, there to take part in
the crescendos and climaxes which "normal" life denies
us? What kind of release is it at the end of all these plays
(which is a happy end only for the conventions of the
period—suitable measures, the restoration of order—),
when we experience the dreamlike executioner's ax which
cuts short such crescendos as so many excesses? We slink
into *Oedipus*; for taboos still exist and ignorance is no
excuse before the law. Into *Othello*; for jealousy still
causes us trouble and everything depends on possession.
Into *Wallenstein*; for we need to be free for the competi-
tive struggle and to observe the rules, or it would peter out.
This deadweight of old habits is also needed for plays like
Ghosts and *The Weavers*, although there the social structure, in the shape of a "setting," presents itself as more
open to question. The feelings, insights, and impulses of
the chief characters are forced on us, and so we learn
nothing more about society than the setting can give.

(35)

We need a type of theatre which not only releases the
feelings, insights, and impulses possible within the partic-

ular historical field of human relations in which the action
takes place, but employs and encourages those thoughts
and feelings which help transform the field itself.

(36)

This field has to be defined in historically relative
terms. In other words we must drop our habit of taking
the different social structures of past periods, then strip-
ping them of everything that makes them different; until
they all look more or less like our own, which then acquires
a certain air of having been there all along, in other words
of permanence pure and simple. Instead we must leave
them their distinguishing marks and keep their imperma-
nence always before our eyes, so that our own period can
be realized to be impermanent too. (It is of course futile
to make use of gaudy coloring and folklore for this, such
as our theatres apply precisely in order to emphasize the
similarities in human behavior at different times. We shall
indicate the theatrical methods below.)

(37)

If we insure that our characters on the stage are moved
by social impulses and that these differ according to the
period, then we make it harder for our spectator to identify himself with them. He cannot just feel: that's how I
would act, but at most can say: if I had lived under those
circumstances. And if we play works dealing with our own
time as though they too were historical, then perhaps the
circumstances under which he himself acts will strike
him as equally odd; and this is where the critical attitude
begins.

(38)

The "historical conditions" must of course not be imagined (nor will they be so constructed) as mysterious
Powers (in the background); on the contrary, they are
created and maintained by men (and will in due course
be altered by them). It is the actions taking place before
us that allow us to see what they are.

(39)

If a character responds in a manner historically in
keeping with his period, and would respond otherwise in

other periods, does that not mean that he is simply "Everyman"? Undoubtedly a man will respond differently according to his circumstances and his class; if he were living at another time, or in his youth, or on the darker side of life, he would infallibly give a different response, though one still determined by the same factors and like anyone else's response in that position at that time. So should we not ask if there are further differences too? Where is the man himself, the living, unmistakable man, who is not quite identical with those identified with him? It is clear that his stage image must bring him to light, and that this particular contradiction is recreated in the image. The image that gives historical definition will retain something of the rough sketching which indicates traces of other movements and features all around the fully worked-out figure. Or imagine a man standing in a valley and making a speech in which he occasionally switches his views or simply utters sentences which contradict one another, so that the accompanying echo as it were confronts them.

(40)

Such images certainly demand a way of acting which will leave the spectator's intellect free and highly mobile. He has again and again to make what one might call hypothetical adjustments to our structure, by mentally switching off the motive forces of our society or by substituting others for them; a process which leads real conduct to acquire an element of "unnaturalness," thus allowing the real motive forces to be shorn of their naturalness and to become capable of manipulation.

(41)

It is the same as when an irrigation expert looks at a river together with its former bed and the various hypothetical courses which it might have followed if there had been a different tilt to the plateau or a different volume of water. And while he in his mind is looking at a new river, the socialist in his is hearing new kinds of talk from the laborers who work by it. Similarly in the theatre, the spectator should find the incidents set among such laborers likewise accompanied by echoes and by traces of sketching.

(42)

The kind of acting which was tried out at the Schiff-
bauerdamm-Theater in Berlin between the first and second
World Wars, with the object of producing such images,
is based on a technique of creating detachment, known
as the Alienation Effect. A representation that creates
detachment is one which allows us to recognize its subject, but at the same time makes it seem unfamiliar. The
classical and medieval theatre defamiliarized its characters by making them wear human or animal masks; the
Asiatic theatre even today uses musical and pantomimic
A Effects. Such devices were certainly a barrier to empathy (*Einfühlung*), and yet this technique owed more,
not less, to hypnotic suggestion than do those by which
empathy is achieved. The social aims of these old devices
were entirely different from our own.

(43)

The old A Effects quite remove the object represented
from the spectator's grasp, turning it into something that
cannot be altered. The new are not odd in themselves,
though the unscientific eye stamps anything strange as
odd. The new detachment is only designed to free socially
conditioned phenomena from that stamp of familiarity
which protects them against our grasp today.

(44)

For it seems impossible to alter what has long not
been altered. We are always coming on things that are
too obvious for us to bother to understand them. What
men experience among themselves they think of as "the"
human experience. A child, living in a world of old men,
learns how things work there. He knows the run of things
before he can walk. If anyone is bold enough to want
something further, he only wants to have it as an exception. Even if he realizes that the arrangements made for
him by "Providence" are only what has been provided by
society he is bound to see society, that vast collection of
beings like himself, as a whole that is greater than the sum
of its parts, and therefore not in any way to be influenced.
Moreover, he is accustomed to things that cannot be

influenced; and who mistrusts what he is used to? To transform himself from general passive acceptance to a corresponding state of suspicious inquiry he needs to develop that detached eye with which the great Galileo observed a swinging chandelier. He was amazed by this pendulum motion, as if he had not expected it and could not understand its occurring, and this enabled him to come on the rules by which it was governed. Here is the outlook, disconcerting but fruitful, which the theatre must provoke with its representations of human social life. It must amaze its public, and it achieves this by a technique of making the familiar seem strange.

(45)

This technique allows the theatre to make use in its representations of the new social scientific method known as dialectical materialism. In order to unearth society's laws of motion this method treats social situations as processes, and traces out all their inconsistencies. It regards nothing as existing except in so far as it changes; in other words, is in disharmony with itself. This also goes for those human feelings, opinions, and attitudes through which at any time the form of human social life finds its expression.

(46)

Our own period, which is transforming nature in so many and different ways, takes pleasure in understanding things so that we can intervene. There is a great deal to man, we say; so a great deal can be made out of him. He does not have to stay the way he is now, nor does he have to be seen only as he is now, but also as he might become. We must not start with him; we must start on him. This means, however, that I must not simply set myself in his place, but must set myself facing him, to represent us all. That is why the theatre must make what it shows seem strange.

(47)

In order to produce A Effects the actor has to discard whatever means he has learned of persuading the audience to identify itself with the characters which he plays. Aiming not to put his audience into a trance, he must not go into a trance himself. His muscles must remain

loose, for a turn of the head, e.g., with tautened neck
muscles, will "magically" lead the spectators' eyes
and even their heads to turn with it, and this can only de-
tract from any speculation or reaction which the gesture
may bring about. His way of speaking has to be free from
ecclesiastical singsong and from all those cadences which
lull the spectator so that the sense gets lost. Even when he
plays a man possessed he must not seem to be possessed
himself, for how can the spectator discover what possesses
the character if he does?

(48)

At no moment must he go so far as to be wholly transformed into the character played. The verdict: "He didn't
act Lear, he was Lear" would be an annihilating blow to
him. He has just to show the character, or rather he
has to do more than just get into it; this does not mean
that if he is playing passionate parts he must himself remain cold. It is only that his feelings must not at bottom
be those of the character, so that the audience's may not
at bottom be those of the character either. The audience
must have complete freedom here.

(49)

This principle—that the actor appears on the stage in
a double role, as Laughton and as Galileo; that the show-
man Laughton does not disappear in the Galileo whom he
is showing; from which this way of acting gets its name of
"epic"—comes to mean simply that the tangible, matter-
of-fact process is no longer hidden behind a veil; that
Laughton is actually there, standing on the stage and
showing us what he imagines Galileo to have been. Of
course the audience would not forget Laughton if he attempted the full change of personality, in that they would
admire him for it; but they would in that case miss his own
opinions and sensations, which would have been completely
swallowed up by the character. He would have taken its
opinions and sensations and made them his own, so that
a single homogeneous pattern would emerge, which he
would then make ours. In order to prevent this abuse the
actor must furthermore put some artistry into the act
of showing. An illustration may help: we find a gesture
which expresses one half of his attitude, that of showing,

if we make him smoke a cigar and then imagine him laying it down now and again in order to show us some further
characteristic attitude of the figure in the play. If we then
subtract all element of hurry from the image, and do
not read slackness into its refusal to be taut, we shall have
an actor who is fully capable of leaving us to our thoughts,
or to his own.

(50)

There needs to be yet a further change in the actor's
communication of these images, and it too makes the
process more "matter-of-fact." Just as the actor no longer
has to persuade the audience that it is the author's character and not he himself who is standing on the stage, so
also he need not pretend that the events taking place on
the stage have never been rehearsed, and are now happening for the first and only time. Schiller's distinction is
no longer valid: that the rhapsodist has to treat his material as wholly in the past; the mime his as wholly here and
now.[6] It should be apparent all through his performance
that "even at the start and in the middle he knows how
it ends" and he must "thus maintain a calm independence
throughout." He narrates the story of his character by
vivid portrayal, always knowing more than it does and
treating its "now" and "here" not as a pretense made
possible by the rules of the game, but as something to be
distinguished from yesterday and some other place, so as
to make visible the knotting together of the events.

(51)

This matters particularly in the portrayal of large-scale
events or ones where the outside world is abruptly changed,
as in wars and revolutions. The spectator can then have
the whole situation and the whole course of events set before him. He can, for instance, hear a woman speaking
and imagine her speaking differently, let us say in a few
weeks' time, or other women speaking differently at that
moment but in another place. This would be feasible if
the actress were to play as though the woman had lived
through the entire period and were now, out of her memory
and her knowledge of what happened next, recalling those

[6] Letter to Goethe, December 26, 1797 (B. B.).

utterances of hers which were important at the time; for
what is important here is what became important. To
make an individual seem unfamiliar in this way, as being
"this particular individual" and "this particular individual
at this particular moment" is only possible if there are
no illusions that the player is identical with the character,
or the performance with the actual event.

(52)

We shall find that this has meant scrapping yet another
illusion: that everybody behaves like the character concerned. "I am doing this" has become "I did this," and
now "he did this" has got to become "he did this, when
he might have done something else." It is an oversimpli-
fication if we make the actions fit the character and the
character fit the actions; the inconsistencies which are to
be found in the actions and characters of real people cannot be shown like that. The laws of motion of a society are
not to be demonstrated by "perfect examples," for "im-
perfection" (inconsistency) is an essential part both of
motion and of the thing moved. It is only necessary—but
absolutely necessary—that there should be something approaching experimental conditions: i.e., that a counter-
experiment should now and then be conceivable. In short,
this is a way of treating society as though all its actions
were performed as experiments.

(53)

Even if empathy, or self-identification with the character, can be usefully indulged in at rehearsals (something to be avoided in a performance), it has to be treated
as just one of a number of methods of observation. It
can help when rehearsing, for even though the contemporary theatre has applied it in an indiscriminate way it
has none the less led to subtle delineation of personality.
But it is the crudest form of empathy when the actor
simply asks: what should I be like if this or that were to
happen to me? what would it look like if I were to say this
and do that?—instead of asking: have I ever heard somebody saying this and doing that? in order to piece together all sorts of elements with which to construct a new

character such as would allow the story to have taken place
—and a good deal else. The coherence of the character
is in fact shown by the way in which its individual qualities
conflict with one another.

(54)

Observation is a major part of acting. The actor observes his fellow-men with all his nerves and muscles, in an
act of imitation which is at the same time a process of
the mind. For pure imitation would only bring out what
had been observed; and this is not enough, because the
original says what it has to say with too subdued a voice.
To achieve a character rather than a caricature, the actor
looks at people as though they were playing him their
actions, in other words as though they were advising him
to give their actions careful consideration.

(55)

Without opinions and objectives one can represent
nothing at all. Without knowledge one can show nothing;
how could one know what would be worth knowing? Unless the actor is satisfied to be a parrot or a monkey he
must master our period's knowledge of human social life
by himself joining in the war of the classes. Some people
may feel this to be degrading, because they rank art, once
the financial side has been settled, among the Highest
Things; but mankind's highest decisions are in fact fought
out on earth, not in the heavens; in the "external" world,
not inside people's heads. Nobody can stand above the
warring classes, for nobody can stand above the human
race. Society cannot share a common communication system so long as it is split into warring classes. For art,
to be "unpolitical" means only that it should ally itself
with the ruling group.

(56)

So the choice of viewpoint is also a major element of
the actor's art, and it has to be decided outside the theatre.
Like the transformation of nature, that of society is a
liberating act; and it is the joys of liberation which the
theatre of a scientific age has got to convey.

(57)

Let us go on to examine how, for instance, this view-point must affect the actor's reading of his part. It be-comes important that he should not "catch on" too quickly. Even if he straightway establishes the most natural cadences for his part, the least awkward way of speaking it, he still cannot regard its actual pronouncement as being ideally natural, but must think twice and take his own gen-eral opinions into account, then consider various other conceivable pronouncements; in short, take up the atti-tude of a man who just wonders. This is not only to pre-vent him from "fixing" a particular character too soon, so that it has to be stuffed out with afterthoughts because he has not waited to register all the other pronouncements, and especially those of the other characters; but also and principally in order to build into the character that element of "Not—But" on which so much depends if society, in the shape of the audience, is to be able to look at what takes place in such a way as to be able to affect it. Each actor, moreover, instead of concentrating on what suits him and calling it "human nature," must go above all for what does not suit him, is not his speciality. And along with his part he must commit to memory his first reactions, reserves, criticisms, shocks, so that they are not destroyed by being "swallowed up" in the final version but are preserved and perceptible; for character and all must not grow on the audience so much as strike it.

(58)

And the learning process must be co-ordinated so that the actor learns as the other actors are learning and develops his character as they are developing theirs. For the smallest social unit is not the single person but two people. In life too we develop one another.

(59)

Here we can learn something from our own theatre's deplorable habit of letting the dominant actor, the star, "come to the front" by getting all the other actors to work for him: he makes his character terrible or wise by forc-ing his partners to make theirs terrified or attentive.

Even if only to secure this advantage for all, and thus to help the story, the actors should sometimes swap roles with their partners during rehearsal, so that the characters can get what they need from one another. But it is also good for the actors when they see their characters copied or portrayed in another form. If the part is played by somebody of the opposite sex, the sex of the character will be more clearly brought out; if it is played by a comedian, whether comically or tragically, it will gain fresh aspects. By helping to develop the parts that correspond to his own, or at any rate standing in for their players, the actor strengthens the all-decisive social standpoint from which he has to present his character. The master is only the sort of master his servant lets him be, and so on.

(60)

A mass of operations to develop the character are carried out when it is introduced among the other characters of the play; and the actor will have to memorize what he himself has anticipated in this connection from his reading of the text. But now he finds out much more about himself from the treatment which he gets at the hands of the characters in the play.

(61)

The realm of attitudes adopted by the characters toward one another is what we call the realm of *Gestus*.[7] Physical attitude, tone of voice, and facial expression are all determined by a social *Gestus:* the characters are cursing, flattering, instructing one another, and so on. The attitudes which people adopt toward one another include even those attitudes which would appear to be quite private, such as the utterances of physical pain in an illness, or of religious faith. These expressions of a *Gestus* are usually highly complicated and self-contradictory, so

[7] This word has been left in German because its most natural English equivalent—the word Gesture—is far more misleading than even Alienation is (as a translation of *Verfremdung*). I quote Mr. Willett (*The Theatre of Bertolt Brecht*, p. 175): ". . . there is no single word by which *Gestus* can be translated. It is at once gesture and gist, attitude and point: one aspect of the relation between two people, studied singly, cut to essentials and physically or verbally expressed . . ." (E. B.).

that they cannot be rendered by any single word, and the
actor must take care that in giving his image the necessary emphasis he does not lose anything but emphasizes
the entire complex.

(62)

The actor masters his character by paying critical attention to its manifold utterances, as also to those of
his counterparts and of all the other characters involved.

(63)

To see what kinds of *Gestus* a play can embrace, let
us run through the opening scenes of a fairly modern
play, my own *Galileo*.[8] Since we wish at the same time to
find out what light the different utterances cast on one another we will assume that it is not our first introduction to
the play. It begins with the man of forty-six having his
morning wash, broken by occasional browsing in books and
by a lesson on the solar system for Andrea Sarti, a small
boy. In order to play this, surely you have got to know
that we shall be ending with the man of seventy-eight
having his supper, just after he has said good-by forever
to the same pupil. He is then more terribly altered than
this passage of time could possibly have brought about.
He wolfs his food with unrestrained greed, no other idea
in his head; he has rid himself of his educational mission
in shameful circumstances, as though it were a burden: he,
who once drank his morning milk without a care, greedy
to teach the boy. But does he really drink it without care?
Isn't the pleasure of drinking and washing all one with the
pleasure which he takes in the new ideas? Don't forget:
he thinks out of self-indulgence. . . . Is that good or bad?
I would advise you to represent it as good, since on this
point you will find nothing in the whole play to harm society, and more especially because you yourself are, I
hope, a gallant child of the scientific age. But take careful note: many horrible things will happen in this connection. The fact that the man who here acclaims the new

[8] Charles Laughton's English version is to be found in my
anthology, *From the Modern Repertoire*, Series Two, Denver,
1952 (and since 1953 distributed by the Indiana University
Press) (E. B.).

age will be forced at the end to beg this age to disown him as contemptible, even to dispossess him—all this is one relevant point. As for the lesson, you may like to decide whether the man's heart is so full that his mouth is over-flowing, so that he has to talk to anybody about it, even a child, or whether the child must first draw the knowledge out of him, by knowing him and showing interest. Again, there may be two of them who cannot restrain themselves, the one from asking, the other from giving the answer: a bond of this sort would be interesting, for one day it is going to be rudely snapped. Of course you will want the demonstration of the earth's rotation round the sun to be conducted quickly, since it is given for nothing, and now the wealthy unknown pupil appears, lending the schol-ar's time a monetary value. He shows no interest, but he has to be served; Galileo lacks resources, so he will stand be-tween the wealthy pupil and the intelligent one, and sigh as he makes his choice. There is little that he can teach his new student, and so he learns from him instead; he hears of the telescope which has been invented in Holland: in his own way he gets something out of the disturbance of his morning's work. The Rector of the university arrives. Galileo's application for an increase in salary has been turned down; the university is reluctant to pay as much for the theories of physics as for those of theology; it wishes him, who after all is operating on a generally ac-cepted low level of scholarship, to produce something use-ful here and now. You will see from the way in which he offers his treatise that he is used to being refused and corrected. The Rector reminds him that the Republic guarantees freedom of research even if she doesn't pay; he replies that he cannot make much of this freedom if he lacks the leisure which good payment permits. Here you should not find his impatience too peremptory, or his poverty will not be given due weight. For shortly after that you find him having ideas which need some explana-tion; the prophet of a new age of scientific truth considers how he can trick the Republic by offering her the telescope as his own invention. All he sees in the new invention, you will be surprised to hear, is a few scudi, and he examines it simply with a view to annexing it for himself. But if you move on to the second scene, you will find that while he is selling the invention to the Venetian *signoria* with a speech that disgraces him by its falsehoods he has al-

ready almost forgotten the money, for he has realized
that the instrument has not only military but astronomical
significance. The article which he has been blackmailed
—let us call it that—into producing proves to have great
qualities for the very research which he had to break off
in order to produce it. If during the ceremony, as he com-
placently accepts the undeserved honors paid him, he
outlines to his learned friend the marvelous discoveries in
view—don't overlook the theatrical way in which he does
this—you will find in him a far more profound excitement
than the thought of monetary gain called forth. Seen in
this light, his charlatanry may not mean much, but it
still shows how determined the man is to take the easy
course, and to apply his reason in a base as well as a noble
way. A more significant test awaits him; and does not
every capitulation bring the next one closer?

(64)

Splitting such material into one *Gestus* after another,
the actor masters his character by first mastering the
story.[9] It is only after walking all around the entire episode
that he can, as it were by a single leap, seize and fix his
character, complete with all its individual features. Once
he has done his utmost to let himself be amazed by the inconsistencies in its various attitudes, knowing that he in
turn will have to make them amaze the audience, then the
story considered as a whole may allow him to pull the inconsistencies together; for the story, being a clearly defined episode, has a specific sense, i.e., only gratifies
a specific fraction of all the interests that might arise.

(65)

Everything hangs on the story; it is the heart of the
theatrical performance. For it is what happens *between*
people that provides them with the material to discuss,
criticize, alter. Even if the particular person represented by the actor has ultimately to fit into more than
just the one episode, it is mainly because the episode
will be all the more striking if it reaches fulfillment in a
particular person. The story is the theatre's great opera-

9 Brecht's word is "Fabel"—the Latin *Fabula* (E. B.).

tion: the whole complex of incidents with each different *Gestus,* embracing the communications and impulses that must now go to make up the audience's entertainment.

(66)

Each single incident has its basic *Gestus: Richard Gloster courts his victim's widow. The child's true mother is found by means of a chalk circle. God has a bet with the Devil for Dr. Faustus' soul. Woyzeck buys a cheap knife in order to do in his wife,* etc. The grouping of the characters on the stage and the movements of the groups must be such that the necessary beauty is attained above all by the elegance with which the material conveying that *Gestus* is set out and laid bare to the understanding of the audience.

(67)

As we cannot invite the audience to fling itself into the story as if it were a river and let itself be carried vaguely hither and thither, the individual episodes have to be knotted together in such a way that the knots are easily noticed. The episodes must not succeed one another indistinguishably but must give us a chance to interpose our judgment. (If it were above all the obscurity of the original interrelations that interested us, then this circumstance would have to be made sufficiently strange.) The parts of the story have to be carefully set off one against another by giving each its own structure as a play within the play. To this end it is best to agree to use titles like those in the preceding paragraph. The titles must include the social point, saying at the same time something about the kind of portrayal wanted, i.e., should copy the tone of a chronicle or a ballad or a newspaper or a morality. For instance, a simple way of making something seem unfamiliar is that which is normally applied to customs and moral principles. A visit, the treatment of an enemy, a lovers' meeting, agreements about politics or business, can be portrayed as though they were simply illustrations of general principles valid for the place in question. Shown thus, the particular and unrepeatable incident acquires a disconcerting look, because it appears as something general, something that has become a principle. As soon as we ask

whether in fact it should have become such, or what about
it should have done so, we are treating the incident as unfamiliar. The poetic approach to history can be studied in
the so-called panoramas at sideshows in fairs. Since this
detached treatment means lending historical perspective,
certain incidents can just be represented as historic, as
though they had for a long while been common knowledge
and care must be taken not to offer the least obstacle to
their further transmission. In short, there are many conceivable ways of telling a story, some of them known and
some still waiting to be discovered.

(68)

What needs to be treated as unfamiliar, and how this
is to be done, depends on the exposition demanded by
the entire episode; and this is where the theatre has to
speak up decisively for the interests of its own time. Let
us take as an example of such exposition the old play
Hamlet. Given the dark and bloody period in which I
am writing—the criminal ruling classes, the widespread
doubt in the power of reason, continually being misused—
I think that I can read the story thus: It is an age of war-
riors. Hamlet's father, King of Denmark, slew the King
of Norway in a successful war of spoliation. While the latter's son Fortinbras is arming for a fresh war, the Danish
king is likewise slain—by his own brother. The slain kings'
brothers, now themselves kings, avert war by arranging that
the Norwegian troops should cross Danish soil to launch
a predatory war against Poland. But at this point the
young Hamlet is summoned by his warrior father's ghost
to avenge the crime committed against him. After at first
being reluctant to answer one bloody deed by another,
and even preparing to go into exile, he meets young Fortinbras at the coast as he is marching with his troops to
Poland. Overcome by this warrior-like example, he turns
back[10] and in a piece of barbaric butchery slaughters his
uncle, his mother, and himself, leaving Denmark to the

[10] But Hamlet in fact does not turn back at that point, nor is it
accurate to say that he slaughters his mother and himself. When
I made some such comments to Brecht, he replied with the
following letter, only part of which has previously been published (in Beatrice Gottlieb's translation of the *Organum*, *Accent*, Urbana, 1951):

Norwegian. These events show the young man, already somewhat stout, making the most ineffective use of the new approach to Reason which he has picked up at the University of Wittenberg. In the feudal business to which he returns it simply hampers him. Faced with irrational practices, his reason is utterly unpractical. He falls a tragic victim to the discrepancy between such reasoning and such action. This way of reading the play, which can be read in more than one way, might in my view interest our audience.

(69)

Whether or no literature presents them as successes, each step forward, every emancipation from nature that is scored in the field of production so as to lead to a

---

Berliner Ensemble
Berlin N.W. 7
31 October, 1949

Dear Bentley,

You are right. Section 68 of the *Short Organum* needs a footnote and a correction.

Correction: Instead of "and in a piece of barbaric butchery slaughters his uncle, his mother, and himself," it must read: "and in a piece of barbaric butchery brings about the death of his uncle, his mother, and himself."

Footnote: The fourth scene of the Fourth Act (A plain in Denmark), in which we see Hamlet for the last time before his return in the flesh, we take to be the turning point. Here he has the great monologue in which he succumbs to Fortinbras' drums of war: "Oh, from this time forth/ My thoughts be bloody or be nothing worth!" True, the letter to Horatio in the scene after next announces that Hamlet has nonetheless taken ship for England. But none of this is acted out, and his report to Horatio on the king's plot against him (II, 2) [*sic.* But V, 2 must be meant.—E. B.] does not give the performer the chance to enact his decision (to go to England).

The Hamlet interpretation is just an example of an *interpretation*—that is, certain emphases and displacements, possibly cuts, and even occasionally (not in this case) interpolations are needed.

Anyhow the *Short Organum* will be read here for the moment chiefly by students. To be sure, more discussion is under way about my demand that the theatres should use our Model Books. You know, of course, the *Antigone* Model, and now Suhrkamp is bringing out the *Courage* Model. And I have also prepared an example of a text on The Building of a Role—Laughton's *Galilei*.

I'd be very glad if you could come over to this side again this winter. Unhappily we cannot do anything for you in the Golden West. Warmly, Your Brecht. (E. B.).

transformation of society, all those explorations in some
new direction which mankind has embarked on in order to
improve its lot, give us a sense of confidence and triumph
and lead us to take pleasure in the possibilities of change
in all things. Galileo expresses this when he says: "It is
my view that the earth is most noble and wonderful, seeing the great number and variety of changes and generations which incessantly take place on it."

(70)

The exposition of the story and its communication by
suitable means of estrangement constitute the main business of the theatre. Not everything depends on the actor,
even though nothing may be done without taking him into
account. The story is set out, brought forward, and
shown by the theatre as a whole, by actors, stage designers,
mask-makers, costumers, composers, and choreographers.
They unite their various arts for the joint operation, without of course sacrificing their independence in the process.

(71)

It emphasizes the general *Gestus* of showing, which
always underlies that which is being shown, when the audience is musically addressed by means of songs. Because
of this the actors ought not to "drop into" song, but
should clearly mark it off from the rest of the text; and
this is best reinforced by a few theatrical methods such
as changing the lighting or inserting a title. For its part,
the music must strongly resist the smooth incorporation
which is generally expected of it and turns it into an un-
thinking slavey. Music does not "accompany" except in the
form of comment. It cannot simply "express itself" by
discharging the emotions with which the incidents of the
play have filled it. Thus Eisler, e.g., helped admirably in
the knotting of the incidents when in the carnival scene
of *Galileo* he set the masked procession of the guilds to
a triumphant and threatening music which showed what
a revolutionary twist the lower orders had given to the
scholar's astronomical theories. Similarly in *The Caucasian
Chalk Circle*[11] the singer, by using a chilly and unemo-

[11] *The Caucasian Chalk Circle* is to be found in the volume
Parables for the Theatre, University of Minnesota Press, 1948
(and since 1957 an Evergreen Paperback) (E. B.).

tional way of singing to describe the servant girl's rescue of the child as it is being mimed on the stage, makes plain the terror of a period in which motherly instincts can become a suicidal weakness. Thus music can make its point in a number of ways and with full independence, and can give its own reaction to the subjects dealt with; at the same time it can also quite simply help to lend variety to the entertainment.

(72)

Just as the composer wins back his freedom by no longer having to create an atmosphere which allows the audience to lose itself unreservedly in the events on the stage, so also the stage designer gets considerable freedom as soon as he no longer needs to give the illusion of a room or a locality when he is building his sets. It is enough for him to give hints, though these must make statements of greater historical or social interest than does the real setting. At the Jewish Theatre in Moscow *King Lear* was rendered unfamiliar by a structure that recalled a medieval tabernacle; Neher set *Galileo* in front of projections of maps, documents, and Renaissance works of art; for *Haitang Erwacht* at the Piscator-Theater in Berlin Heartfield used a background of reversible flags bearing inscriptions, to mark changes in the political situation of which the persons on the stage were sometimes unaware.

(73)

For choreography, too, there are once again tasks of a realistic kind. It is a relatively recent error to suppose that it has nothing to do with the representation of "people as they really are." If art reflects life it does so with special mirrors. Art does not become unrealistic by changing the proportions but by changing them in such a way that if the audience took its representations as a practical guide to insights and impulses it would go astray in real life. It is of course essential that stylization should not remove the natural element but should heighten it. Anyhow, a theatre where everything depends on the *Gestus* cannot do without choreography. Elegant movement and graceful grouping, for a start, promote detachment, and inventive miming greatly helps the story.

(74)

So let us invite all the sister arts of the drama, not in order to create an "integrated work of art" (*Gesamtkunstwerk*) in which they all offer themselves up and are lost, but so that together with the drama they may further the common task in their different ways; and their relations with one another consist in this: that they lead to mutual detachment.

(75)

And here once again let us recall that their task is to entertain the children of the scientific age, and to do so with sensuousness and humor. This is something that we Germans cannot tell ourselves too often, for with us everything easily slips into the insubstantial and unapproachable, and we begin to talk of a World View (*Weltanschauung*) when the world in question has already dissolved. Even materialism is little more than an idea with us. Sexual pleasure with us turns into marital obligations, the pleasures of art subserve culture, and by learning we mean not an enjoyable process of finding out, but the forcible shoving of our nose into something. Our activity has none of the pleasure of exploration, and if we want to make our mark we do not say how much fun we have got out of something but how much effort it has cost us.

(76)

One more thing: the delivery to the audience of what has been built up in the rehearsals. Here it is essential that the actual playing should be infused with the *Gestus* of handing over a finished article. What now comes before the spectator is the most frequently repeated of what has not been rejected, and so the finished representations have to be delivered with the eyes fully open, so that they may be received with the eyes open too.

(77)

That is to say, our representations must take second place to what is represented—people's life together in society—and the pleasure felt in their perfection must be converted into the higher pleasure felt when the rules emerging from this life in society are treated as imperfect and provisional. In this way the theatre leaves its spectators productively disposed even after the spectacle is over. Let us hope that their theatre may allow them to enjoy as entertainment that terrible and never-ending labor which should insure their maintenance, together with the terror of their unceasing transformation. Let them here produce their own lives in the simplest way; for the simplest way of living is in art.

THORNTON WILDER
(b. 1897)

Some Thoughts on Playwriting[1] (1941)

FOUR FUNDAMENTAL conditions of the drama separate it from the other arts. Each of these conditions has its advantages and disadvantages, each requires a particular aptitude from the dramatist, and from each there are a number of instructive consequences to be derived. These conditions are:

1. The theatre is an art which reposes upon the work of many collaborators;
2. It is addressed to the group-mind;
3. It is based upon a pretense and its very nature calls out a multiplication of pretenses;
4. Its action takes place in a perpetual present time.

I. THE THEATRE IS AN ART WHICH REPOSES UPON THE WORK OF MANY COLLABORATORS

We have been accustomed to think that a work of art is by definition the product of one governing selecting will.

A landscape by Cézanne consists of thousands of brushstrokes each commanded by one mind. *Paradise Lost* and *Pride and Prejudice,* even in cheap frayed copies, bear the immediate and exclusive message of one intelligence.

It is true that in musical performance we meet with intervening executants, but the element of intervention is slight compared to that which takes place in drama. Illustrations:

1. One of the finest productions of *The Merchant of Venice* in our time showed Sir Henry Irving as Shylock, a noble, wronged, and indignant being, of such stature

---

[1] Thornton Wilder, "Some Thoughts on Playwriting," in *The Intent of the Artist,* edited by Augusto Centeno. Copyright Princeton University Press, 1941, pp. 83–98.

that the Merchants of Venice dwindled before him into irresponsible schoolboys. He was confronted in court by a gracious, even queenly, Portia, Miss Ellen Terry. At the Odéon in Paris, however, Gémier played Shylock as a vengeful and hysterical buffoon, confronted in court by a Portia who was a *gamine* from the Paris streets with a lawyer's quill three feet long over her ear; at the close of the trial scene Shylock was driven screaming about the auditorium, behind the spectators' back and onto the stage again, in a wild Elizabethan revel. Yet for all their divergences both were admirable productions of the play.

2. If there were ever a play in which fidelity to the author's requirements were essential in the representation of the principal role, it would seem to be Ibsen's *Hedda Gabler,* for the play is primarily an exposition of her character. Ibsen's directions read: "Enter from the left Hedda Gabler. She is a woman of twenty-nine. Her face and figure show great refinement and distinction. Her complexion is pale and opaque. Her steel-gray eyes express an unruffled calm. Her hair is of an attractive medium brown, but is not particularly abundant; and she is dressed in a flowing loose-fitting morning gown." I once saw Eleonora Duse in this role. She was a woman of sixty and made no effort to conceal it. Her complexion was pale and transparent. Her hair was white, and she was dressed in a gown that suggested some medieval empress in mourning. And the performance was very fine.

One may well ask: why write for the theatre at all? Why not work in the novel where such deviations from one's intentions cannot take place?

There are two answers:

1. The theatre presents certain vitalities of its own so inviting and stimulating that the writer is willing to receive them in compensation for this inevitable variation from an exact image.

2. The dramatist through working in the theatre gradually learns not merely to take account of the presence of the collaborators, but to derive advantage from them; and he learns, above all, to organize the play in such a way that its strength lies not in appearances beyond his control, but in the succession of events and in the unfolding of an idea, in narration.

The gathered audience sits in a darkened room, one end of which is lighted. The nature of the transaction at which it is gazing is a succession of events illustrating a general idea — the stirring of the idea; the gradual feeding out of information; the shock and countershock of circumstances; the flow of action; the interruption of action; the moments of allusion to earlier events; the preparation of surprise, dread, or delight — all that is the author's and his alone.

For reasons to be discussed later — the expectancy of the group-mind, the problem of time on the stage, the absence of the narrator, the element of pretense — the theatre carries the art of narration to a higher power than the novel or the epic poem. The theatre is unfolding action and in the disposition of events the authors may exercise a governance so complete that the distortions effected by the physical appearance of actors, by the fancies of scene painters and the misunderstandings of directors, fall into relative insignificance. It is just because the theatre is an art of many collaborators, with the constant danger of grave misinterpretation, that the dramatist learns to turn his attention to the laws of narration, its logic and its deep necessity of presenting a unifying idea stronger than its mere collection of happenings. The dramatist must be by instinct a storyteller.

There is something mysterious about the endowment of the storyteller. Some very great writers possessed very little of it, and some others, lightly esteemed, possessed it in so large a measure that their books survive down the ages, to the confusion of severer critics. Alexandre Dumas had it to an extraordinary degree; while Melville, for all his splendid quality, had it barely sufficiently to raise his work from the realm of non-fiction. It springs, not, as some have said, from an aversion to general ideas, but from an instinctive coupling of idea and illustration; the idea, for a born storyteller, can only be expressed imbedded in its circumstantial illustration. The myth, the parable, the fable are the fountainhead of all fiction and in them is seen most clearly the didactic, moralizing employment of a story. Modern taste shrinks from emphasizing the central idea that hides behind the fiction, but it exists there nevertheless, supplying the unity to fantasizing, and offering a justification to what otherwise we would repudiate as mere arbitrary contrivance, pretentious lying, or individualistic emotional association spinning. For all their magnificent intellectual endowment, George Meredith

and George Eliot were not born storytellers; they chose
fiction as the vehicle for their reflections, and the passing
of time is revealing their error in that choice. Jane Austen
was pure storyteller and her works are outlasting those
of apparently more formidable rivals. The theatre is
more exacting than the novel in regard to this faculty,
and its presence constitutes a force which compensates
the dramatist for the deviations which are introduced into
his work by the presence of his collaborators.

The chief of these collaborators are the actors.

The actor's gift is a combination of three separate
faculties or endowments. Their presence to a high degree in any one person is extremely rare, although the
ambition to possess them is common. Those who rise
to the height of the profession represent a selection and
a struggle for survival in one of the most difficult and
cruel of the artistic activities. The three endowments
that compose the gift are observation, imagination, and
physical co-ordination.

1. An observant and analyzing eye for all modes of
behavior about us, for dress and manner, and for the
signs of thought and emotion in one's self and in others.

2. The strength of imagination and memory whereby
the actor may, at the indication in the author's text,
explore his store of observations and represent the details of appearance and the intensity of the emotions —
joy, fear, surprise, grief, love, and hatred, and through
imagination extend them to intenser degrees and to
differing characterizations.

3. A physical co-ordination whereby the force of
these inner realizations may be communicated to voice,
face, and body.

An actor must *know* the appearances and the mental
states; he must *apply* his knowledge to the role; and he
must physically *express* his knowledge. Moreover, his
concentration must be so great that he can effect this
representation under conditions of peculiar difficulty —
in abrupt transition from the non-imaginative conditions behind the stage; and in the presence of fellow-
actors who may be momentarily destroying the reality
of the action.

A dramatist prepares the characterization of his personages in such a way that it will take advantage of the
actor's gift.

Characterization in a novel is presented by the author's dogmatic assertion that the personage was such, and by an analysis of the personage with generally an account of his or her past. Since, in the drama, this is replaced by the actual presence of the personage before us and since there is no occasion for the intervening all-knowing author to instruct us as to his or her inner nature, a far greater share is given in a play to (1) highly characteristic utterances and (2) concrete occasions in which the character defines itself under action and (3) a conscious preparation of the text whereby the actor may build upon the suggestions in the role according to his own abilities.

Characterization in a play is like a blank check which the dramatist accords to the actor for him to fill in — not entirely blank, for a number of indications of individuality are already there, but to a far less definite and absolute degree than in the novel.

The dramatist's principal interest being the movement of the story, he is willing to resign the more detailed aspects of characterization to the actor and is often rewarded beyond his expectation.

The sleepwalking scene from *Macbeth* is a highly compressed selection of words whereby despair and remorse rise to the surface of indirect confession. It is to be assumed that had Shakespeare lived to see what the genius of Sarah Siddons could pour into the scene from that combination of observation, self-knowledge, imagination, and representational skill, even he might have exclaimed, "I never knew I wrote so well!"

II. THE THEATRE IS AN ART ADDRESSED TO A GROUP-MIND

Painting, sculpture, and the literature of the book are certainly solitary experiences; and it is likely that most people would agree that the audience seated shoulder to shoulder in a concert hall is not an essential element in musical enjoyment.

But a play presupposes a crowd. The reasons for this go deeper than (1) the economic necessity for the support of the play and (2) the fact that the temperament of actors is proverbially dependent on group attention.

It rests on the fact that (1) the pretense, the fiction, on the stage would fall to pieces and absurdity without the support accorded to it by a crowd, and (2) the excitement induced by pretending a fragment of life is such that it partakes of ritual and festival, and requires a throng.

Similarly the fiction that royal personages are of a mysteriously different nature from other people requires audiences, levees, and processions for its maintenance. Since the beginnings of society, satirists have occupied themselves with the descriptions of kings and queens in their intimacy and delighted in showing how the prerogatives of royalty become absurd when the crowd is not present to extend to them the enhancement of an imaginative awe.

The theatre partakes of the nature of festival. Life imitated is life raised to a higher power. In the case of comedy, the vitality of these pretended surprises, deceptions, and *contretemps* becomes so lively that before a spectator, solitary or regarding himself as solitary, the structure of so much event would inevitably expose the artificiality of the attempt and ring hollow and unjustified; and in the case of tragedy, the accumulation of woe and apprehension would soon fall short of conviction. All actors know the disturbing sensation of playing before a handful of spectators at a dress rehearsal or performance where only their interest in pure craftsmanship can barely sustain them. During the last rehearsals the phrase is often heard: "This play is hungry for an audience."

Since the theatre is directed to a group-mind, a number of consequences follow:

1. A group-mind presupposes, if not a lowering of standards, a broadening of the fields of interest. The other arts may presuppose an audience of connoisseurs trained in leisure and capable of being interested in certain rarefied aspects of life. The dramatist may be prevented from exhibiting, for example, detailed representations of certain moments in history that require specialized knowledge in the audience, or psychological states in the personages which are of insufficient general interest to evoke self-identification in the majority. In the Second Part of Goethe's *Faust* there are long passages dealing with the theory of paper money. The exposition of the nature of misanthropy (so much more drastic than Molière's) in Shakespeare's *Timon of Athens* has never been a suc-

cess. The dramatist accepts this limitation in subject matter and realizes that the group-mind imposes upon him the necessity of treating material understandable by the larger number.

2. It is the presence of the group-mind that brings another requirement to the theatre—forward movement.

Maeterlinck said that there was more drama in the spectacle of an old man seated by a table than in the majority of plays offered to the public. He was juggling with the various meanings in the word "drama." In the sense whereby drama means the intensified concentration of life's diversity and significance he may well have been right; if he meant drama as a theatrical representation before an audience he was wrong. Drama on the stage is inseparable from forward movement, from action.

Many attempts have been made to present Plato's dialogues, Gobineau's fine series of dialogues, *La Renaissance,* and the *Imaginary Conversations* of Landor; but without success. Through some ingredient in the group-mind, and through the sheer weight of anticipation involved in the dressing up and the assumption of fictional roles, an action is required, and an action that is more than a mere progress in argumentation and debate.

III. THE THEATRE IS A WORLD OF PRETENSE

It lives by conventions: a convention is an agreed-upon falsehood, a permitted lie.

Illustrations: Consider at the first performance of the *Medea,* the passage where Medea meditates the murder of her children. An anecdote from antiquity tells us that the audience was so moved by this passage that considerable disturbance took place.

The following conventions were involved:

1. Medea was played by a man.

2. He wore a large mask on his face. In the lip of the mask was an acoustical device for projecting the voice. On his feet he wore shoes with soles and heels half a foot high.

3. His costume was so designed that it conveyed

to the audience, by convention: woman of royal birth and Oriental origin.

4. The passage was in metric speech. All poetry is an "agreed-upon falsehood" in regard to speech.

5. The lines were sung in a kind of recitative. All opera involves this "permitted lie" in regard to speech.

Modern taste would say that the passage would convey much greater pathos if a woman "like Medea" had delivered it — with an uncovered face that exhibited all the emotions she was undergoing. For the Greeks, however, there was no pretense that Medea was on the stage. The mask, the costume, the mode of declamation, were a series of signs which the spectator interpreted and reassembled in his own mind. Medea was being re-created within the imagination of each of the spectators.

The history of the theatre shows us that in its greatest ages the stage employed the greatest number of conventions. The stage is fundamental pretense and it thrives on the acceptance of that fact and in the multiplication of additional pretenses. When it tries to assert that the personages in the action "really are," really inhabit such and such rooms, really suffer such and such emotions, it loses rather than gains credibility. The modern world is inclined to laugh condescendingly at the fact that in the plays of Racine and Corneille the gods and heroes of antiquity were dressed like the courtiers under Louis XIV; that in the Elizabethan age scenery was replaced by placards notifying the audience of the location; and that a whip in the hand and a jogging motion of the body indicated that a man was on horseback in the Chinese theatre; these devices did not spring from naïveté, however, but from the vitality of the public imagination in those days and from an instinctive feeling as to where the essential and where the inessential lay in drama.

The convention has two functions:

1. It provokes the collaborative activity of the spectator's imagination; and

2. It raises the action from the specific to the general.

This second aspect is of even greater importance than the first.

If Juliet is represented as a girl "very like Juliet" — it was not merely a deference to contemporary prejudices that assigned this role to a boy in the Elizabethan age — moving about in a "real" house with marble staircases, rugs, lamps, and furniture, the impression is irresistibly conveyed that these events happened to this one girl, in one place, at one moment in time. When the play is staged as Shakespeare intended it, the bareness of the stage releases the events from the particular and the experience of Juliet partakes of that of all girls in love, in every time, place and language.

The stage continually strains to tell this generalized truth and it is the element of pretense that reinforces it. Out of the lie, the pretense, of the theatre proceeds a truth more compelling than the novel can attain, for the novel by its own laws is constrained to tell of an action that "once happened" — "once upon a time."

IV. THE ACTION ON THE STAGE TAKES PLACE IN A PERPETUAL PRESENT TIME

Novels are written in the past tense. The characters in them, it is true, are represented as living moment by moment their present time, but the constant running commentary of the novelist ("Tess slowly descended into the valley"; "Anna Karenina laughed") inevitably conveys to the reader the fact that these events are long since past and over.

The novel is a past reported in the present. On the stage it is always now. This confers upon the action an increased vitality which the novelist longs in vain to incorporate into his work.

This condition in the theatre brings with it another important element:

In the theatre we are not aware of the intervening storyteller. The speeches arise from the characters in an apparently pure spontaneity.

A play is what takes place.

A novel is what one person tells us took place.

A play visibly represents pure existing. A novel is what one mind, claiming to omniscience, asserts to have existed.

Many dramatists have regretted this absence of the narrator from the stage, with his point of view, his pow-

ers of analyzing the behavior of the characters, his ability to interfere and supply further facts about the past,
about simultaneous actions not visible on the stage, and
above *all* his function of pointing the moral and emphasizing the significance of the action. In some periods
of the theatre he has been present as chorus, or prologue and epilogue or as *raisonneur*. But surely this
absence constitutes an additional force to the form, as
well as an additional tax upon the writer's skill. It is the
task of the dramatist so to co-ordinate his play, through
the selection of episodes and speeches, that, though he
is himself not visible, his point of view and his governing intention will impose themselves on the spectator's
attention, not as dogmatic. assertion or motto, but as
self-evident truth and inevitable deduction.

Imaginative narration — the invention of souls and
destinies — is to a philosopher an all but indefensible
activity.

Its justification lies in the fact that the communication of ideas from one mind to another inevitably
reaches the point where exposition passes into illustration, into parable, metaphor, allegory, and myth.

It is no accident that when Plato arrived at the height
of his argument and attempted to convey a theory of
knowledge and a theory of the structure of man's nature he passed over into story telling, into the myths of
the Cave and the Charioteer; and that the great religious teachers have constantly had recourse to the
parable as a means of imparting their deepest intuitions.

The theatre offers to imaginative narration its highest possibilities. It has many pitfalls and its very vitality
betrays it into service as mere diversion and the enhancement of insignificant matter; but it is well to
remember that it was the theatre that rose to the highest place during those epochs that aftertime has chosen
to call "great ages" and that the Athens of Pericles and
the reigns of Elizabeth, Philip II, and Louis XIV were
also the ages that gave to the world the greatest dramas
it has known.

JEAN-PAUL SARTRE
(b. 1905)

Forgers of Myths[1] (1946)

IN READING the newspaper reviews of Katharine Cornell's production of Jean Anouilh's *Antigone,* I had the impression that the play had created a certain amount of discomfort in the minds of the New York drama critics. Many expressed surprise that such an ancient myth should be staged at all. Others reproached Antigone with being neither alive nor credible, with not having what, in theatre jargon, is called "character." The misunderstanding, I believe, was due to the fact that the critics were not informed of what many young authors in France—each along differing lines and without concerted aim—are attempting to do.

There has been a great deal of discussion in France about "a return to tragedy," about the "rebirth of the philosophic play." The two labels are confusing and they should both be rejected. Tragedy is, for us, an historic phenomenon which flourished between the sixteenth and eighteenth centuries; we have no desire to begin that over again. Nor are we anxious to produce philosophic plays, if by that is meant works deliberately intended to set forth on the stage the philosophy of Marx, St. Thomas, or existentialism. Nevertheless there is some truth attached to these two labels: in the first place, it is a fact that we are less concerned with making innovations than with returning to a tradition; it is likewise true that the problems we wish to deal with in the theatre are very different from those we habitually dealt with before 1940.

The theatre, as conceived of in the period between the

[1] Jean-Paul Sartre, "Forgers of Myths," translated by Rosamond Gilder, *Theatre Arts Anthology,* edited by Rosamond Gilder, Hermine Rich Isaacs and others (New York: Theatre Arts Books, 1951), pp. 135–42. Copyright 1946 by Theatre Arts, Inc., 1950 by Theatre Arts Books.

two world wars, and as it is perhaps still thought of in the
United States today, is a theatre of characters. The analysis
of characters and their confrontation was the theatre's
chief concern. The so-called "situations" existed only for
the purpose of throwing the characters into clearer relief.
The best plays in this period were psychological studies of
a coward, a liar, an ambitious man or a frustrated one.
Occasionally a playwright made an effort to outline the
workings of a passion—usually love—or to analyze an
inferiority complex.

Judged by such principles Anouilh's Antigone is not a
character at all. Nor is she simply a peg on which to hang
a passion calculated to develop along the approved lines
of whatever psychology might be in style. She represents
a naked will, a pure, free choice; in her there is no distinguishing between passion and action. The young playwrights of France do not believe that men share a ready-
made "human nature" which may alter under the impact of a given situation. They do not think that individuals
can be seized with a passion or a mania which can be
explained purely on the grounds of heredity, environment,
and situations. What is universal, to their way of thinking,
is not nature but the situations in which man finds himself; that is, not the sum total of his psychological traits
but the limits which enclose him on all sides.

For them man is not to be defined as a "reasoning
animal," or a "social" one, but as a free being, entirely
indeterminate, who must choose his own being when confronted with certain necessities, such as being already
committed in a world full of both threatening and favorable
factors among other men who have made their choices
before him, who have decided in advance the meaning
of those factors. He is faced with the necessity of having
to work and die, of being hurled into a life already complete which yet is his own enterprise and in which he
can never have a second chance; where he must play his
cards and take risks no matter what the cost. That is why
we feel the urge to put on the stage certain situations
which throw light on the main aspects of the condition
of man and to have the spectator participate in the free
choice which man makes in these situations.

Thus, Anouilh's Antigone may have seemed abstract
because she was not portrayed as a young Greek princess,
formed by certain influences and some ghastly memories,

but rather as a free woman without any features at all until she chooses them for herself in the moment when she asserts her freedom to die despite the triumphant tyrant. Similarly, when the burgomaster of Vauxelles in Simone de Beauvoir's *Les Bouches Inutiles* has to decide whether to save his beleaguered town by cutting off half its citizens (women, children, and old men) or to risk making them all perish in an effort to save them all, we do not care whether he is sensual or cold, whether he has an Oedipus complex, or whether he is of an irritable or jolly disposition. No doubt if he is rash or incautious, vain or pusillanimous, he will make the wrong decision. But we are not interested in arranging in advance the motivations or reasons which will inevitably force his choice. Rather, we are concerned in presenting the anguish of a man who is both free and full of good will, who in all sincerity is trying to find out the side he must take, and who knows that when he chooses the lot of others he is at the same time choosing his own pattern of behavior and is deciding once and for all whether he is to be a tyrant or a democrat.

If one of us happens to present character on the boards, it is only for the purpose of getting rid of it at once. For instance, Caligula, at the outset of Albert Camus' play of that name, has a character. One is led to believe he is gentle and well behaved, and no doubt he actually is both. But that gentleness and that modesty suddenly melt away in the face of the prince's horrifying discovery of the world's absurdity. From then on he will choose to be the man to persuade other men of that absurdity, and the play becomes only the story of how he carries out his purpose.

A man who is free within the circle of his own situations, who chooses, whether he wishes to or not, for everyone else when he chooses for himself—that is the subject matter of our plays. As a successor to the theatre of characters we want to have a theatre of situation; our aim is to explore all the situations that are most common to human experience, those which occur at least once in the majority of lives. The people in our plays will be distinct from one another—not as a coward is from a miser or a miser from a brave man, but rather as actions are divergent or clashing, as right may con-

flict with right. In this it may well be said that we derive
from the Corneillean tradition.

It is easy to understand, therefore, why we are not
greatly concerned with psychology. We are not searching
for the right "word" which will suddenly reveal the whole
unfolding of a passion, nor yet the "act" which will seem
most lifelike and inevitable to the audience. For us psychology is the most abstract of the sciences because it
studies the workings of our passions without plunging
them back into their true human surroundings, without
their background of religious and moral values, the taboos
and commandments of society, the conflicts of nations and
classes, of rights, of wills, of actions. For us a man is a
whole enterprise in himself. And passion is a part of
that enterprise.

In this we return to the concept of tragedy as the
Greeks saw it. For them, as Hegel has shown, passion was
never a simple storm of sentiment but fundamentally always the assertion of a right. The fascism of Creon, the
stubbornness of Antigone for Sophocles and Anouilh, the
madness of Caligula for Camus, are *at one and the same
time* transports of feeling which have their origin deep
within us and expressions of impregnable will which are
affirmations of systems of values and rights such as the
rights of citizenship, the rights of the family, individual
ethics, collective ethics, the right to kill, the right to
reveal to human beings their pitiable condition, and so
forth. We do not reject psychology, that would be
absurd; we integrate life.

For fifty years one of the most celebrated subjects for
dissertation in France has been formulated as follows:
"Comment on La Bruyère's saying: Racine draws man as
he is; Corneille, as he should be." We believe the statement should be reversed. Racine paints psychologic man,
he studies the mechanics of love, of jealousy in an abstract,
pure way; that is, without ever allowing moral considerations or human will to deflect the inevitability of their
evolution. His dramatis personae are only creatures of
his mind, the end results of an intellectual analysis. Corneille, on the other hand, showing will at the very core
of passion, gives us back man in all his complexity, in
his complete reality.

The young authors I am discussing take their stand on

Corneille's side. For them the theatre will be able to present man in his entirety only in proportion to the theatre's willingness to be *moral*. By that we do not mean that it should put forward examples illustrating the rules of deportment or the practical ethics taught to children, but rather that the study of the conflict of characters should be replaced by the presentation of the conflict of rights. It was not a question of the opposition of *character* between a Stalinist and a Trotskyite; it was not in their characters that an anti-Nazi of 1933 clashed with an S.S. guard; the difficulties in international politics do not derive from the characters of the men leading us; the strikes in the United States do not reveal conflicts of character between industrialists and workers. In each case it is, in the final analysis and in spite of divergent interests, the system of values, of ethics and of concepts of man which are lined up against each other.

Therefore, our new theatre definitely has drawn away from the so-called "realistic theatre" because "realism" has always offered plays made up of stories of defeat, laissez-faire, and drifting; it has always preferred to show how external forces batter a man to pieces, destroy him bit by bit, and ultimately make of him a weathervane turning with every change of wind. But we claim for ourselves the *true* realism because we know it is impossible, in everyday life, to distinguish between fact and right, the real from the ideal, psychology from ethics.

This theatre does not give its support to any one "thesis" and is not inspired by any preconceived idea. All it seeks to do is to explore the state of man in its entirety and to present to the modern man a portrait of himself, his problems, his hopes, and his struggles. We believe our theatre would betray its mission if it portrayed individual personalities, even if they were as universal types as a miser, a misanthrope, a deceived husband, because, if it is to address the masses, the theatre must speak in terms of their most general preoccupations, dispelling their anxieties in the form of myths which anyone can understand and feel deeply.

My first experience in the theatre was especially fortunate. When I was a prisoner in Germany in 1940, I wrote, staged, and acted in a Christmas play which, while pulling wool over the eyes of the German censor

by means of simple symbols, was addressed to my fellow-
prisoners. This drama, biblical in appearance only, was
written and put on by a prisoner, was acted by prisoners
in scenery painted by prisoners; it was aimed exclusively
at prisoners (so much so that I have never since then
permitted it to be staged or even printed), and it addressed
them on the subject of their concerns as prisoners. No
doubt it was neither a good play nor well acted: the work
of an amateur, the critics would say, a product of special
circumstances. Nevertheless, on this occasion, as I addressed my comrades across the footlights, speaking to
them of their state as prisoners, when I suddenly saw
them so remarkably silent and attentive, I realized what
theatre ought to be—a great collective, religious phenomenon.

To be sure, I was, in this case, favored by special
circumstances; it does not happen every day that your
public is drawn together by one great common interest, a
great loss or a great hope. As a rule, an audience is made
up of the most diverse elements; a big businessman sits
beside a traveling salesman or a professor, a man next to a
woman, and each is subject to his own particular preoccupations. Yet this situation is a challenge to the playwright: he must create his public, he must fuse all the
disparate elements in the auditorium into a single unity by
awakening in the recesses of their spirits the things which
all men of a given epoch and community care about.

This does not mean that our authors intend to make use
of symbols in the sense that symbols are the expression
either indirect or poetic of a reality one either cannot
or will not grasp directly. We would feel a profound
distaste today for representing happiness as an elusive
bluebird, as Maeterlinck did. Our times are too austere
for child's play of that sort. Yet if we reject the theatre
of symbols, we still want ours to be one of myths; we
want to attempt to show the public the great myths of
death, exile, love. The characters in Albert Camus' *Le
Malentendu* are not symbols, they are flesh and blood:
a mother and *a* daughter, *a* son who comes back from a
long journey; their tragic experiences are complete in
themselves. And yet they are mythical in the sense that
the misunderstanding which separates them can serve as
the embodiment of all misunderstandings which separate
man from himself, from the world, from other men.

The French public makes no mistake about this, as has been proved by the discussions engendered by certain plays. With *Les Bouches Inutiles,* for instance, criticism was not confined to discussing the story of the play which was based on actual events that took place frequently in the Middle Ages: it recognized in the play a condemnation of fascist procedures. The Communists, on the other hand, saw in it a condemnation of their own procedures: "The conclusion," so they said in their newspapers, "is couched in terms of petty bourgeois idealism. All useless mouths should have been sacrificed to save the city." Anouilh also stirred up a storm of discussion with *Antigone,* being charged on the one hand with being a Nazi, on the other with being an anarchist. Such violent reactions prove that our plays are reaching the public just where it is important that it should be reached.

Yet these plays are austere. To begin with, since the situation is what we care about above all, our theatre shows it at the very point where it is about to reach its climax. We do not take time out for learned research, we feel no need of registering the imperceptible evolution of a character or a plot: one does not reach death by degrees, one is suddenly confronted with it—and if one approaches politics or love by slow degrees, then acute problems, arising suddenly, call for no progression. By taking our dramatis personae and precipitating them, in the very first scene, into the highest pitch of their conflicts we turn to the well-known pattern of classic tragedy, which always seizes upon the action at the very moment it is headed for catastrophe.

Our plays are violent and brief, centered around one single event; there are few players and the story is compressed within a short space of time, sometimes only a few hours. As a result they obey a kind of "rule of the three unities," which has been only a little rejuvenated and modified. A single set, a few entrances, a few exits, intense arguments among the characters who defend their individual rights with passion—this is what sets our plays at a great distance from the brilliant fantasies of Broadway. Yet some of them find that their austerity and intensity have not lacked appreciation in Paris. Whether New York will like them is a question.

Since it is their aim to forge myths, to project for the audience an enlarged and enhanced image of its own

sufferings, our playwrights turn their backs on the constant preoccupation of the realists, which is to reduce
as far as possible the distance which separates the spectator from the spectacle. In 1942, in Gaston Baty's production of *The Taming of the Shrew,* there were steps
going from the stage to the auditorium so that certain
characters could go down among the orchestra seats.
We are very far away from such concepts and methods.
To us a play should not seem too *familiar.* Its greatness
derives from its social and, in a certain sense, religious
functions: it must remain a rite; even as it speaks to the
spectators of themselves it must do it in a tone and with
a constant reserve of manner which, far from breeding
familiarity, will increase the distance between play and
audience.

That is why one of our problems has been to search
out a style of dialogue which, while utterly simple and
made up of words on everyone's lips, will still preserve
something of the ancient dignity of our tongue. We have
all barred from our plays the digressions, the set speeches,
and what we in France like to call the "*poésie de
réplique*"; all this chitchat debases a language. It seems
to us that we shall recapture a little of the pomp of
ancient tragedies if we practice the most rigorous economy
of words. As for me, in *Morts Sans Sépulture,* my latest
play, I did not deny myself the use of familiar turns of
phrase, swearwords, even slang, whenever I felt that such
speech was germane to the characters. But I did attempt
to preserve, through the pace of the dialogue, an extreme
conciseness of statement—ellipses, brusque interruptions,
a sort of inner tension in the phrases which at once set
them apart from the easygoing sound of everyday talk.
Camus' style in *Caligula* is different in kind but it is
magnificently sober and taut. Simone de Beauvoir's language in *Les Bouches Inutiles* is so stripped that it is
sometimes accused of dryness.

Dramas which are short and violent, sometimes reduced to the dimensions of a single long act (*Antigone*
lasts an hour and a half, my own play, *Huis-Clos,* an
hour and twenty minutes without intermission), dramas
entirely centered on one event—usually a conflict of rights,
bearing on some very general situation—written in a
sparse, extremely tense style, with a small cast not pre-

sented for their individual characters but thrust into a conjunction where they are forced to make a choice— in brief this is the theatre, austere, moral, mythic, and ceremonial in aspect, which has given birth to new plays in Paris during the occupation and especially since the end of the war. They correspond to the needs of a people exhausted but tense, for whom liberation has not meant a return to abundance and who can live only with the utmost economy.

The very severity of these plays is in keeping with the severity of French life; their moral and metaphysical topics reflect the preoccupation of a nation which must at one and the same time reconstruct and re-create and which is searching for new principles. Are they the product of local circumstances or can their very austerity of form enable them to reach a wider public in more fortunate countries? This is a question we must ask ourselves frankly before we try to transplant them.

Why Verse?[1] (1955)

... THERE ARE many people to whom verse in the theatre is an irritating, or boring, or distracting, or pretentious flight of fashion; and in certain moods I can pish and tush with the best of them. This point is not held so strongly about literature in general. It isn't often said that there should be no such thing as poetry at all. When Wordsworth writes:

> Felt in the blood, and felt along the heart

we should think twice, perhaps, before we asked him why he didn't write the passage in prose. "Felt in the blood, and felt along the heart" is a good example, by the way, of the speed and economy with which poetry can express what would take prose far longer.

What reason is there for limiting the theatre to one form of communication? It is even believed that the prose play and the verse play are in opposition, or that the one precludes the other; there appears to be a kind of color bar in the matter. Such rivalry is nonsense. Indeed, prose and verse existing side by side counter each other's dangers. If they pass altogether out of each other's reach they cease to be themselves, becoming on the one hand journalese, official cant, or any other string of sentences; and on the other, a vagueness, an abstraction, a preciousness. This interplay of difference, one touching the hand of the other as it separates, like men and women dancing the Grand Chain, is what keeps each in its own state of grace.

One explanation of our impatience with a verse play is that the spring of theatre is action, and any insistence upon words is felt to hang like heavy clothes on the body of an

[1] Christopher Fry, "Why Verse?", *Vogue,* March, 1955, pp. 136–37. Copyright 1955 by Christopher Fry. Reprinted by permission of the author.

athlete. When we go to the theatre we go to be interested by a story of lives living out their conflicts in a
concentration of time. We do not go to hear them discuss
the matter; we go to see and hear them live it.

But we know that words and actions are not unrelated.
One illuminates the other; and the full significance of action
can be explored only by words. If we compare the murder
of Maria Marten in the Red Barn, with the murder of
Duncan in Macbeth's castle, we see that in each the
physical action is roughly the same, but the significance
of the action is entirely different. The one is merely done,
the other is experienced, and the experience is in the
words. What is more, the experience is the true nature
of the action. The experience ultimately is the action. The
action is not the dagger in Duncan's breast, or the blood
on Macbeth's hand, but rather the limitless experience of
the words arising out of them: the experience of

> Macbeth does murder sleep!

of:

> . . . this my hand will rather
> The multitudinous seas incarnadine,
> Making the green one red.

The three words "this my hand," in the context, so
deepen our thoughts about the human hand and what it
performs, that the action is not only true of this one
human, and this one deed; it becomes also an elemental
action, done in the beginning of the fallen world. In
sounds alone, "multitudinous," which heaves like a wil-
derness of molten lava, set against the three monosyllables
"this my hand," gives us, or should give us, an experience
of being. We begin to feel there is not one action, but two,
not two, but twenty in the course of a speech.

You may be prepared to agree with me that words
give us a larger, or deeper, experience of action, but still
you may say, "Why verse? Why this formality of syllables?
Why this unnatural division of sentences into lines?"

I suggest we forget the questions, and go on as though
verse plays, like wasps, are apparently with us for some
reason which they don't reveal. I only ask you to allow
me to suppose an organic discipline, pattern, or proportion
in the universe, evident in all that we see, which is a

government uniting the greatest with the least, form with behavior, natural event with historic event, which stamps its mark through us and through our perceptions, as the name of Brighton is marked through a stick of rock candy. When Milton says: "Elephants endors'd with towers," or when Wordsworth says: "A noticeable man with large gray eyes," they are not being so true to that organic discipline as, for instance, Chaucer, when he says:

> Now with his love, now in the colde grave
> Allone, withouten any companye.

I ask you to allow me to suppose a shaping but undogmatical presence "felt in the blood, and felt along the heart," which is of a kind with the law of gravity, and the moral law, and the law which gives us two legs and not six. From the way I am going on you would think I was talking about the Eleusinian mysteries, not about a theatre in which you propose to spend an entertaining evening. It is the fault of the question "Why Verse?" I should really write a play which would be so good that the question would never arise, a play which would please not some of the people some of the time, but all of the people all of the time, which would be both the immediate appearance of things and the eternal nature of things, combined with felicity.

I wish I could promise any such thing. Every few generations have to shape afresh the language which will express both these things together; and some of us find, like the donkey, that communication with our fellow being is something not easily achieved. We may think we have avoided all misconception, and then overhear a member of the audience making his comment, as after a performance of *The Dark Is Light Enough* (a play about the Austro-Hungarian war, taking place near Vienna) when a gentleman said, with charitable resignation, "I never can understand these Russian plays."

It is no good asking poetry to tell us what it says; it simply *is* what it says. In the theatre it must have a direct surface meaning, an immediate impact of sense, but half its work should be going on below that meaning, drawing the ear, consciously or unconsciously, into a certain experience of being.

This has been an age of signposts, of ideologies, of patent cures, of battle cries; we must take up our positions, draw clear lines between this or that, label, analyze, dissect; we must live the letter, for the letter is the law. But we have been looking at the possibility that poetry has another, deeper law. The truth of poetry deepens under your eye. It is never absolute. There is no moment when we can trumpet it abroad as finally understood.

In a play I wrote called *A Sleep Of Prisoners*, Cain and Abel throw dice together, and Abel prays as he shakes the dice:

> Deal me high, deal me low
> Make my deeds
> My nameless needs.
> I know I do not know.

In our anxiety to be in the know we defend our scraps of knowledge and decision so passionately that over the centuries we have burned, tortured, imprisoned, shot, and blown up those who contradicted or doubted us. But the spirit of our scrap of knowledge was in the contradiction and doubt, as much as in the belief. What we were torturing and blowing up was the spirit of truth.

Poetry in the theatre is the action of listening. It is an unrolling exploration, following your nose, or it would be better to say following your ear, for sound itself, pure sound, has logic, as we know in music, and what does that logic accord to if not the universal discipline felt along the heart? What part this logic plays in our life here on the earth is beyond calculation. If it wakens harmony, modulation, and the resolving of discord in us, we are nearer to our proper natures.

> The man that hath no music in himself,
> Nor is not moved with concord of sweet sounds,
> Is fit for treasons, stratagems and spoils;
> The motions of his spirit are dull as night,
> And his affections dark as Erebus:
> Let no such man be trusted.
> Mark the music.

Mark the music. Even in the broad give-and-take of the theatre our ears should be able to accept the interplay of the vowel sounds of a line of poetry, and know them as indications of the universal discipline, and consider the comma in the line with almost as much purpose as the comma on the underwing of the butterfly. But this precision has to exist within the broad and tough character

of the theatre; it has to hold its own against distractions
of many kinds: against coughs in the auditorium, failings
in the author, even—on rare occasions—against irregu-
larities of the actor's memory; just as in life our awareness of our larger natures has to hold its own against
a host of distractions within and without.

> Such harmony is in immortal souls;
> But whilst this muddy vesture of decay
> Doth grossly close it in, we can not hear it.

So the general lines of the play, the shape of the story,
the disposition of the characters, should point and impli-
cate by their actions and their wider uses the texture of
the poetry. The large pattern of the action should have a
meaning in itself, above and beyond the story; the kind
of meaning which gives everlasting truth to myths and
legends, and makes the fairy story into a sober fact; a
meaning not so conscious as a parable or so contrived as
an allegory, but as it were tracing a figure which the
poetry can naturally and inevitably fill.

This is all very well, you may now say, this fine theory;
but we have to put up with verse plays as they are, not
as ideally they should be; it seems to us that a good deal
of these plays could be written at least as well, and more
honestly, in prose. Why, for instance, should you present
to us as verse a speech such as this:

> I sometimes think
> His critical judgment is so exquisite
> It leaves us nothing to admire except his opinion.
> He should take into account
> The creative value of the fault.

I have no answer to satisfy you if you believe that human
nature, or human personality, is divided into two parts,
of whatever proportion, the prosaic and the poetic. I
think we live always with a foot in each camp, or rather,
that there is no moment when we can safely say that
we belong entirely to one or the other. There is no moment when we can certainly say that even our apparently most insignificant actions have not a significance
greatly beyond ourselves.

It is this tension between two meanings which verse
conveys, favoring sometimes one, sometimes the other.
The prosaic or colloquial can be rhythmically just sufficiently charged to resolve into the implication of verse at

a moment's notice, even halfway through a sentence, and
back again, without disturbing the unity of the speech,
in the way that the spirit and the flesh work in ourselves
without noticeably sawing us in half. The writer's responsibility is to know when he can safely break free of this,
and relax for contrast into the rhythms of prose.

In *The Dark Is Light Enough* there comes a moment
when the situation reduces everyone to silence; when
there seems no way of the scene going on without bringing
the curtain down. And then the Countess begins to speak.
I will tell you what she says, not because the verse does
what I want it to do, but it says something to our
purpose.

> How shall we manage, with time at a standstill?
> We can't go back to where nothing has been said;
> And no heart is served, caught in a moment
> Which has frozen. Since no words will set us free—
> Not at least now, until we can persuade
> Our thoughts to move—
> Music would unground us best,
> As a tide in the dark comes to boats at anchor
> And they begin to dance. My father told me
> How he went late one night, a night
> Of some Hungarian anxiety,
> To the Golden Bull at Buda, and there he found
> The President of your House of Deputies
> Alone and dancing in his shirtsleeves
> To the music of the band, himself
> Put far away, bewitched completely
> By the dance's custom; and so it went on,
> While my father drank and talked with friends,
> Three or four hours without a pause:
> This weighty man of seventy, whose whole
> Recognition of the world about him
> During those hours, was when occasionally
> He turned his eyes to the gipsy leader
> And the music changed, out of a comprehension
> As wordless as the music.
> It was dancing that came up out of the earth
> To take the old man's part against anxiety.

A comprehension as wordless as the music. It is this
comprehension which poetry tries to speak, this revelation
of discipline that comes up out of the earth, or is felt
along the heart; it is this which verse has to offer.

FRIEDRICH DUERRENMATT
(b. 1921)

Problems of the Theatre[1] (1955)

BEHOLD THE DRIVE for purity in art as art is practiced these days. Behold this writer striving for the purely poetic, another for the purely lyrical, the purely epic, the purely dramatic. The painter ardently seeks to create the pure painting, the musician pure music, and someone even told me pure radio represents the synthesis between Dionysus and Logos. Even more remarkable for our time, not otherwise renowned for its purity, is that each and everyone believes he has found his unique and the only true purity. Each vestal of the arts has, if you think of it, her own kind of chastity. Likewise, too numerous to count, are all the theories of the theatre, of what is pure theatre, pure tragedy, pure comedy. There are so many modern theories of the drama, what with each playwright keeping three or four at hand, that for this reason, if no other, I am a bit embarrassed to come along now with my theories of the problems of the theatre.

Furthermore, I would ask you not to look upon me as the spokesman of some specific movement in the theatre or of a certain dramatic technique, nor to believe that I knock at your door as the traveling salesman of one of the philosophies current on our stages today, whether as existentialist, nihilist, expressionist, or satirist, or any other label put on the compote dished up by literary criticism. For me, the stage is not a battlefield for theories, philoso-

---

[1] Friedrich Duerrenmatt, "Problems of the Theatre," translated by Gerhard Nellhaus, *Tulane Drama Review,* October, 1958, pp. 3–26. Copyright 1955 by Peter Schifferli, Verlags AG. Die Arche, Zurich. Reprinted by permission of the author's representative, Kurt Hellmer, 52 Vanderbilt Avenue, New York 17, New York, and Gerhard Nellhaus. This version was prepared for publication from the manuscript of a lecture delivered by Friedrich Duerrenmatt in the fall of 1954 and the spring of 1955 in different cities of Switzerland and West Germany.

phies, and manifestos, but rather an instrument whose possibilities I seek to know by playing with it. Of course, in my plays there are people and they hold to some belief or philosophy—a lot of blockheads would make for a dull piece—but my plays are not for what people have to say: what is said is there because my plays deal with people, and thinking and believing and philosophizing are all, to some extent at least, a part of human behavior. The problems I face as playwright are practical, working problems, problems I face not before, but during the writing. To be quite accurate about it, these problems usually come up after the writing is done, arising out of a certain curiosity to know how I did it. So what I would like to talk about now are these problems, even though I risk disappointing the general longing for something profound and creating the impression that an amateur is talking. I haven't the faintest notion of how else I should go about it, of how not to talk about art like an amateur. Consequently I speak only to those who fall asleep listening to Heidegger.

What I am concerned with are empirical rules, the possibilities of the theatre. But since we live in an age when literary scholarship and criticism flourish, I can not quite resist the temptation of casting a few side glances at some of the theories of the art and practice of the theatre. The artist indeed has no need of scholarship. Scholarship derives laws from what exists already; otherwise it would not be scholarship. But the laws thus established have no value for the artist, even when they are true. The artist can not accept a law he has not discovered for himself. If he can not find such a law, scholarship can not help him with one it has established; and when the artist does find one, then it does not matter that the same law was also discovered by scholarship. But scholarship, thus denied, stands behind the artist like a threatening ogre, ready to leap forth whenever the artist wants to talk about art. And so it is here. To talk about problems of the theatre is to enter into competition with literary scholarship. I undertake this with some misgivings. Literary scholarship looks on the theatre as an object; for the dramatist it is never something purely objective, something separate from him. He participates in it. It is true that the playwright's activity makes drama into something objective (that is exactly his job), but he destroys the object he has created again and again, forgets it, rejects it, scorns it, reevaluates it, all in order to make room for something new. Scholarship sees only the result; the process, which led to this result, is what the playwright can not forget. What he says has to be taken with a grain of salt. What he thinks about his art changes as he creates his art; his thoughts are always subject to his mood and the moment. What alone really counts for him is what he is doing at a given moment; for its sake he can betray what he did just a little while ago. Perhaps a writer should never talk about his art, but once he starts, then it is not altogether a waste of time to listen to him. Literary scholars who have not the faintest notion of the difficulties of writing and of the hidden rocks that force the stream of art into oft unsuspected channels run the danger of merely asserting and stupidly proclaiming laws that do not exist.

Doubtless the unities of time, place, and action which Aristotle—so it was supposed for a long time—derived from Greek tragedy constitute the ideal of drama. From a logical and hence also aesthetic point of view, this thesis is incontestable, so incontestable indeed, that the question arises if it does not set up the framework once and for all within which each dramatist must work. Aristotle's three unities demand the greatest precision, the greatest economy, and the greatest simplicity in the handling of the dramatic material. The unities of time, place, and action ought to be a basic dictate put to the dramatist by literary scholarship, and the only reason scholarship does not hold the artist to them is that Aristotle's unities have not been obeyed by anyone for ages. Nor can they be obeyed, for reasons which best illustrate the relationship of the art of writing plays to the theories about that art.

The unities of time, place, and action in essence presuppose Greek tragedy. Aristotle's unities do not make Greek tragedy possible; rather, Greek tragedy allows his unities. No matter how abstract an aesthetic law may appear to be, the work of art from which it was derived is contained in that law. If I want to set about writing a dramatic action which is to unfold and run its course in the same place inside of two hours, for instance, then this action must have a history behind it, and that history is the story which took place before the stage action commenced, a story which alone makes the action on the stage possible. Thus the history behind Hamlet is, of course, the murder of his father; the drama lies in the discovery of that murder. As a rule, too, the stage action is much shorter in time than the event depicted; it often starts out right in the middle of the event, or indeed toward the end of it. Before Sophocles' tragedy could begin, Oedipus had to have killed his father and married his mother. The stage action condenses an event to the extent to which Aristotle's unities are fulfilled; the closer a playwright adheres to the three unities, the more important is the background history of the action.

It is, of course, possible to invent a history and hence a dramatic action that would seem particularly favorable for keeping to Aristotle's unities. But this brings into force the rule that the more invented a story is and the more unknown it is to the audience, the more careful must its exposition, the unfolding of the background, be. Greek tragedy was possible only because it did not have to invent its historical background, because it already possessed one. The spectators knew the myths with which each drama dealt; and because these myths were public, ready coin, part of religion, they made the feats of the Greek tragedians possible, feats never to be attained again; they made possible their abbreviations, their straightforwardness, their stichomythy and choruses, and hence also Aristotle's unities. The audience knew what the play was all about; its curiosity was not focused on the story so much as on its treatment. Aristotle's unities presupposed the general appreciation of the subject matter—a genial exception in more recent times is Kleist's *The Broken Jug*—presupposed a religious theatre based on myths. Therefore as soon as the theatre lost its religious, its mythical significance, the unities had to be reinterpreted or discarded. An audience facing an unknown story will pay more attention to the story than to its treatment, and by necessity then such a play has to be richer in detail and circumstances than one with a known action. The feats of one playwright can not be the feats of another. Each art exploits the chances offered by its time, and it is hard to imagine a time without chances. Like every other form of art, drama creates its world; but not every world can be created in the same fashion. This is the natural limitation of every aesthetic rule, no matter how self-evident such a rule may be. This does not mean that Aristotle's unities are obsolete; what was once a rule has become an exception, a case that may occur again at any time. The one-act play obeys the unities still, even though under a different condition. The plot is dominated by a situation instead of by history, and thus unity is once again achieved.

. . . the task of art, insofar as art can have a task at all, and hence also the task of drama today, is to create something concrete, something that has form. This can be accomplished best by comedy. Tragedy, the strictest genre in art, presupposes a formed world. Comedy—insofar as it is not just satire of a particular society as in Molière —supposes an unformed world, a world being made and turned upside down, a world about to fold like ours. Tragedy overcomes distance; it can make myths originating in times immemorial seem like the present to the Athenians. But comedy creates distance; the attempt of the Athenians to gain a foothold in Sicily is translated by comedy into the birds undertaking to create their own empire before which the gods and men will have to capitulate. How comedy works can be seen in the most primitive kind of joke, in the dirty story, which, though it is of very dubious value, I bring up only because it is the best illustration of what I mean by creating distance. The subject of the dirty story is the purely sexual, and, because it is purely sexual, it is formless and without objective distance. To achieve form the purely sexual is transmuted, as I have already mentioned, into the dirty joke. Therefore this type of joke is a kind of original comedy, a transposition of the sexual onto the plain of the comical. In this way it is possible today in a society dominated by John Doe, to talk in an accepted way about the purely sexual. Thus the dirty story demonstrates that the comical exists in forming what is formless, in creating order out of chaos.

The means by which comedy creates distance is the conceit. Tragedy is without conceit. Hence there are few tragedies whose subjects were invented. By this I do not mean to imply that the ancient tragedians lacked inventive ideas of the sort that are written today, but the marvel of their art was that they had no need of these

inventions, of conceits. That makes all the difference.
Aristophanes, on the other hand, lives by conceits. The
stuff of his plays are not myths but inventions, which take
place not in the past but the present. They drop into their
world like bombshells which, by poking holes into the
landscape, change the present into the comic and thus
scatter the dirt for everyone to see. This, of course, does
not mean that drama today can only be comical. Tragedy
and comedy are but formal concepts, dramatic attitudes,
figments of the aesthetic imagination which can embrace
one and the same thing. Only the conditions under which
each is created are different, and these conditions have
their basis only in small part in art.

Tragedy presupposes guilt, despair, moderation, lucid-
ity, vision, a sense of responsibility. In the Punch-and-
Judy show of our century, in this backsliding of the
white race, guilty and, hence, responsible men no longer
exist. On all sides we hear: "We couldn't help it," "We
didn't really want that to happen." And indeed, things
happen without anyone in particular being responsible for
them. Everything is swept along and everyone gets caught
up somehow in the current of events. We are all
collectively guilty, collectively bogged down in the sins of
our fathers and of our forefathers. We are the offspring
of children. That is our misfortune, but not our guilt;
guilt can exist only as a personal achievement, as a religious deed. What is right for us is comedy. Our world
has led to the grotesque as well as to the atom bomb,
and Jeronimo's madness is with us again, the apocalyp-
tic vision has become the grotesquely real. But the grotesque is only a way of expressing in a tangible manner,
of making us perceive physically the paradoxical, the
form of the unformed, the face of a world without face;
and just as in our thinking today we seem to be unable
to do without the concept of the paradox, so also in
art, and in our world which at times seems still to exist
only because the atom bomb exists: out of fear of the
bomb.

But the tragic is still possible even if pure tragedy is
not. We can achieve the tragic out of comedy. We can
bring it forth as a frightening moment, as an abyss that
opens suddenly; indeed many of Shakespeare's tragedies
are already really comedies out of which the tragic arises.

All this then might easily lead to the conclusion that

comedy is the expression of despair, but this conclusion is not inevitable. To be sure, whoever realizes the sense-lessness, the hopelessness of this world might well despair, but this despair is not a result of this world. Rather it is an answer given by an individual to this world; another answer would be not to despair, would be an individual's decision to endure this world in which we live like Gulli-ver among the giants. He also achieves distance, he also steps back a pace or two who takes measure of his opponent, who prepares himself to fight his opponent or to escape him. It is still possible to show man as a courageous being.

In truth this is a principal concern of mine. The blind men, Romulus, Uebelohe, Akki, are all men of courage. The lost world order is restored within them; the universal escapes my grasp. I refuse to find the universal in a doc-trine. The universal for me is chaos. The world (hence the stage which represents this world) is for me something monstrous, a riddle of misfortunes which must be accep-ted but before which one must not capitulate. The world is far bigger than any man, and perforce threatens him constantly. If one could but stand outside the world, it would no longer be threatening. But I have neither the right nor the ability to be an outsider to this world. To find solace in poetry can also be all too cheap; it is more honest to retain one's human point of view. Brecht's thesis, that the world is an accident, which he developed in "Die Strassenszene"[2] where he shows how this accident happened, may yield—as it in fact did—some magnificent theatre; but he did it by concealing most of the evidence! Brecht's thinking is inexorable, because inexorably there are many things he will not think about.

And lastly it is through the conceit, through comedy that the anonymous audience becomes possible as an audience, becomes a reality to be counted on, and, also, one to be taken into account. The conceit easily trans-forms the crowd of theatregoers into a mass which can be attacked, deceived, outsmarted into listening to things it would otherwise not so readily listen to. Comedy is a mousetrap in which the public is easily caught and in which it will get caught over and over again. Tragedy, on

[2] An article from *Schriften Zum Theater,* available in an English translation by Eric Bentley under the title "A Model for Epic Theatre."

the other hand, predicates a true community, a kind of
community whose existence in our day is but an embarrassing fiction. Nothing is more ludicrous, for instance,
than to sit and watch the mystery plays of the Anthro-
posophists when one is not a participant.

Granting all this, there is still one more question to
be asked: is it permissible to go from a generality to a
particular form of art, to do what I just did when I
went from my assertion that the world was formless to
the particular possibility for writing comedies today? I
doubt that this is permissible. Art is something personal,
and something personal should never be explained in
generalities. The value of a work of art does not depend
on whether more or less good reasons for its existence
can be found. Hence I have also tried to avoid certain
problems, as, for example, the argument which is very
lively today, whether or not plays ought to be written in
verse or in prose. My own answer lies simply in writing
prose, without any intentions of thereby deciding the issue.
A man has to choose to go one way, after all, and why
should one way always be worse than another? As far
as my concepts of comedy are concerned, I believe that
here, too, personal reasons are more important than
more general ones that are always open to argument.
What logic in matters of art could not be refuted! One
talks best about art when one talks of one's own art.
The art one chooses is an expression of freedom without
which no art can exist, and at the same time also of
necessity without which art can not exist either. The
artist always represents his world and himself. If at one
time philosophy taught men to arrive at the particular
from the general, then unlike Schiller, who started out
believing in general conclusions, I can not construct a
play as he did when I doubt that the particular can
ever be reached from the general. But my doubt is mine
and only mine, and not the doubt and problems of a
Catholic for whom drama holds possibilities non-Catholics
do not share. This is so even if, on the other hand, a
Catholic who takes his religion seriously, is denied those
possibilities which other men possess. The danger inherent in this thesis lies in the fact that there are always
those artists who for the sake of finding some generalities to believe in accept conversion, taking a step which

is the more to be wondered at for the sad fact that it really will not help them. The difficulties experienced by a Protestant in writing a drama are just the same difficulties he has with his faith. Thus it is my way to mistrust what is ordinarily called the building of the drama, and to arrive at my plays from the unique, the sudden idea or conceit, rather than from some general concept or plan. Speaking for myself, I need to write off into the blue, as I like to put it so that I might give critics a catchword to hang onto. They use it often enough, too, without really understanding what I mean by it.

But these matters are my own concerns and hence it is not necessary to invoke the whole world and to make out as if what are my concerns are the concerns of art in general (lest I be like the drunk who goes back to Noah, the Flood, original sin, and the beginning of the world to explain what is, after all, only his own weakness). As in everything and everywhere, and not just in the field of art, the rule is: No excuses, please! . . .

JOHN OSBORNE
(b. 1929)

Declaration[1] (1958)

WHENEVER I sit down to write, it is always with dread in my heart. But never more than when I am about to write straightforward prose, because I know then that my failure will be greater and more obvious. There will be no exhilarating skirmishes, no small victories on the way to defeat. When I am writing for the theatre I know these small victories: when the light on my desk is too bright and my back aches, but I go on writing because I am afraid that my pen will lose the words that come into my head; when I watch an actor on an empty stage deliver something that proves to me that my sense of timing has been exact, after all. Timing is an artistic problem, it is the prime theatrical problem. You can learn it, but it cannot be taught. It must be felt. Things like this—composition, sonata form, the line that is unalterable—there are small victories to be won from them, because these are things that seem worth doing for themselves. If you are any good at all at what you set out to do, you know whether it is good and rely on no one to tell you so. You depend on no one.

It is not true to say that a play does not "come alive" until it is actually in performance. Of course it comes alive—to the man who has written it, just as those three symphonies must have come alive to Mozart during those last six weeks. One is sure to fail, but there are usually enough perks to be picked up on the way to make it bearable. It is the pattern of life itself, and it is acceptable. But whenever I sit down to write in prose about my present feelings and attitudes, my dread is enormous be-

[1] John Osborne, "They Call it Cricket," *Declaration,* edited by Tom Maschler (New York: E. P. Dutton, 1958), pp. 45–66. Copyright 1957 by MacGibbon and Kee. Reprinted by permission of E. P. Dutton and Co., Inc., and MacGibbon and Kee, London.

cause I know that there will be no perks to pick up, or
if there are, that they will be negligible. . . .

Part of my job is to try and keep people interested in
their seats for about two and a half hours; it is a very
difficult thing to do, and I am proud of having been even
fairly successful at it. *Look Back in Anger* has been playing to large audiences all over the country for months,
at a time when touring is all but finished. Provincial
audiences (who, on the whole, are far more receptive
than West End audiences) don't remember what the posh
papers said about plays, even if they read them. They
go to the theatre because the guvnor's wife went on Mon-
day night and said it was a jolly good show. I simply
want to point out that my job has not been an easy one
to learn, merely because I have had what looks like an
easy success. I shall go on learning as long as there is a
theatre standing in England, but I didn't learn the job
from the *Daily Mail* or the *Spectator*.

I want to make people feel, to give them lessons in
feeling. They can think afterward. In some countries this
could be a dangerous approach, but there seems little
danger of people feeling too much—at least not in England as I am writing. I am an artist—whether or not I
am a good one is beside the point now. For the first
time in my life I have a chance to get on with my job,
and that is what I intend to do. I shall do it in the
theatre and, possibly, in films. I shall not try and hand
out my gospel version of the Labour party's next manifesto to prop up any journalist who wants a bit of easy
copy or to give some reviewer another smart clue for
his weekly written-up crossword game. I shall simply fling
down a few statements—you can take your pick. They
will be what are often called "sweeping statements" but
I believe we are living at a time when a few "sweeping
statements" may be valuable. It is too late for caution.

When my play *The Entertainer* was produced, it was
complained that one of the characters was "vaguely anti-
queen." Now if this character was vague in the way she
expressed herself, it was because the existence of the Lord
Chamberlain's office compelled it. I should have been delighted if she could have been more explicit, although,
in this case, I was anxious that this particular point should
not be made too literally. The bigger point that this

character was trying to make was something like: "What kind of symbols do we live by? *Are* they truthful and worthwhile?" But in expressing herself in anti-queen terms, which was a relevant and colorful image—or so I thought—I believe she was asking an important question. I still believe it to be an important question.

Recently I read an article by David Marquand called *"Lucky Jim* and the Labour Party." . . . The principal figures seem to have been Kingsley Amis, John Wain —and myself. A great deal of the *Lucky Jim* gibberish has been promoted by a few words I put into the mouth of Jimmy Porter [*Look Back in Anger*]. These were: "There aren't any good, brave causes left." Immediately they heard this, all the shallow heads with their savage thirst for trimmed-off explanations got to work on it, and they had enough new symbols to play about with happily and fill their columns for half a year. They believed him, just as some believed Archie Rice [*The Entertainer*] when he said, "I don't feel a thing" or "I may be an old pouf, but I'm not right-wing." They were incapable of recognizing the texture of ordinary despair, the way it expresses itself in rhetoric and gestures that may perhaps look shabby, but are seldom simple. It is too simple to say that Jimmy Porter himself believed that there were no good, brave causes left, any more than Archie didn't feel a thing.

At this I can hear all kinds of impatient inflections. "Well, if your characters only mean what they say some of the time, when are we supposed to know what they're getting at? What are *you* getting at? What do you *mean?* How do you *explain* these characters, these situations?" At every performance of any of my plays, there are always some of these deluded pedants, sitting there impatiently, waiting for the plugs to come singing in during natural breaks in the action. If the texture is too complex, they complain that too much is going on for them to follow. There they sit, these fashionable turnips, the death's heads of imagination and feeling, longing for the interval and its overprojected drawls of ignorance. Like the B.B.C. critics, they either have no ear at all, or they can never listen to themselves.

I offer no explanations to such people. All art is organized evasion. You respond to Lear or Max Miller— or you don't. I can't teach the paralyzed to move their limbs. Shakespeare didn't describe symptoms or offer explanations. Neither did Chekhov. Neither do I.

It is an inescapable fact that when the middle classes discuss experience that is not dominated by their own emotional values, they hedge and bluster with all they've got. A few weeks ago, a reviewer wrote: "One is compelled to believe that if they [the characters] have indeed been drawn from life, Mr. Osborne has set them down with shamelessly pointed accuracy." This, at least, is refreshingly honest. There is no pretense at being capable of judging whether the characters have been indeed drawn from life—just a shrug at shamelessly pointed accuracy. The boys in the orchestra at the Royal Court Theatre were capable of judging, and they did: *"We've been through it and we know what it is like."* This is what audiences have muttered beneath their heartbeat as they have watched Oedipus or Lear or Willy Loman. "It's still a bitter truth of life," says the same writer, "that the most wretched human beings become bores when they start moaning—even the sick, the aged, and afflicted." This sentence sums up fairly neatly a prevalent class attitude to the pain and struggle of other people. I do not accept it for one moment. It is true that the middle classes do not talk about their private troubles. But like working people they do moan a great deal about the way they think they are being cheated out of their inheritance, submerged by taxes and unfair checks on their "incentive"—in other words they are not allowed to make enough money to buy themselves their traditional privileges—the education that will assure them of the best places in the sun. But, on the whole, they scrupulously avoid discussing their personal problems. Even with their friends.

I am not going to define my own socialism. Socialism is an experimental idea, not a dogma; an attitude to truth and liberty, the way people should live and treat each other. Individual definitions are unimportant. The difference between socialist and Tory values should have been made clear enough by this time. I am a writer and my own contribution to a socialist society is to demonstrate those values in my own medium, not to discover the best ways of implementing them. I don't need to step outside my own home to canvass for the Labour party. Years ago, T.S.

Eliot wrote: "In a society like ours, worm-eaten with Liberalism, the only thing possible for a person with strong convictions is to state a point of view and leave it at that." Substitute Toryism for Liberalism, and I'd say that this very roughly sums up my present socialist attitude—an experimental attitude to feeling. All the fields of experiment must be tackled by their own experts—economists and sociologists, town planners and educationists, industrial psychologists, observers, lawmakers, and truth seekers.

Nobody can be very interested in my contribution to a problem like the kind of houses people should have built for them, the kind of school they should send their children to, or the pensions they should be able to look forward to. But there are other questions to be asked— how do people live inside those houses? What is their relationship with one another, and with their children, with their neighbors and the people across the street, or on the floor above? What are the things that are important to them, that make them care, give them hope and anxiety? What kind of language do they use to one another? What is the meaning of the work they do? Where does the pain lie? What are their expectations? What moves them, brings them together, makes them speak out? Where is the weakness, the loneliness? Where are the things that are unrealized? Where is the strength? Experiment means asking questions, and these are all the questions of socialism.

EUGENE IONESCO
(b. 1912)

The Starting Point[1] (1955)

ALL MY PLAYS have their origin in two fundamental states
of consciousness: now the one, now the other is predom-
inant, and sometimes they are combined. These basic
states of consciousness are an awareness of evanescence
and of solidity, of emptiness and of too much presence,
of the unreal transparency of the world and its opacity,
of light and of thick darkness. Each of us has surely
felt at moments that the substance of the world is dreamlike, that the walls are no longer solid, that we seem to
be able to see through everything into a spaceless universe made up of pure light and color; at such a moment
the whole of life, the whole history of the world, becomes
useless, senseless, and impossible. When you fail to go
beyond this first stage of *dépaysement*—for you really
do have the impression you are waking to a world unknown
—the sensation of evanescence gives you a feeling of
anguish, a form of giddiness. But all this may equally
well lead to euphoria: the anguish suddenly turns into release; nothing counts now except the wonder of being, that
new and amazing consciousness of life in the glow of a
fresh dawn, when we have found our freedom again; the
fact of being astonishes us, in a world that now seems all
illusion and pretense, in which all human behavior tells of
absurdity and all history of absolute futility; all reality
and all language appear to lose their articulation, to dis-
integrate and collapse, so what possible reaction is there
left, when everything has ceased to matter, but to laugh
at it all? I myself at one such moment felt so completely
free, so released, that I had the impression I could do
anything I wished with the language and the people of a

[1] Eugene Ionesco, Foreword, *Plays*, translated by Donald
Watson (London: John Calder, 1959), I, vii–ix. Reprinted by
courtesy of Eugene Ionesco and Donald Watson.

world that no longer seemed to me anything but a base-
less and ridiculous sham.

Of course this state of consciousness is very rare; this
joy and wonder at being alive, in a universe that troubles
me no more and *is* no more, can only just hold; more
commonly the opposite feeling prevails: what is light grows
heavy, the transparent becomes dense, the world op-
presses, the universe is crushing me. A curtain, an impassable wall stands between me and the world, between
me and myself; matter fills every corner, takes up all the
space and its weight annihilates all freedom; the horizon
closes in and the world becomes a stifling dungeon.
Language breaks down in a different way and words drop
like stones or dead bodies; I feel I am invaded by heavy
forces, against which I can only fight a losing battle.

This was definitely the starting point of those of my
plays that are generally considered the more dramatic:
Amédée and *Victims of Duty*. Given such a state of
mind, words, their magic gone, are obviously replaced by
objects, by properties: countless mushrooms sprout in
the flat of Amédée and Madeleine; a dead body suffering from "geometrical progression" grows there too and
turns the tenants out; in *Victims of Duty,* when coffee is
to be served to three of the characters, there is a
mounting pile of hundreds of cups; the furniture in *The
New Tenant* first blocks up every staircase in the building,
then clutters the stage, and finally entombs the character
who came to take a room in the house; in *The Chairs*
the stage is filled with dozens of chairs for invisible guests;
and in *Jacques* several noses appear on the face of a
young girl. When words are worn out, the mind is worn
out. The universe, encumbered with matter, is then empty
of presence: "too much" links up with "not enough"
and objects are the materialization of solitude, of the
victory of the anti-spiritual forces, of everything we are
struggling against. But in this anxious situation I do
not quite give up the fight, and if, as I hope, I manage in
spite of the anguish to introduce into the anguish, humor
—which is a happy symptom of the other presence—this
humor is my outlet, my release, and my salvation.

I have no intention of passing judgment on my plays.
It is not for me to do so. I have simply tried to give
some indication of what emotional material went into their
making, of what was at their source: a mood and not an

ideology, an impulse not a program; the cohesive unity that grants formal structure to emotions in their primitive state satisfies an inner need and does not answer the logic of some structural order imposed from without; not submission to some predetermined action, but the exteriorization of a psychic dynamism, a projection onto the stage of internal conflict, of the universe that lies within: but as the microcosm is in the likeness of the macrocosm and each one of us is all the others, it is in the deepest part of myself, of my anguish and my dreams, it is in my solitude that I have the best chance of rediscovering the universal, the common ground.

The Bald Soprano is the only one of my plays the critics consider to be "purely comic." And yet there again the comic seems to me to be an expression of the unusual. But in my view the unusual can spring only from the dullest and most ordinary daily routine and from our everyday prose, when pursued beyond their limits. To feel the absurdity, the improbability of everyday experience and of our attempts at communication is already to have gone a stage further; before you do this, you must first saturate yourself. The comic is the unusual pure and simple; nothing surprises me more than banality; the "surreal" is there, within our reach, in our daily conversation.

PART 2 Creations

HENRIK IBSEN
(1828-1906)

A Doll's House[1] (1878)

NOTES FOR THE MODERN TRAGEDY

THERE ARE two kinds of spiritual law, two kinds of con-science, one in man and another, altogether different, in woman. They do not understand each other; but in practical life the woman is judged by man's law, as though she were not a woman but a man.

The wife in the play ends by having no idea of what is right or wrong; natural feeling on the one hand and belief in authority on the other have altogether bewildered her.

A woman cannot be herself in the society of the present day, which is an exclusively masculine society, with laws framed by men and with a judicial system that judges feminine conduct from a masculine point of view.

She has committed forgery, and she is proud of it; for she did it out of love for her husband, to save his life. But this husband with his commonplace principles of

[1] Henrik Ibsen, *From Ibsen's Workshop,* translated by A. G. Chater, *The Works of Henrik Ibsen.* (New York: Charles Scrib-ner's Sons, 1912), XII, pp. 91–95 (*A Doll's House*), pp. 185–86 (*Ghosts*). "This volume contains all the notes, sketches, drafts, and other 'foreworks' (as he used to call them) for Ibsen's plays from *Pillars of Society* onwards. . . . The papers here translated throw invaluable light upon the genesis of his ideas and the development of his technique. They are an indispensable aid to the study of his intellectual processes during that part of his career which made him world famous. . . . Nowhere else, so far as I am aware, do we obtain so clear a view of the processes of a great dramatist's mind" (from the introduction by William Archer). "Of *A Doll's House* we possess a first brief memoran-dum, a fairly detailed scenario, a complete draft, in quite acta-ble form, and a few detached fragments of dialogue" (Archer).

honor is on the side of the law and looks at the question from the masculine point of view.

Spiritual conflicts. Oppressed and bewildered by the belief in authority, she loses faith in her moral right and ability to bring up her children. Bitterness. A mother in modern society, like certain insects who go away and die when she has done her duty in the propagation of the race. Love of life, of home, of husband and children and family. Now and then a womanly shaking off of her thoughts. Sudden return of anxiety and terror. She must bear it all alone. The catastrophe approaches, inexorably, inevitably. Despair, conflict, and destruction.

(Krogstad has acted dishonorably and thereby become well-to-to-do; now his prosperity does not help him, he cannot recover his honor.)

SCENARIO: FIRST ACT

A room comfortably, but not showily, furnished. A door to the right in the back leads to the hall; another door to the left in the back leads to the room or office of the master of the house, which can be seen when the door is opened. A fire in the stove. Winter day.

She enters from the back, humming gaily; she is in outdoor dress and carries several parcels, has been shopping. As she opens the door, a porter is seen in the hall, carrying a Christmas tree. She: Put it down there for the present. (Taking out her purse) How much? Porter: Fifty öre. She: Here is a crown. No, keep the change. The porter thanks her and goes. She continues humming and smiling contentedly as she opens several of the parcels she has brought. Calls off to find out if he is home. Yes! At first, conversation through the closed door; then he opens it and goes on talking to her while continuing to work most of the time, standing at his desk. There is a ring at the hall door; he does not want to be disturbed; shuts himself in. The maid opens the door to her mistress's friend, just arrived in town. Happy surprise. Mutual explanation of the state of affairs. He has received the post of manager in the new joint-stock bank and is to begin at New Year's; all financial worries are at an end. The friend has come to town to look for some small employment in an office or whatever may present itself. Mrs. Stenborg encourages her, is certain that all will turn out well. The maid opens the front door to the debt collector. Mrs. Stenborg terrified; they exchange a few words; he is shown into the office. Mrs. Stenborg and her friend; the circumstances of the collector are touched upon. Stenborg enters in his overcoat; has sent the collector out the other way. Conversation about the friend's affairs; hesitation on his part. He and the friend go out; his wife follows them into the hall; the Nurse enters with the children. Mother and children play. The collector enters. Mrs. Stenborg sends the children out to the left. Big scene between her and him. He goes. Stenborg enters; has met him on the stairs; displeased; wants to know what he came back for? Her support? No intrigues. His wife cautiously tries to pump him. Strict legal answers. Exit to his room. *She:* (repeating her words when the collector went out) But that's impossible. Why, I did it from love!

SECOND ACT

The last day of the year. Midday. Nora and the old Nurse. Nora, driven by anxiety, is putting on her things to go out. Anxious random questions of one kind and another intimate that thoughts of death are in her mind. Tries to banish these thoughts, to make light of it, hopes that something or other may intervene. But what? The Nurse goes off to the left. Stenborg enters from his room. Short dialogue between him and Nora. The Nurse re-enters; looks for Nora; the youngest child is crying. Annoyance and questioning on Stenborg's part; exit the Nurse; Stenborg is going in to the children. Doctor enters. Scene between him and Stenborg. Nora soon re-enters; she has turned back; anxiety has driven her home again. Scene between her, the Doctor, and Stenborg. Stenborg goes into his room. Scene between Nora and the Doctor. The Doctor goes out. Nora alone. Mrs. Linde enters. Scene between her and Nora. Lawyer Krogstad enters. Short scene between him, Mrs. Linde, and Nora. Mrs. Linde in to the children. Scene between Krogstad and Nora. She entreats and implores him for the sake of her little children; in vain. Krogstad goes out. The letter is seen to fall from outside into the letter box. Mrs. Linde re-enters after a short pause. Scene between her and Nora. Half confession. Mrs. Linde goes out. Nora alone. Stenborg enters. Scene between him and Nora. He wants to empty the letter box. Entreaties, jests, half-playful persuasion. He promises to let business wait till after New Year's Day; but at 12 o'clock midnight . . . ! Exit. Nora alone. *Nora:* (looking at the clock) It is five o'clock. Five; seven hours till midnight. Twenty-four hours till the next midnight. Twenty-four and seven—thirty-one. Thirty-one hours to live.

THIRD ACT

A muffled sound of dance music is heard from the floor above. A lighted lamp on the table. Mrs. Linde sits in an armchair and absently turns the pages of a book, tries to read, but seems unable to fix her attention; once or twice she looks at her watch. Nora comes down from the party; so disturbed she was compelled to leave; surprise at finding Mrs. Linde, who pretends that she wanted to see Nora in her costume. Helmer, displeased at her going away, comes to fetch her back. The Doctor also enters, to say good-by. Meanwhile Mrs. Linde has gone into the side room on the right. Scene between the Doctor, Helmer, and Nora. He is going to bed, he says, never to get up again; they are not to come and see him; there is ugliness about a deathbed. He goes out. Helmer goes upstairs again with Nora, after the latter has exchanged a few words of farewell with Mrs. Linde. Mrs. Linde alone. Then Krogstad. Scene and explanation between them. Both go out. Nora and the children. Then she alone. Then Helmer. He takes the letters out of the letter box. Short scene; good night; he goes into his room. Nora in despair prepares for the final step, is already at the door when Helmer enters with the open letter in his hand. Big scene. A ring. Letter to Nora from Krogstad. Final scene. Divorce. Nora leaves the house.

Ghosts[2]

THE PLAY is to be like a picture of life. Belief undermined. But it does not do to say so. "The Orphanage"—

[2] "Of the studies for *Ghosts* only a few brief fragments have been preserved. The most important of these are mere casual memoranda, some of them written on the back of an envelope

for the sake of others. They are to be happy—but this too is only an appearance—everything is ghosts.

A leading point: She has been a believer and romantic —this is not entirely obliterated by the standpoint reached later—"Everything is ghosts."

Marriage for external reasons, even when these are religious or moral, brings a Nemesis upon the offspring.

She, the illegitimate child, can be saved by being married to—the son—but then—?

¶ He was dissipated and his health was shattered in his youth; then she appeared, the religious enthusiast; she saved him; she was rich. He was going to marry a girl who was considered unworthy. He had a son by his wife, then he went back to the girl; a daughter.

¶ These modern women, ill-used as daughters, as sisters, as wives, not educated according to their gifts, prevented from following their calling, deprived of their inheritance, embittered in temper—it is these who furnish the mothers of the new generation. What will be the result?

¶ The keynote is to be: The prolific growth of our intellectual life, in literature, arts, etc.—and in contrast to this: all of mankind gone astray.

The complete human being is no longer a product of nature, he is an artificial product like grain, and fruit trees, and the Creole race and thoroughbred horses and dogs, the vine, etc.

The fault lies in that all mankind has failed. If a man claims to live and develop in a human way, it is megalomania. All mankind, and especially the Christian part of it, suffers from megalomania.

¶ Among us, monuments are erected to the *dead,* since we have a duty toward them; we allow lepers to marry; but their offspring . . . ? The unborn . . . ?

---

addressed to 'Madame Ibsen.' These memoranda fall into six sections, of which the fourth and fifth seem to have as much bearing on other plays—for instance, on *An Enemy of the People* and *The Lady From the Sea* as on *Ghosts.* I should take them rather for detached jottings than for notes specially referring to that play" (Archer).

Hedda Gabler[3]

(1)

¶ This married woman more and more imagines that she is an important personality, and as a consequence feels compelled to create for herself a sensational past—

¶ If an interesting female character appears in a new story or in a play, she believes that it is she who is being portrayed.

¶ The masculine environment helps to confirm her in this belief.

¶ The two lady friends agree to die together. One of them carries out her end of the bargain. But the other one who realizes what lies in store for her loses her courage. This is the reversal—

---

[3] More preliminary notes have been preserved for *Hedda Gabler* than for almost any other play by Ibsen. These notes afford the student of playwriting a rare opportunity to trace the growth of a masterpiece from the first embryonic thoughts through its birth as a full-length draft. Nearly all of these preliminary notes are given here, grouped in seven sets to indicate their different sources: scattered loose sheets, notebooks, even a calling card. Of greatest interest are the notes in sets 1 and 5 taken from a little black book, now in the possession of Tancred Ibsen, which Ibsen carried about with him. According to Else Høst, *Hedda Gabler: En monografi* (Oslo: 1958), pp. 78 ff., the notes in set 1 were probably jotted down in the fall of 1889 and comprise the abortive ideas for a play about a prominent woman novelist, Camilla Collett, who imagined that Ibsen had used her as a model for the heroine of *The Lady from the Sea*. Ibsen made no progress with this play, but among the notes for it he had planted the seeds of another play: a play about a cowardly woman, the woman's jealousy of a man with a mission in life, and a misplaced manuscript which represents that mission. The lengthy sequence of notes in set 5, almost certainly in chronological order, was probably made during the winter and spring of 1890 and reveals the convolutions of Ibsen's thought as the characters, plot, and motives of *Hedda Gabler* take shape. In late July or early August, Ibsen began to write a full-length draft, most of which is translated in *From Ibsen's Workshop*, Vol. XII of the Archer edition of Ibsen's Collected Works. This draft was thoroughly revised in October, fair copied in October and November, and *Hedda Gabler* was published on December 4, 1890, in time for the Christmas season. The notes are arranged in the order given in the Centennial Edition of Ibsen's works (21 vols.; Oslo: 1928–1957), ed. Francis Bull, Halvdan Koht, and Didrik Arup Seip, XI, pp. 496–516. (Translator's note.)

¶ "He has such a disgusting way of walking when one sees him from behind."

¶ She hates him because he has a goal, a mission in life. The lady friend has one too, but does not dare to devote herself to it. Her personal life treated in fictional form.

¶ In the second act the manuscript that is left behind—

¶ "The lost soul" apologizes for the man of culture. The wild horse and the race horse. Drinks—eats paprika. House and clothes. Revolution against the laws of nature —but nothing stupid, not until the position is secure.

(2)

¶ The pale, apparently cold beauty. Expects great things of life and the joy of life.

The man who has now finally won her, plain and simple in appearance, but an honest and talented, broad-minded scholar.

(3)

¶ The manuscript that H. L. leaves behind contends that man's mission is: Upward, toward the bearer of light. Life on the present foundations of society is not worth living. Therefore he escapes from it through his imagination. By drinking, etc.—Tesman stands for correct behavior. Hedda for blasé oversophistication. Mrs. R. is the nervous-hysterical modern individual. Brack represents the personal bourgeois point of view.

¶ Then H. departs this world. And the two of them are left sitting there with the manuscript they cannot interpret. And the aunt is with them. What an ironic comment on humanity's striving for progress and development.

¶ But Holger's double nature intervenes. Only by realizing the basely bourgeois can he win a hearing for his great central idea.

¶ Mrs. Rising is afraid that H., although "a model of propriety," is not normal. She can only guess at his way of thinking but cannot understand it. Quotes some of his remarks—

¶ One talks about building railways and highways for the cause of progress. But no, no, that is not what is needed. Space must be cleared so that the spirit of man can make its great turnabout. For it has gone astray. The spirit of man has gone astray.

¶ *Holger:* I have been out. I have behaved obscenely. That doesn't matter. But the police know about it. That's what counts.

¶ H. L.'s despair lies in that he wants to master the world but cannot master himself.

¶ Tesman believes that it is he who has in a way seduced H. L. into indulging in excesses again. But that is not so. It is as Hedda has said: that it was *he* she dreamed of when she talked about "the famous man." But she does not dare tell Tesman this.

¶ To aid in understanding his own character, L. has made notes in "the manuscript." These are the notes the two of them should interpret, want to interpret, but *cannot* possibly.

¶ Brack is inclined to live as a bachelor, and then gain admittance to a good home, become a friend of the family, indispensable—

¶ They say it is a law of nature. Very well then, raise an opposition to it. Demand its repeal. Why give way. Why surrender unconditionally—

¶ In conversations between T. and L. the latter says that he lives for his studies. The former replies that in that case he can compete with him.—(T. lives *on* his studies) that's the point.

¶ L. (Tesman) says: I couldn't step on a worm! "But now I can tell you that I too am seeking the professorship. We are rivals."

(4)

¶ She has respect for his knowledge, an eye for his noble character, but is embarrassed by his insignificant, ridiculous appearance, makes fun of his conduct and remarks.

(5)

¶ The aunt asks all sorts of ambiguous questions to find out about those things that arouse her imagination the most.

¶ NOTES: One evening as Hedda and Tesman, together with some others, were on their way home from a party, Hedda remarked as they walked by a charming house that was where she would like to live. She meant it, but she said it only to keep the conversation with Tesman going. "He simply cannot carry on a conversation."

The house was actually for rent or sale. Tesman had been pointed out as the coming young man. And later when he proposed, and let slip that he too had dreamed of living there, she accepted.

He too had liked the house very much.

They get married. And they rent the house.[4]

But when Hedda returns as a young wife, with a vague sense of responsibility, the whole thing seems distasteful to her. She conceives a kind of hatred for the house just because it has become her home. She confides this to Brack. She evades the question with Tesman.

¶ The play shall deal with "the impossible," that is, to aspire to and strive for something which is against all the conventions, against that which is acceptable to conscious minds—Hedda's included.

¶ The episode of the hat makes Aunt Rising lose her composure. She leaves—That it could be taken for the maid's hat—no, that's going too far!

That my hat, which I've had for over nine years, could be taken for the maid's—no, that's really too much!

¶ *Hedda:* Yes, once I thought it must be wonderful to live here and own this house.

Brack: But now you are contradicting yourself.

Hedda: That may be so. But that's how it is anyway.

¶ *Hedda:* I don't understand these self-sacrificing people. Look at old Miss Rising. She has a paralyzed sister in her house, who has been lying in bed for years. Do you suppose she thinks it is a sacrifice to live for that poor creature, who is a burden even to herself? Far from it! Just the opposite. I don't understand it.

¶ *Hedda:* And how greedy they are for married

[4] Both of them, each in his and her own way, have seen in their common love for this house a sign of their mutual understanding. As if they sought and were drawn to a common home. Then he rents the house. They get married and go abroad. He orders the house bought and his aunt furnishes it at his expense. Now it is their home. It is theirs and yet it is not, because it is not paid for. Everything depends on his getting the professorship. (Ibsen's note.)

men. Do you know what, Judge Brack? You don't do yourself any good by not getting married.

Brack: Then I can practically consider myself married.

Hedda: Yes, you certainly can—in one way—in many ways even—

Brack: In many ways? What do you mean by that?

Hedda: No thanks. I won't tell you.

¶ When Mrs. Elvsted says that the first part of Lövborg's book deals with the historical development of "Sociology," and that another volume will appear later, Tesman looks at her a little startled.

¶ Very few true parents are to be found in the world. Most people grow up under the influence of aunts or uncles—either neglected and misunderstood or else spoiled.

¶ Hedda rejects him because he does not dare expose himself to temptation. He replies that the same is true of her. The wager! . . . He loses . . . ! Mrs. Elvsted is present. Hedda says: No danger—He loses.

¶ Hedda feels herself demoniacally attracted by the tendencies of the times. But she lacks courage. Her thoughts remain theories, ineffective dreams.[5]

¶ The feminine imagination is not active and independently creative like the masculine. It needs a bit of reality as a help.

¶ Lövborg has had inclinations toward "the bohemian life." Hedda is attracted in the same direction, but she does not dare to take the leap.

¶ Buried deep within Hedda there is a level of poetry. But the environment frightens her. Suppose she were to make herself ridiculous!

¶ Hedda realizes that she, much more than Thea, has abandoned her husband.

¶ The newly wedded couple return home in September —as the summer is dying. In the second act they sit in the garden—but with their coats on.

¶ Being frightened by one's own voice. Something strange, foreign.

¶ NEWEST PLAN: The festivities in Tesman's garden —and Lövborg's defeat—already prepared for in the 1st act. Second act: the party—

---

[5] This note is omitted in the Centennial Edition. It is translated from Else Høst, *Hedda Gabler: En monografi* (Oslo: 1958), p. 82.

¶ Hedda energetically refuses to serve as hostess. She will not celebrate their marriage because (in her opinion, it isn't a marriage)

¶ *Holger:* Don't you see? I am the cause of your marriage—

¶ Hedda is the type of woman in her position and with her character. She marries Tesman but she devotes her imagination to Eilert Lövborg. She leans back in her chair, closes her eyes, and dreams of his adventures. . . . This is the enormous difference: Mrs. Elvsted "works for his moral improvement." But for Hedda he is the object of cowardly, tempting daydreams. In reality she does not have the courage to be a part of anything like that. Then she realizes her condition. Caught! Can't comprehend it. Ridiculous! Ridiculous!

¶ The traditional delusion that one man and one woman are made for each other. Hedda has her roots in the conventional. She marries Tesman but she dreams of Eilert Lövborg. . . . She is disgusted by the latter's flight from life. He believes that this has raised him in her estimation. . . . Thea Elvsted is the conventional, sentimental, hysterical Philistine.

¶ Those Philistines, Mrs. E. and Tesman, explain my behavior by saying first I drink myself drunk and that the rest is done in insanity. It's a flight from reality which is an absolute necessity to me.

¶ *E. L.:* Give me something—a flower—at our parting. Hedda hands him the revolver.

Then Tesman arrives: Has he gone? "Yes." Do you think he will still compete against me? No, I don't think so. You can set your mind at rest.

¶ Tesman relates that when they were in Gratz she did not want to visit her relatives—

He misunderstands her real motives.

¶ In the last act as Tesman, Mrs. Elvsted, and Miss Rysing are consulting, Hedda plays in the small room at the back. She stops. The conversation continues. She appears in the doorway—Good night—I'm going now. Do you need me for anything? Tesman: No, nothing at all. Good night, my dear! . . . The shot is fired—

¶ CONCLUSION: All rush into the back room. Brack sinks as if paralyzed into a chair near the stove: But God have mercy—people don't *do* such things!

¶ When Hedda hints at her ideas to Brack, he says: Yes, yes, that's extraordinarily amusing—Ha ha ha! He does not understand that she is quite serious.

¶ Hedda is right in this: There is no love on Tesman's part. Nor on the aunt's part. However full of love she may be.

Eilert Lövborg has a double nature. It is a fiction that one loves only *one* person. He loves two—or many —alternately (to put it frivolously). But how can he explain his position? Mrs. Elvsted, who forces him to behave correctly, runs away from her husband. Hedda, who drives him beyond all limits, draws back at the thought of a scandal.

¶ Neither he nor Mrs. Elvsted understands the point. Tesman reads in the manuscript that was left behind about "the two ideals." Mrs. Elvsted can't explain to him what E. L. meant. Then comes the burlesque note: both T. and Mrs. E. are going to devote their future lives to interpreting the mystery.

¶ Tesman thinks that Hedda hates E. L.

Mrs. Elvsted thinks so too.

Hedda sees their delusion but dares not disabuse them of it. There is something beautiful about having an aim in life. Even if it is a delusion —

She cannot do it. Take part in someone else's.

That is when she shoots herself.

The destroyed manuscript is entitled "The ~~Philosophy~~ Ethics of Future Society."

¶ Tesman is on the verge of losing his head. All this work meaningless. New thoughts! New visions! A whole new world! Then the two of them sit there, trying to find the meaning in it. Can't make any sense of it. . . .

¶ The greatest misery in this world is that so many have nothing to do but pursue happiness without being able to find it.

¶ "From Jochum Tesman there developed a Jørgen Tesman—but it will be a long, long time before this Jørgen gives rise to a George."

¶ The simile: The journey of life = the journey on a train.

H.: One doesn't usually jump out of the compartment. No, not when the train is moving.

Nor stand still when it is stationary. There's always someone on the platform, staring in.

¶ *Hedda:* Dream of a scandal—yes, I understand that well enough. But commit one—no, no, no.

¶ *Lövborg:* Now I understand. My ideal was an illusion. You aren't a bit better than I. Now I have nothing left to live for. Except pleasure—dissipation—as you call it. . . Wait, here's a present (The pistol)

¶ Tesman is nearsighted. Wears glasses. My, what a beautiful rose! Then he stuck his nose in the cactus. Ever since then—!

¶ NB: The mutual hatred of women. Women have no influence on external matters of government. Therefore they want to have an influence on souls. And then so many of them have no aim in life (the lack thereof is inherited)—

¶ Lövborg and Hedda bent over the photographs at the table.

He: How is it possible? *She:* Why not? *L.:* Tesman! You couldn't find words enough to make fun of him. . . . Then comes the story about the general's "disgrace," dismissal, etc. The worst thing for a lady at a ball is not to be admired for her own sake. . . *L.:* And Tesman? He took you for the sake of your person. That's just as unbearable to think about.

¶ Just by marrying Tesman it seems to me I have gotten so unspeakably far away from him.

¶ *He:* Look at her. Just look at her! . . . *Hedda:* (stroking her hair) Yes, isn't she beautiful!

¶ Men and women don't belong to the same century. . . . What a great prejudice that one should love only *one!*

¶ Hedda and Brack talk about traveling to the small university towns. *Hedda:* Now I'm not counting that little trip through the Tyrol—

¶ *Brack:* (to Tesman) Are you blind and deaf? Can't you see? Can't you hear—

Tesman: Ah. Take the manuscript. Read to me!

¶ The demoniacal element in Hedda is this: She wants to exert her influence on someone—But once she has done so, she despises him. . . . The manuscript?

¶ In the third act Hedda questions Mrs. Elvsted. But if he's like that, why is he worth holding on to. . . . Yes, yes, I know—

¶ Hedda's discovery that her relations with the maid cannot possibly be proper.

¶ In his conversation with Hedda, Lövborg says: Miss H—Miss—You know, I don't believe that you are married.

¶ *Hedda:* And now I sit here and talk with these Philistines—And the way we once could talk to each other—No, I won't say any more. . . Talk? How do you mean? Obscenely? Ish. Let us say indecently.

¶ NB!! The reversal in the play occurs during the big scene between Hedda and E. L. *He:* What a wretched business it is to conform to the existing morals. It would be ideal if a man of the present could live the life of the future. What a miserable business it is to fight over a professorship!

Hedda—that lovely girl! *H.:* No! *E. L.:* Yes, I'm going to say it. That lovely, cold girl—cold as marble.

I'm not dissipated fundamentally. But the life of reality isn't livable—

¶ In the fifth act: *Hedda:* How hugely comic it is that those two harmless people, Tesman and Mrs. E., should try to put the pieces together for a monument to E. L. The man who so deeply despised the whole business—

¶ Life becomes for Hedda a ridiculous affair that isn't "worth seeing through to the end."

¶ The happiest mission in life is to place the people of today in the conditions of the future.

L.: Never put a child in this world, H.!

¶ When Brack speaks of a "triangular affair," Hedda thinks about what is going to happen and refers ambiguously to it. Brack doesn't understand.

¶ Brack cannot bear to be in a house where there are small children. "Children shouldn't be allowed to exist until they are fourteen or fifteen. That is, girls. What about boys? Shouldn't be allowed to exist at all—or else they should be raised outside the house."

¶ H. admits that children have always been a horror to her too.

¶ Hedda is strongly but imprecisely opposed to the idea that one should love "the family." The aunts mean nothing to her.

¶ It liberated Hedda's spirit to serve as a confessor to E. L. Her sympathy has secretly been on his side—But it became ugly when the public found out everything. Then she backed out.

¶ MAIN POINTS:

1. They are not all made to be mothers.

2. They are passionate but they are afraid of scandal.

3. They perceive that the times are full of missions worth devoting one's life to, but they cannot discover them.

¶ And besides Tesman is not exactly a professional, but he is a specialist. The Middle Ages are dead—

¶ *T.:* Now there you see also the great advantages to my studies. I can lose manuscripts and rewrite them— no inspiration needed—

¶ Hedda is completely taken up by the child that is to come, but when it is born she dreads what is to follow—

¶ Hedda must say somewhere in the play that she did not like to get out of her compartment while on the trip. Why not? I don't like to show my legs. . . . Ah, Mrs. H., but they do indeed show themselves. Nevertheless, I don't.

¶ Shot herself! Shot herself!

Brack (collapsing in the easy chair): But great God— people don't *do* such things!

¶ NB!! Eilert Lövborg believes that a comradeship must be formed between man and woman out of which the truly spiritual human being can arise. Whatever else the two of them do is of no concern. This is what the people around him do not understand. To them he is dissolute. Inwardly he is not.

¶ If a man can have several male friends, why can't he have several lady friends?

¶ It is precisely the sensual feelings that are aroused while in the company of his female "friends" or "comrades" that seek release in his excesses.

¶ Now I'm going. Don't you have some little remembrance to give me—? You have flowers—and so many other things—(The story of the pistol from before)— But you won't use it anyhow—

¶ In the fourth act when Hedda finds out that he has shot himself, she is jubilant. . . . He had courage.

Here is the rest of the manuscript.

¶ CONCLUSION: Life isn't tragic. . . . Life is ridiculous. . . . And that's what I can't bear.

¶ Do you know what happens in novels? All those who kill themselves—through the head—not in the stomach. . . . How ridiculous—how baroque—

¶ In her conversation with Thea in the first act, Hedda

remarks that she cannot understand how one can fall in love with an unmarried man—or an unengaged man —or an unloved man—on the other hand—⁶

¶ Brack understands well enough that it is Hedda's repression, her hysteria that motivates everything she does.

¶ On her part, Hedda suspects that Brack sees through her without believing that she understands.

¶ *H.:* It must be wonderful to take something from someone.

¶ When H. talks to B. in the fifth act about those two sitting there trying to piece together the manuscript without the spirit being present, she breaks out in laughter. . . . Then she plays the piano—then—d—

¶ Men—in the most indescribable situations how ridiculous they are.

¶ NB! She really wants to live a *man's* life wholly. But then she has misgivings. Her inheritance, what is implanted in her.

¶ Loving and being loved by aunts . . . Most people who are born of old maids, male and female.

¶ This deals with the "underground forces and powers." Woman as a minor. Nihilism. Father and mother belonging to different eras. The female underground revolution in thought. The slave's fear of the outside world.

¶ NB!! Why should I conform to social morals that I know won't last more than half a generation. When I run wild, as they call it, it's my escape from the present. Not that I find any joy in my excesses. I'm up to my neck in the established order. . . .

¶ What is Tesman working on?

¶ *Hedda:* It's a book on the domestic industries of Brabant during the Middle Ages.

¶ I have to play the part of an idiot in order to be understood. Pretend that I want to rehabilitate myself in the eyes of the mob—today's mob.

¶ When I had finished with my latest book, I conceived the idea for a brilliant new work. You must help me with it. I need women, Hedda—! In the Middle Ages

⁶ 1. But, my heavens, Tesm. was unmarried. *H.:* Yes, he was. *Th.:* But you married him. *H.:* Yes, I did. *Th.:* Then how can you say that . . . Well now—
2. But now he's married. *H.:* Yes, but not to someone else.

the female conscience was so constituted that if she discovered she had married her nephew, she was filled with rancor——

¶ Shouldn't the future strive for the great, the good, and the beautiful as Tesman says it should? Yes! But the great, the good, the beautiful of the future won't be the same as it is for us——

¶ *H.:* I remember especially a red-headed girl whom I have seen on the street. *Br.:* I know whom you mean— *H.:* You called her—it was such a pretty name— *Br.:* I know her name too. But how do you know it was pretty? *H.:* Oh, Judge Brack, you are an idiot.

¶ The passenger and his trunk at the railway station. P. decides where he is going, buys his ticket. The trunk is attended to——

¶ Hedda: Slender figure of average height. Nobly shaped, aristocratic face with fine, wax-colored skin. The eyes have a veiled expression. Hair medium brown. Not especially abundant hair. Dressed in a loose-fitting dressing gown, white with blue trimmings. Composed and relaxed in her manners. The eyes steel-gray, almost lusterless.

¶ Mrs. Elvsted: weak build. The eyes round, rather prominent, almost as blue as water. Weak face with soft features. Nervous gestures, frightened expression——

¶ See above. E. L.'s idea of comradeship between man and woman. . . . The idea is a life-saver!

¶ If society won't let us live morally with them (women), then we'll have to live with them immorally——

¶ *Tesman:* The new idea in E. L.'s book is that of progress resulting from the comradeship between man and woman.

¶ Hedda's basic demand is: I want to know everything, but keep myself clean.

¶ I want to know everything—everything—everything— *H.:—— —*

H.: If only I could have lived like him!

¶ Is there something about Brabant? *B.:* What on earth is that? . . .

¶ The wager about the use of both pistols.

¶ *Miss T.:* Yes, this is the house of life and health. Now I shall go home to a house of sickness and death. God bless both of you. From now on I'll come out here every day to ask Bertha how things are——

¶ In the third act H. tells E. L. that she is not interested in the great questions—nor the great ideas—but in the great freedom of man. . . . But she hasn't the courage.

¶ The two ideals! *Tesman:* What in the name of God does he mean by that? What? What do we have to do with ideals?

¶ The new book treats of "the two ideals." Thea can give no information.

(6)

¶ NB! Brack had always thought that Hedda's short engagement to Tesman would come to nothing.

Hedda speaks of how she felt herself set aside, step by step, when her father was no longer in favor, when he retired and died without leaving anything. Then she realized, bitterly, that it was for his sake she had been made much of. And then she was already between twenty-five and twenty-six. In danger of becoming an old maid.

She thinks that in reality Tesman only feels a vain pride in having won her. His solicitude for her is the same as is shown for a thoroughbred horse or a valuable sporting dog. This, however, does not offend her. She merely regards it as a fact.

Hedda says to Brack that she does not think Tesman can be called ridiculous. But in reality she finds him so. Later on she finds him pitiable as well.

Tesman: Could you not call me by my Christian name?

Hedda: No, indeed I couldn't—unless they have given you some other name than the one you have.

Tesman puts Lövborg's manuscript in his pocket so that it may not be lost. Afterward it is Hedda who, by a casual remark, with tentative intention, gives him the idea of keeping it.

Then he reads it. A new line of thought is revealed to him. But the strain of the situation increases. Hedda awakens his jealousy.

¶ In the third act one thing after another comes to light about Lövborg's adventures in the course of the night. At last he comes himself, in quiet despair. "Where is the manuscript?" "Did I not leave it behind me here?" He does not know that he has done so.

But after all, of what use is the manuscript to him now!
He is writing of the "moral doctrine of the future"! When
he has just been released by the police!

¶ Hedda's despair is that there are doubtless so many
chances of happiness in the world, but that she cannot
discover them. It is the want of an object in life that
torments her.

When Hedda beguiles T. into leading E. L. into ruin,
it is done to test T.'s character.

¶ It is in Hedda's presence that the irresistible craving
for excess always comes over E. L.

Tesman cannot understand that E. L. could wish to
base his future on injury to another.

¶ *Hedda:* Do I hate T.? No, not at all. I only find
him boring.

¶ *Brack:* But nobody else thinks so.

Hedda: Neither is there any one but myself who is
married to him.

Brack: . . . not at all boring.

Hedda: Heavens, you always want me to express myself
so correctly. Very well then, T. is not boring, but I am
bored by living with him.

Hedda: . . . had no prospects. Well, perhaps you
would have liked to see me in a convent (home for unmarried ladies).

Hedda: . . . then isn't it an honorable thing to profit
by one's person? Don't actresses and others turn their
advantages into profit. I had no other capital. Marriage
—I thought it was like buying an annuity.

Hedda: Remember that I am the child of an old man
—and a worn-out man too—or past his prime at any
rate—perhaps that has left its mark.

Brack: Upon my word, I believe you have begun to
brood over problems.

Hedda: Well, what cannot one take to doing when one
has gone and got married.

(7)

¶ *E. L.:* It's impossible for me to call you Mrs. T.
You will always be H. G. to me.

¶ Both Miss T. and B. have seen what lies in store for
Hedda. . . . T. on the other hand cries out: My God,
I had no idea.

¶ When E. L. tells H. that he cannot possibly confess to Thea that her and his book has been lost, H. says: I don't believe a word of that. *E.L.:* No, but I know how terribly dismayed she will be.

Translated by Evert Sprinchorn
(Section 6 translated by A. G. Chater)

THE PRIMACY OF CHARACTER[7]

Before I write down one word, I have to have the character in mind through and through. I must penetrate into the last wrinkle of his soul. I always proceed from the individual; the stage setting, the dramatic ensemble, all of that comes naturally and does not cause me any worry, as soon as I am certain of the individual in every aspect of his humanity. But I have to have his exterior in mind also, down to the last button, how he stands and walks, how he conducts himself, what his voice sounds like. Then I do not let him go until his fate is fulfilled.

As a rule, I make three drafts of my dramas which differ very much from each other in characterization, not in action. When I proceed to the first sketch of the material I feel as though I had the degree of acquaintance with my characters that one acquires on a railway journey; one has met and chatted about this or that. With the next draft I see everything more clearly, I know characters just about as one would know them after a few weeks' stay in a spa; I have learned the fundamental traits in their characters as well as their little peculiarities; yet it is not impossible that I might make an error in some essential matter. In the last draft, finally, I stand at the limit of knowledge; I know my people from close and long association—they are my intimate friends, who will not disappoint me in any way; in the manner in which I see them now, I shall always see them.

[7] A. E. Zucker, *Ibsen: The Master Builder* (New York: Henry Holt, 1929), pp. 194, 208. Copyright 1929, Henry Holt and Company. Reprinted by permission of Henry Holt and Company.

AUGUST STRINDBERG
(1849-1912)

Miss Julie[1] (1888)

THEATRE HAS long seemed to me—in common with much other art—a *Biblia Pauperum*, a Bible in pictures for those who cannot read what is written or printed; and I see the playwright as a lay preacher peddling the ideas of his time in popular form, popular enough for the middle classes, mainstay of theatre audiences, to grasp the gist of the matter without troubling their brains too much. For this reason theatre has always been an elementary school for the young, the semieducated, and for women who still have a primitive capacity for deceiving themselves and letting themselves be deceived—who, that is to say, are susceptible to illusion and to suggestion from the author. I have therefore thought it not unlikely that in these days, when that rudimentary and immature thought process operating through fantasy appears to be developing into reflection, research, and analysis, that theatre, like religion, might be discarded as an outworn form for whose appreciation we lack the necessary conditions. This opinion is confirmed by the major crisis still prevailing in the theatres of Europe, and still more by the fact that in those countries of culture, producing the greatest thinkers of the age, namely England and Germany, drama—like other fine arts—is dead.

Some countries, it is true, have attempted to create a new drama by using the old forms with up-to-date contents, but not only has there been insufficient time for these new ideas to be popularized, so that the audience can grasp them, but also people have been so wrought up by the taking of sides that pure, disinterested appreciation has become impossible. One's deepest impressions are up-

[1] August Strindberg, Author's foreword to *Miss Julie*, in *Six Plays of Strindberg*, translated by Elizabeth Sprigge (New York: Doubleday Anchor Books, 1955), *Miss Julie*, pp. 61–73; *A Dream Play*, p. 193. Copyright 1955 by Elizabeth Sprigge. Reprinted by permission of Willis Kingsley Wing.

set when an applauding or a hissing majority dominates
as forcefully and openly as it can in the theatre. Moreover,
as no new form has been devised for these new contents,
the new wine has burst the old bottles.

In this play I have not tried to do anything new, for
this cannot be done, but only to modernize the form to
meet the demands which may, I think, be made on this
art today. To this end I chose—or surrendered myself to—
a theme which claims to be outside the controversial
issues of today, since questions of social climbing or falling, of higher or lower, better or worse, of man and woman, are, have been, and will be of lasting interest. When I
took this theme from a true story told me some years ago,
which made a deep impression, I saw it as a subject for
tragedy, for as yet it is tragic to see one favored by
fortune go under, and still more to see a family heritage
die out, although a time may come when we have grown
so developed and enlightened that we shall view with
indifference life's spectacle, now seeming so brutal, cynical,
and heartless. Then we shall have dispensed with those
inferior, unreliable instruments of thought called feelings,
which become harmful and superfluous as reasoning
develops.

The fact that my heroine rouses pity is solely due to
weakness; we cannot resist fear of the same fate over-
taking us. The hypersensitive spectator may, it is true,
go beyond this kind of pity, while the man with belief in
the future may actually demand some suggestion for
remedying the evil—in other words some kind of policy.
But, to begin with, there is no such thing as absolute evil;
the downfall of one family is the good fortune of another,
which thereby gets a chance to rise, and, fortune being
only comparative, the alternation of rising and falling is
one of life's principal charms. Also, to the man of policy,
who wants to remedy the painful fact that the bird of
prey devours the dove, and lice the bird of prey, I should
like to put the question: why should it be remedied? Life
is not so mathematically idiotic as only to permit the big
to eat the small; it happens just as often that the bee kills
the lion or at least drives it mad.

That my tragedy depresses many people is their own
fault. When we have grown strong as the pioneers of the
French Revolution, we shall be happy and relieved to see
the national parks cleared of ancient rotting trees which

have stood too long in the way of others equally entitled
to a period of growth—as relieved as we are when an in-
curable invalid dies.

My tragedy *The Father* was recently criticized for being
too sad—as if one wants cheerful tragedies! Everybody
is clamoring for this supposed "joy of life," and theatre
managers demand farces, as if the joy of life consisted
in being ridiculous and portraying all human beings as
suffering from St. Vitus's dance or total idiocy. I myself
find the joy of life in its strong and cruel struggles, and
my pleasure in learning, in adding to my knowledge. For
this reason I have chosen for this play an unusual situation, but an instructive one—an exception, that is to say,
but a great exception, one proving the rule, which will no
doubt annoy all lovers of the commonplace. What will
offend simple minds is that my plot is not simple, nor its
point of view single. In real life an action—this, by the
way, is a somewhat new discovery—is generally caused by
a whole series of motives, more or less fundamental, but
as a rule the spectator chooses just one of these—the one
which his mind can most easily grasp or that does most
credit to his intelligence. A suicide is committed. Business
troubles, says the man of affairs. Unrequited love, say
the women. Sickness, says the invalid. Despair, says the
down-and-out. But it is possible that the motive lay in all
or none of these directions, or that the dead man concealed
his actual motive by revealing quite another, likely to
reflect more to his glory.

I see Miss Julie's tragic fate to be the result of many
circumstances: the mother's character, the father's mistaken upbringing of the girl, her own nature, and the
influence of her fiancé on a weak, degenerate mind. Also,
more directly, the festive mood of Midsummer Eve, her
father's absence, her monthly indisposition, her preoccupation with animals, the excitement of dancing, the magic
of dusk, the strongly aphrodisiac influence of flowers, and
finally the chance that drives the couple into a room alone
—to which must be added the urgency of the excited man.

My treatment of the theme, moreover, is neither exclusively physiological nor psychological. I have not put the
blame wholly on the inheritance from her mother, nor on
her physical condition at the time, nor on immorality. I
have not even preached a moral sermon; in the absence of
a priest I leave this to the cook.

I congratulate myself on this multiplicity of motives as being up-to-date, and if others have done the same thing before me, then I congratulate myself on not being alone in my "paradoxes," as all innovations are called.

In regard to the drawing of the characters, I have made my people somewhat "characterless" for the following reasons. In the course of time the word character has assumed manifold meanings. It must have originally signified the dominating trait of the soul complex, and this was confused with temperament. Later it became the middle-class term for the automaton, one whose nature had become fixed or who had adapted himself to a particular role in life. In fact a person who had ceased to grow was called a character, while one continuing to develop—the skillful navigator of life's river, sailing not with sheets set fast, but veering before the wind to luff again—was called characterless, in a derogatory sense, of course, because he was so hard to catch, classify, and keep track of. This middle-class conception of the immobility of the soul was transferred to the stage where the middle class has always ruled. A character came to signify a man fixed and finished: one who invariably appeared either drunk or jocular or melancholy, and characterization required nothing more than a physical defect such as a clubfoot, a wooden leg, a red nose; or the fellow might be made to repeat some such phrase as: "That's capital!" or: "Barkis is willin'!" This simple way of regarding human beings still survives in the great Molière. Harpagon is nothing but a miser, although Harpagon might have been not only a miser, but also a first-rate financier, an excellent father, and a good citizen. Worse still, his "failing" is a distinct advantage to his son-in-law and his daughter, who are his heirs, and who therefore cannot criticize him, even if they have to wait a while to get to bed. I do not believe, therefore, in simple stage characters; and the summary judgments of authors—this man is stupid, that one brutal, this jealous, that stingy, and so forth—should be challenged by the Naturalists who know the richness of the soul complex and realize that vice has a reverse side very much like virtue.

Because they are modern characters, living in a period of transition more feverishly hysterical than its predecessor at least, I have drawn my figures vacillating, disintegrated, a blend of old and new. Nor does it seem to me unlikely that, through newspapers and conversations, modern ideas may have filtered down to the level of the domestic servant.

My souls (characters) are conglomerations of past and present stages of civilization, bits from books and newspapers, scraps of humanity, rags and tatters of fine clothing, patched together as is the human soul. And I have added a little evolutionary history by making the weaker steal and repeat the words of the stronger, and by making the characters borrow ideas or "suggestions" from one another.

Miss Julie is a modern character, not that the half-woman, the man-hater, has not existed always, but because now that she has been discovered she has stepped to the front and begun to make a noise. The half-woman is a type who thrusts herself forward, selling herself nowadays for power, decorations, distinctions, diplomas, as formerly for money. The type implies degeneration; it is not a good type and it does not endure; but it can unfortunately transmit its misery, and degenerate men seem instinctively to choose their mates from among such women, and so they breed, producing offspring of indeterminate sex to whom life is torture. But fortunately they perish, either because they cannot come to terms with reality, or because their repressed instincts break out uncontrollably, or again because their hopes of catching up with men are shattered. The type is tragic, revealing a desperate fight against nature, tragic too in its Romantic inheritance now dissipated by Naturalism, which wants nothing but happiness—and for happiness strong and sound species are required.

But Miss Julie is also a relic of the old warrior nobility now giving way to the new nobility of nerve and brain. She is a victim of the discord which a mother's "crime" has produced in a family, a victim too of the day's complaisance, of circumstances, of her own defective constitution, all of which are equivalent to the Fate or Universal Law of former days. The Naturalist has abolished guilt with God, but the consequences of the action—punishment, imprisonment, or the fear of it—he cannot abolish, for the simple reason that they remain whether he is acquitted or not. An injured fellow-being is not so complacent as outsiders, who have not been injured, can afford to be. Even if the father had felt impelled to take no vengeance, the daughter would have taken vengeance on herself, as she does here, from that innate or acquired sense of honor which the upper classes inherit—whether from barbarism or Aryan forebears, or from the chivalry of the Middle Ages, who knows? It is a very beautiful thing, but it has become a danger nowadays to the preservation of the race. It is the nobleman's hara-kiri, the Japanese law of inner conscience which compels him to cut his own stomach open at the insult of another, and which survives in modified form in the duel, a privilege of the nobility. And so the valet Jean lives on, but Miss Julie cannot live without honor. This is the thrall's advantage over the nobleman, that he lacks this fatal preoccupation with honor. And in all of us Aryans there is something of the nobleman, or the Don Quixote, which makes us sympathize with the man who commits suicide because he has done something ignoble and lost his honor. And we are noblemen enough to suffer at the sight of fallen greatness littering the earth like a corpse— yes, even if the fallen rise again and make restitution by honorable deeds. Jean, the valet, is a race-builder, a man of marked characteristics. He was a laborer's son who has educated himself toward becoming a gentleman. He has learned easily, through his well-developed senses (smell, taste, vision)—and he also has a sense of beauty. He has already bettered himself, and is thick-skinned enough to have no scruples about using other people's services. He is already foreign to his associates, despising them as part of the life he has turned his back on, yet also fearing and fleeing from them because they know his secrets, pry into his plans, watch his rise with envy, and look forward with pleasure to his fall. Hence his dual, indeterminate character, vacillating between love of the heights and hatred of those who have already achieved them. He is, he says himself, an aristocrat; he has learned the secrets of good society. He is polished, but vulgar within; he already wears his tails with taste, but there is no guarantee of his personal cleanliness.

He has some respect for his young lady, but he is frightened of Kristin, who knows his dangerous secrets, and he is sufficiently callous not to allow the night's events to wreck his plans for the future. Having both the slave's brutality and the master's lack of squeamishness, he can see blood without fainting and take disaster by the horns

Consequently he emerges from the battle unscathed, and probably ends his days as a hotelkeeper. And even if *he* does not become a Roumanian count, his son will doubtless go to the university and perhaps become a county attorney.

The light which Jean sheds on a lower-class conception of life, life seen from below, is on the whole illuminating —when he speaks the truth, which is not often, for he says what is favorable to himself rather than what is true. When Miss Julie suggests that the lower classes must be oppressed by the attitude of their superiors, Jean naturally agrees, as his object is to gain her sympathy; but when he perceives the advantage of separating himself from the common herd, he at once takes back his words.

It is not because Jean is now rising that he has the upper hand of Miss Julie, but because he is a man. Sexually he is the aristocrat because of his virility, his keener senses, and his capacity for taking the initiative. His inferiority is mainly due to the social environment in which he lives, and he can probably shed it with his valet's livery.

The slave mentality expresses itself in his worship of the Count (the boots), and his religious superstition; but he worships the Count chiefly because he holds that higher position for which Jean himself is striving. And this worship remains even when he has won the daughter of the house and seen how empty is that lovely shell.

I do not believe that a love relationship in the "higher" sense could exist between two individuals of such different quality, but I have made Miss Julie imagine that she is in love, so as to lessen her sense of guilt, and I let Jean suppose that if his social position were altered he would truly love her. I think love is like the hyacinth which has to strike roots in darkness *before* it can produce a vigorous flower. In this case it shoots up quickly, blossoms, and goes to seed all at the same time, which is why the plant dies so soon.

As for Kristin, she is a female slave, full of servility and sluggishness acquired in front of the kitchen fire, and stuffed full of morality and religion, which are her cloak and scapegoat. She goes to church as a quick and easy way of unloading her household thefts onto Jesus and taking on a fresh cargo of guiltlessness. For the rest she is a minor character, and I have therefore sketched her in the same manner as the pastor and the doctor in *The Father,* where I wanted ordinary human beings, as are most country pastors and provincial doctors. If these minor characters seem abstract to some people, this is due to the fact that ordinary people are to a certain extent abstract in pursuit of their work; that is to say, they are without individuality, showing, while working, only one side of themselves. And as long as the spectator does not feel a need to see them from other sides, there is nothing wrong with my abstract presentation.

In regard to the dialogue, I have departed somewhat from tradition by not making my characters catechists who ask stupid questions in order to elicit a smart reply. I have avoided the symmetrical, mathematical construction of French dialogue, and let people's minds work irregularly, as they do in real life where, during a conversation, no topic is drained to the dregs, and one mind finds in another a chance cog to engage in. So too the dialogue wanders, gathering in the opening scenes material which is later picked up, worked over, repeated, expounded, and developed like the theme in a musical composition.

The plot speaks for itself, and as it really only concerns two people, I have concentrated on these, introducing only one minor character, the cook, and keeping the unhappy spirit of the father above and behind the action. I have done this because it seems to me that the psychological process is what interests people most today. Our inquisitive souls are no longer satisfied with seeing a thing happen; we must also know how it happens. We want to see the wires themselves, to watch the machinery, to examine the box with the false bottom, to take hold of the magic ring in order to find the join, and look at the cards to see how they are marked.

In this connection I have had in view the documentary novels of the brothers de Goncourt, which appeal to me more than any other modern literature.

As far as the technical side of the work is concerned, I have made the experiment of abolishing the division into acts. This is because I have come to the conclusion that our capacity for illusion is disturbed by the intervals, during which the audience has time to reflect and escape from the suggestive influence of the author-hypnotist. My play will probably take an hour and a half, and as one can listen to a lecture, a sermon, or a parliamentary debate for as long as that or longer, I do not think a theatrical performance will be fatiguing in the same length of time. As early as 1872, in one of my first dramatic attempts, *The Outlaw,* I tried this concentrated form, although with scant success. The play was written in five acts, and only when finished did I become aware of the restless, disjointed effect that it produced. The script was burned and from the ashes rose a single well-knit act— fifty pages of print, playable in one hour. The form of the present play is, therefore, not new, but it appears to be my own, and changing tastes may make it timely. My hope is one day to have an audience educated enough to sit through a whole evening's entertainment in one act, but one would have to try this out to see. Meanwhile, in order to provide respite for the audience and the players, without allowing the audience to escape from the illusion, I have introduced three art forms: monologue, mime, and ballet. These are all part of drama, having their origins in classic tragedy, monody having become monologue and the chorus, ballet.

Monologue is now condemned by our realists as unnatural, but if one provides motives for it one makes it natural, and then can use it to advantage. It is, surely, natural for a public speaker to walk up and down the room practicing his speech, natural for an actor to read his part aloud, for a servant girl to talk to her cat, a mother to prattle to her child, an old maid to chatter to her parrot, and a sleeper to talk in his sleep. And in order that the actor may have a chance, for once, of working independently, free from the author's direction, it is better that the monologue should not be written, but only indicated. For since it is of small importance what is said in one's sleep or to the parrot or to the cat—none of it influences the action—a talented actor, identifying himself with the atmosphere and the situation, may improvise better than the author, who cannot calculate ahead how much may be said or how long taken without waking the audience from the illusion.

Some Italian theatres have, as we know, returned to improvisation, thereby producing actors who are creative, although within the bounds set by the author. This may well be a step forward, or even the beginning of a new art form worthy to be called *productive.*

In places where monologue would be unnatural I have used mime, leaving here an even wider scope for the actor's imagination, and more chance for him to win independent laurels. But so as not to try the audience beyond endurance, I have introduced music—fully justified by the Midsummer Eve dance—to exercise its powers of persuasion during the dumb show. But I beg the musical director to consider carefully his choice of compositions, so that conflicting moods are not induced by selections from the current operetta or dance show, or by folk tunes of too local a character.

The ballet I have introduced cannot be replaced by the usual kind of "crowd scene," for such scenes are too badly played—a lot of grinning idiots seizing the opportunity to show off and thus destroying the illusion. And as peasants cannot improvise their taunts, but use ready-made phrases with a double meaning, I have not composed their lampoon, but taken a little-known song and dance which I myself noted down in the Stockholm district. The words are not quite to the point, but this too is intentional, for the cunning, i.e., weakness, of the slave prevents him from direct attack. Nor can there be clowning in a serious action, or coarse joking in a situation which nails the lid on a family coffin.

As regards the scenery, I have borrowed from impressionist painting its asymmetry and its economy; thus, I think, strengthening the illusion. For the fact that one does not see the whole room and all the furniture leaves scope for conjecture—that is to say imagination is roused and complements what is seen. I have succeeded too in getting rid of those tiresome exits through doors, since scenery doors are made of canvas, and rock at the slightest touch. They cannot even express the wrath of an irate head of the family who, after a bad dinner, goes out slamming the door behind him, "so that the whole house shakes." On the stage it rocks. I have also kept to a single set, both in order to let the characters develop in their métier and to break away from overdecoration. When one has only one set, one may expect it to be realistic; but as a matter of fact nothing is harder than to get a stage room that looks something like a room, however easily the scene painter can produce flaming volcanoes and waterfalls. Presumably the walls must be of canvas; but it seems about time to dispense with painted shelves and cooking utensils. We are asked to accept so many stage conventions that we might at least be spared the pain of painted pots and pans.

I have set the back wall and the table diagonally so that the actors may play full face and in half-profile when they are sitting opposite one another at the table. In the opera *Aïda* I saw a diagonal background, which led the eye to unfamiliar perspectives and did not look like mere reaction against boring straight lines.

Another much-needed innovation is the abolition of footlights. This lighting from below is said to have the purpose of making the actors' faces fatter. But why, I ask, should all actors have fat faces? Does not this underlighting flatten out all the subtlety of the lower part of the face, specially the jaw, falsify the shape of the nose and throw shadows up over the eyes? Even if this were not so, one thing is certain: that the lights hurt the performers' eyes, so that the full play of their expression is lost. The footlights strike part of the retina usually protected—except in sailors who have to watch sunlight on water—and therefore one seldom sees anything other than a crude rolling of the eyes, either sideways or up toward the gallery, showing their whites. Perhaps this too causes that tiresome blinking of the eyelashes, especially by actresses. And when anyone on the stage wants to speak with his eyes, the only thing he can do is to look straight at the audience, with whom he or she then gets into direct communication, outside the framework of the set—a habit called, rightly or wrongly, "greeting one's friends."

Would not sufficiently strong side lighting, with some kind of reflectors, add to the actor's powers of expression by allowing him to use the face's greatest asset—the play of the eyes?

I have few illusions about getting the actors to play *to* the audience instead of *with* it, although this is what I want. That I shall see an actor's back throughout a critical scene is beyond my dreams, but I do wish crucial scenes could be played, not in front of the prompter's box, like duets expecting applause, but in the place required by the action. So, no revolutions, but just some small modifications, for to make the stage into a real room with the fourth wall missing would be too upsetting altogether.

I dare not hope that the actresses will listen to what

I have to say about make-up, for they would rather be beautiful than lifelike, but the actor might consider whether it is to his advantage to create an abstract character with grease paints, and cover his face with it like a mask. Take the case of a man who draws a choleric charcoal line between his eyes and then, in this fixed state of wrath, has to smile at some repartee. What a frightful grimace the result is! And equally, how is that false forehead, smooth as a billiard ball, to wrinkle when the old man loses his temper?

In a modern psychological drama, where the subtlest reactions of a character need to be mirrored in the face rather than expressed by sound and gesture, it would be worth while experimenting with powerful side lighting on a small stage and a cast without make-up, or at least with the minimum.

If, in addition, we could abolish the visible orchestra, with its distracting lamps and its faces turned toward the audience; if we could have the stalls raised so that the spectators' eyes were higher than the players' knees; if we could get rid of the boxes (the center of my target), with their tittering diners and supper parties, and have total darkness in the auditorium during the performance; and if, first and foremost, we could have a *small* stage and a *small* house, then perhaps a new dramatic art might arise, and theatre once more become a place of entertainment for educated people. While waiting for such a theatre it is as well for us to go on writing so as to stock that repertory of the future.

I have made an attempt. If it has failed, there is time enough to try again.

A Dream Play (1902)

IN THIS dream play, as in his former dream play *To Damascus*, the Author has sought to reproduce the disconnected but apparently logical form of a dream. Anything can happen; everything is possible and probable. Time and space do not exist; on a slight groundwork of reality, imagination spins and weaves new patterns made up of memories, experiences, unfettered fancies, absurdities, and improvisations.

The characters are split, double, and multiply; they evaporate, crystallize, scatter, and converge. But a single consciousness holds sway over them all—that of the dreamer. For him there are no secrets, no incongruities, no scruples and no law. He neither condemns nor acquits, but only relates, and since, on the whole, there is more pain than pleasure in the dream, a tone of melancholy, and of compassion for all living things, runs through the swaying narrative. Sleep, the liberator, often appears as a torturer, but when the pain is at its worst, the sufferer awakes—and is thus reconciled with reality. For, however agonizing real life may be, at this moment, compared with the tormenting dream, it is a joy.

NOTES FOR AN EFFECTIVE PLAY[2]

An effective play should contain or make use of:
hints and intimations

a secret made known to the audience either at the beginning or toward the end. If the spectator but not the actors know the secret, the spectator enjoys their game of blindman's buff. If the spectator is not in on the secret, his curiosity is aroused and his attention held.

an outburst of emotion, rage, indignation

a discovery

a punishment (nemesis), a humiliation

a careful resolution, either with or without a reconciliation

a *quid pro quo*

a parallelism

a reversal (*revirement*), an upset, a well-prepared surprise.

---

[2] August Strindberg, *Samlade otryckta skrifter* (Stockholm: 1919), II, p. 172. These notes have been translated by Evert Sprinchorn especially for inclusion in this volume.

ANTON CHEKHOV
(1860-1904)

Ivanov[1]

ALEX. CHEKHOV, OCTOBER, 1887

I WROTE the play unexpectedly, after a certain conversation with Korsh. Went to bed, thought up a theme, and wrote it down. I spent less than two weeks on it. I cannot judge the merits of the play. It is to come out in a surprisingly short time. Everybody likes it. Korsh did not find a single error or sin against the stage, which is a sad indication of how good and attentive my judges are. I write a play for the first time, ergo mistakes should be therein. The plot is complicated and not silly. I finish up each act as if it were a story: the action goes on quietly and peacefully, and at the end I give the audience a heavy jolt. All my energy was spent on a few really brisk, forceful climaxes; but the bridges joining these are insignificant, loose, and not startling. Still, I am glad; no matter how bad the play is, I created a type that has literary value; I have produced a role which only as great a talent as Davidov will undertake to play, a role in which an actor can reveal himself, and display true ability. . . .

My play has fourteen characters, five of them women. I feel that my ladies, with the exception of one, are not thoroughly well developed.

Modern playwrights begin their plays with angels, scoundrels, and clowns exclusively. Well, go seek these elements in all Russia! Yes, you may find them, but not in such extreme types as the playwrights need. Unwillingly, you begin forging them out of the mind and the imagination, you perspire, and give the matter up. I wanted to be

1 Anton Chekhov, *Letters on the Short Story, the Drama and other Literary Topics,* selected and edited by Louis S. Friedland (New York: Minton, Balch & Co., 1924), pp. 119–41.

original: I did not portray a single villain, not a single angel (though I could not refrain when it came to the clown), did not accuse anyone, or exculpate. Whether all this is well done, I do not know.

A. S. SOUVORIN, DECEMBER 19, 1888

I give you my word that I shall write no more of such intellectual and sickly plays as *Ivanov*. If *Ivanov* does not succeed I shall not be surprised, and shall not lay it to intrigues and plots.

A. S. SOUVORIN, DECEMBER 23, 1888

The absence of Sasha in the fourth act was very noticeable, you say. So it should be. Let the whole audience know that Sasha is not there. You insist on her appearing: the laws, forsooth, demand it. Very well, let her appear, but what will she say? Such young ladies (she is not a girl but a woman) cannot and should not speak. The former Sasha could speak and was sympathetic, but the new one will only irritate the public by appearing. She cannot really fall on Ivanov's neck and say, "I love you!" She does not love and has confessed it. To bring her on the stage at the end she would have to be completely remodeled. You say that there is not a single woman in the closing scenes, and that this makes the ending dry. I agree with you. Only two women could appear at the close and speak for Ivanov; only two women who really loved him: his mother and the Jewess. But as both of them are dead, that is out of the question. An orphan, let him remain an orphan, the devil take him.

A. S. SOUVORIN, DECEMBER 26, 1888

You want me at all costs to free Sasha. But *Ivanov* is not likely to prove a success. If it is, I shall do as you wish, but, pardon me, I shall let her have it, the nasty woman! You say that women love through sympathy and compassion, that they marry through this feeling. . . . And men? I do not like realistic novelists to slander women, but I dislike it even more when they lift woman by the shoulders—as U—— does—and try to show that, even if she is worse than man, yet man is a scoundrel and woman an angel. Neither women nor men are worth a brass farthing, but man is more intelligent and more just.

A. S. SOUVORIN, DECEMBER 30, 1888

. . . The manager thinks Ivanov a superfluous man, in the manner of Turgenev; Savina asks, "Why is Ivanov a scoundrel?" You write, "It is necessary to add something that will make it clear why two women cling to Ivanov, and why he is a scoundrel, and the doctor,—a great man." If the three of you have so understood me that my Ivanov has no good in him at all, then I suppose my wits forsook me, and I did not succeed in writing what I intended. If Ivanov appears in my play as a scoundrel or a super-fluous man, and the doctor as a great man, if it is not clear why Sarra and Sasha love Ivanov, then evidently the play has not turned out as I wished, and to stage it is out of the question. This is how I understand my characters. Ivanov is a gentleman, a university man, and not remarkable in any way. He is excitable, hotheaded, easily carried away, honest, and straightforward like most people of his class. He has lived on his estate and served on the Zemstvo. What he has been doing and how he has behaved, what he has been interested in and enthusiastic over, can be seen from the following words of his addressed to the doctor (Act I, scene 5): "Don't marry Jewesses or neurotic women or bluestockings . . . don't fight with thousands singlehanded, don't wage war on windmills, don't batter your head against the wall. . . . God preserve you from scientific farming, wonderful schools, enthusiastic speeches. . . ." This is what he has in his past. Sarra, who has seen his scientific farming and other crazes, says about him to the doctor, "He is a remarkable man, doctor, and I am sorry you did not meet him two or three years ago. Now he is depressed and melancholy, he doesn't talk or do anything—but in the old days . . . how charming he was!" (Act I, scene 7). His past is beautiful, as is generally the case with educated Russians. There is not, or there hardly is, a single Rus-sian gentleman or university man who does not boast of his past. The present is always worse than the past. Why? Because Russian excitability has one specific character-istic: it is quickly followed by exhaustion. A man has scarcely left the classroom before he rushes to take up a burden beyond his strength; he tackles at once the schools, the peasants, scientific farming, and the *Viestnik Evropi,* he makes speeches, writes to the minister, combats evil, applauds good, falls in love, not in an ordinary, simple way, but selects either a bluestocking, or a neurotic, or a Jewess, or even a prostitute whom he tries to save, and so on, and so on. But by the time he is thirty or thirty-five he begins to feel tired and bored. He has not got decent mustaches yet, but he already says with authority, "Don't marry, my dear fellow. . . . Trust my experience," or, "After all, what does Liberalism come to? Between ourselves, Katkov was often right. . . ." He is ready to reject the Zemstvo and scientific farming, and science and love. My Ivanov says to the doctor (Act I, scene 5), "You took your degree only last year, my dear friend, you are still young and vigorous, while I am thirty-five. I have a right to advise you. . . ." That is how these prematurely exhausted people talk. Further down, sighing authoritatively, he advises, "Don't you marry in this or that way [see above], but choose something commonplace, gray, with no vivid colors or superfluous flourishes. Altogether, build your life according to the conventional pattern. The grayer and more monotonous the background, the better. . . . The life that I have led—how tiring it is! Ah, how tiring!"

Conscious of physical exhaustion and boredom, he does not understand what is the matter with him, and what has happened. Horrified, he says to the doctor (Act I, scene 3), "Here you tell me she is going to die and I feel neither love nor pity, but a sort of emptiness and weariness. . . . If one looks at me from outside it must be horrible. I don't understand what is happening to my soul." Finding themselves in such a position, narrow and unconscientious people generally throw the whole blame on their environment, or write themselves down as Hamlets and superfluous people, and are satisfied with that. But Ivanov, a straightforward man, openly says to the doctor and to the public that he does not understand his own mind. "I don't understand! I don't understand!" That he really doesn't understand can be seen from his long monologue in Act III, where, tête-à-tête with the public, he opens his heart to it and even weeps.

The change that has taken place in him offends his sense of what is fitting. He looks for the causes outside himself and fails to find them; he begins to look for them inside and finds only an indefinite feeling of guilt. It is a Russian feeling. Whether there is a death or illness in his family, whether he owes money or lends it, a Russian always feels guilty. Ivanov talks all the time about being to blame in some way, and the feeling of guilt increases in him at every juncture. In Act I he says, "Suppose I am terribly to blame, yet my thoughts are in a tangle, my soul is in bondage to a sort of sloth, and I am incapable of understanding myself. . . ." In Act II, he says to Sasha, "My conscience aches day and night, I feel that I am profoundly to blame, but in what exactly I have done wrong I cannot make out."

To exhaustion, boredom, and the feeling of guilt add one more enemy: loneliness. Were Ivanov an official, an actor, a priest, a professor, he would have grown used to his position. But he lives on his estate. He is in the country. His neighbors are either drunkards or fond of cards, or are of the same type as the doctor. None of them cares about his feelings or the change that has taken place in him. He is lonely. Long winters, long evenings, an empty garden, empty rooms, the grumbling Count, the ailing wife. . . . He has nowhere to go. This is why he is every minute tortured by the question: what is he to do with himself?

Now about his fifth enemy. Ivanov is tired and does not understand himself, but life has nothing to do with that! It makes its legitimate demands upon him, and whether he will or no, he must settle problems. His sick wife is a problem, his numerous debts are a problem, Sasha flinging herself on his neck is a problem. The way in which he settles all these problems must be evident from his monologue in Act III, and from the contents of the last two acts. Men like Ivanov do not solve difficulties, but collapse under their weight. They lose their heads, gesticulate, become nervous, complain, do silly things, and finally, giving rein to their flabby, undisciplined nerves, lose the ground under their feet and enter the class of the "broken down" and "misunderstood."

Disappointment, apathy, nervous limpness, and exhaustion are the inevitable consequences of extreme excitability, and such excitability is extremely characteristic of our young people. Take literature. Take the present time . . . Socialism is one of the forms of this excitement. But where is socialism? You see it in Tikhomirov's letter to the Tsar. The socialists are married and they criticize the Zemstvo. Where is Liberalism? Mikhailovsky himself says that all the labels have been mixed up now. And what are all the Russian enthusiasms worth? The war has wearied us, Bulgaria has wearied us till we can only be ironical about it. Zucchi has wearied us and so has the comic opera.

Exhaustion (Dr. Bertenson will confirm this) finds expression not only in complaining or the sensation of boredom. The life of an overtired man cannot be represented like this: ~~~~~~~~~~~~~~~~~~~~~~~~~~~~~~~~~~~
It is very unequal. Overtired people never lose the capacity for becoming extremely excited, but cannot keep it up for long, and each excitement is followed by still greater apathy. . . . Graphically, it could be represented like this:

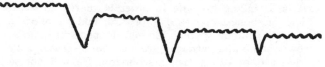

The fall as you see, is not continuous but broken. Sasha declares her love and Ivanov cries out in ecstasy, "A new life!"—and next morning he believes in this new life as little as he does in spooks (the monologue in Act III); his wife insults him, and, fearfully worked up and beside himself with anger, he flings a cruel insult at her. He is called a scoundrel. This is either fatal to his tottering brain, or stimulates him to a fresh paroxysm, and he pronounces sentence on himself.

Not to tire you out altogether I pass now to Dr. Lvov. He is the type of an honest, straightforward, hotheaded, but narrow and uncompromising man. Clever people say of such men, "He is stupid, but his heart is in the right place." Anything like breadth of outlook or unreflecting feeling is foreign to Lvov. He is the embodiment of a program, a walking tendency. He looks through a narrow frame at every person and event, he judges everything according to preconceived notions. Those who shout, "Make way for honest labor!" are an object of worship to him; those who do not shout it are scoundrels and exploiters. There is no middle. He has been brought up on Mikhailov's novels; at the theatre he has seen on the stage "new men," i.e., the exploiters and sons of our age, painted by the modern playwrights. He has stored it all up, and so much so, that when he reads *Rudin* he is sure to be asking himself, "Is Rudin a scoundrel or not?" Literature

and the stage have so educated him that he approaches
every character in real life and in fiction with this question. . . . If it were given him to see your own play, he
would blame you for not saying clearly: are Mmes. Kotel-
nikov, Sabinin, Adashev, Matvella, scoundrels, or not?
That question is to him of first importance. It is not
enough for him that all men are sinners. He wants saints
and villains.

He was prejudiced before he came to the district. He
at once classed all the rich peasants as exploiters, and
Ivanov, whom he could not understand, as a scoundrel.
Why, the man has a sick wife and he goes to see a rich
lady neighbor—of course he is a scoundrel! It is obvious
that he is killing his wife in order to marry an heiress.

Lvov is honest and straightforward, and he blurts out
the truth without sparing himself. If necessary, he will
throw a bomb at a carriage, give a school inspector a blow
in the face, or call a man a scoundrel. He will not stop
at anything. He never feels remorse—it is his mission as
"an honest worker" to fight "the powers of darkness"!

Such people are useful, and are for the most part attractive. To caricature them, even in the interests of the
play, is unfair and, indeed, unnecessary. True, a caricature is more striking, and therefore easier to understand,
but it is better to put your color on too faint than too
strong.

Now about the women. What do they love Ivanov for?
Sarra loves him because he is a fine man, because he has
enthusiasm, because he is brilliant and speaks with as
much heat as Lvov (Act I, scene 7). She loves him while
he is excited and interesting; but when he begins to grow
misty in her eyes, and to lose definiteness of outline,
she ceases to understand him, and at the end of Act III
speaks out plainly and sharply.

Sasha is a young woman of the newest type. She is
well educated, intelligent, honest, and so on. In the realm
of the blind a one-eyed man is king, and so she favors
Ivanov in spite of his being thirty-five. He is better than
anyone else. She knew him when she was a child and saw
his work close at hand, at the period before he was exhausted. He is a friend of her father's.

She is a female who is not won by the vivid plumage
of the male, not by their courage and dexterity, but by
their complaints, whinings, and failures. She is the sort

of girl who loves a man when he is going downhill. The moment Ivanov loses heart the young lady is on the spot! That's just what she was waiting for. Just think of it, she now has such a holy, such a grateful task before her! She will raise up the fallen one, set him on his feet, make him happy. . . . It is not Ivanov she loves, but this mission. Argenton[2] in Daudet's book says, "Life is not a novel." Sasha does not know this. She does not know that for Ivanov love is only a fresh complication, an extra stab in the back. And what comes of it? She struggles with him for a whole year and, instead of being raised, he sinks lower and lower.

If all of this is not in the play, there can be no question of producing it. It seems that I did not write what I wished. Remove it from the boards. I do not want to preach heresy on the stage. If the audience will leave the theatre with the conviction that Ivanovs are scoundrels and that Doctors Lvov are great men, then I'll have to give up and fling my pen to the devil. You won't get anywhere with corrections and insertions. No corrections can bring down a great man from his pedestal, and no insertions can change a scoundrel into an ordinary sinful mortal. You may bring Sasha on the stage at the end, but to Ivanov and Lvov I can add nothing more. I simply don't know how. And if I should add anything, it will spoil the effect still more. Trust in my intuition; it is an author's, you know. If the public does not understand "iron in the blood," then to the devil with it, i.e., with the blood in which there is no iron.

. . . Characteristically, Ivanov often lets fall the word "Russian." Don't be cross about it. When I was writing the play I had in mind only the things that really matter —that is, only the typical Russian characteristics. Thus the extreme excitability, the feeling of guilt, the liability to become exhausted are purely Russian. Germans are never excited, and that is why Germany knows nothing of disappointed, superfluous, or overtired people. . . . The excitability of the French is always maintained at one and the same level, and makes no sudden bounds or falls, and so a Frenchman is normally excited down to a decrepit old age. In other words, the French do not have to waste their strength in overexcitement; they spend their powers sensibly, and do not go bankrupt.

[2] In Alphonse Daudet's *Jack*.

It is understood that in the play I did not use such terms as "Russian," "excitability," etc., in the full expectation that the reader and spectator would be attentive and that for them it would not be necessary to underscore these. I tried to express myself simply, was not subtle, and was far from the suspicion that the readers and spectators would fasten my characters to a phrase, would emphasize the conversations about the dowry, etc. I suppose I could not write the play. Of course, it is a pity. Ivanov and Lvov appear to my imagination to be living people. I tell you honestly, in all conscience, these men were born in my head, not by accident, not out of sea foam, or preconceived "intellectual" ideas. They are the result of observing and studying life. They stand in my brain, and I feel that I have not falsified the truth or exaggerated it a jot. If on paper they have not come out clear and living, the fault is not in them but in me, for not being able to express my thoughts. It shows it is too early for me to begin writing plays.

WILLIAM ARCHER
(1856-1924)
BERNARD SHAW
(1856-1950)

Widowers' Houses: A Collaboration[1] (1893)

[WILLIAM ARCHER]

PARTLY to facilitate the labours of Mr George Bernard Shaw's biographers, and partly by way of relieving my own conscience, I think I ought to give a short history of the genesis of Widowers' Houses. Far away back in the olden days [1885], while as yet the Independent Theatre slumbered in the womb of Time, together with the New Drama, the New Criticism, the New Humour, and all the other glories of our renovated world, I used to be a daily frequenter of the British Museum Reading Room. Even more assiduous in his attendance was a young man of tawny complexion and attire, beside whom I used frequently to find myself seated. My curiosity was piqued by the odd conjunction of his subjects of research. Day after day for weeks he had before him two books, which he studied alternately, if not simultaneously—Karl Marx's Das Kapital (in French), and an orchestral score of Tristan und Isolde. I did not know then how exactly this quaint juxtaposition symbolised the main interests of his life. Presently I met him at the house of a common acquaintance, and we conversed for the first time. I learned from himself that he was the author of several unpublished masterpieces of fiction. Construction, he owned with engaging modesty, was not his strong point, but his dialogue was incomparable. Now, in those days, I had still a certain hankering after the rewards, if not the glories, of the playwright. With a modesty in no way inferior to Mr Shaw's, I had realised that I could not write dialogue a bit; but I still considered myself a born constructor. So I proposed,

[1] Bernard Shaw, *Prefaces* (London: Constable & Co. Ltd., 1934), pp. 667-71. Reprinted by permission of The Public Trustee and The Society of Authors.

and Mr Shaw agreed to, a collaboration. I was to provide
him with one of the numerous plots I kept in stock, and he
was to write the dialogue. So said, so done. I drew out, scene
by scene, the scheme of a twaddling cup-and-saucer comedy
vaguely suggested by Augier's Ceinture Dorée. The details I forget, but I know it was to be called Rhinegold,
was to open, as Widowers' Houses actually does, in a
hotel-garden on the Rhine, and was to have two heroines,
a sentimental and a comic one, according to the accepted
Robertson-Byron-Carton formula. I fancy the hero was to
propose to the sentimental heroine, believing her to be the
poor niece instead of the rich daughter of the sweater,
or slum-landlord, or whatever he may have been; and I
know he was to carry on in the most heroic fashion, and
was ultimately to succeed in throwing the tainted treasure
of his father-in-law, metaphorically speaking, into the
Rhine. All this I gravely propounded to Mr Shaw, who
listened with no less admirable gravity. Then I thought the
matter had dropped, for I heard no more of it for many
weeks. I used to see Mr Shaw at the Museum, laboriously
writing page after page of the most exquisitely neat
shorthand at the rate of about three words a minute; but
it did not occur to me that this was our play. After about
six weeks he said to me, 'Look here, I've written half the
first act of that comedy, and I've used up all your plot.
Now I want some more to go on with.' I told him that my
plot was a rounded and perfect organic whole, and that
I could no more eke it out in this fashion than I could provide him or myself with a set of supplementary arms and
legs. I begged him to extend his shorthand and let me see
what he had done; but this would have taken him far too
long. He tried to decipher some of it orally, but the
process was too lingering and painful for endurance. So he
simply gave me an outline in narrative of what he had
done; and I saw that, so far from having used up my
plot, he had not even touched it. There the matter rested
for months and years. Mr Shaw would now and then hold
out vague threats of finishing 'our play,' but I felt no
serious alarm. I thought (judging from my own experience
in other cases) that when he came to read over in cold
blood what he had written, he would see what impossible
stuff it was. Perhaps my free utterance of this view
piqued him; perhaps he felt impelled to remove from
the Independent Theatre the reproach of dealing solely

in foreign products. The fire of his genius, at all events, was not to be quenched by my persistent applications of the wet blanket. He finished his play; Mr Grein, as in duty bound, accepted it; and the result was the performance of Friday last [9th Dec. 1892] at the Independent Theatre.

[BERNARD SHAW]

To this history I have little to add. The circumstances occurred, in the main, as Mr Archer states them. But I most strenuously deny that there is any such great difference between his Rhinegold and Widowers' Houses as he supposes. I appeal to the impartial public, which has now both my play and Mr Archer's story before it, to judge whether I did not deal faithfully with him. The Rhine hotel garden, the hero proposing to the heroine in ignorance of the source of her father's wealth, the "tainted treasure of the father-in-law," the renunciation of it by the lover: all these will be found as prominently in the pages of the play as in Mr Archer's description of the fable which he persists in saying I did "not even touch." As a matter of fact the dissolution of partnership between us came when I told him that I had finished up the renunciation and wanted some more story to go on with, as I was only in the middle of the second act. He said that according to his calculation the renunciation ought to have landed me at the end of the play. I could only reply that his calculation did not work out, and that he must supply further material. This he most unreasonably refused to do; and I had eventually to fish up the tainted treasure out of the Rhine, so to speak, and make it last out another act and a half, which I had to invent all by myself. Clearly, then, he was the defaulter; and I am the victim.

It will have been noted by the attentive reader that what I have called a story, Mr Archer calls a plot; and that he mentions two heroines, introduced for the sole purpose of being mistaken for one another. Now, I confess to discarding the second daughter. She was admittedly a mere joist in the plot; and I had then, have now, and have always had, an utter contempt for "constructed" works of art. How any man in his senses can deliberately take as his model the sterile artifice of Wilkie Collins or Scribe, and repudiate the natural artistic activity of Fielding, Goldsmith, Defoe and Dickens, not to mention Aeschylus and Shakespear, is beyond argument with me: those who entertain such preferences are obviously incapable people, who prefer a "well made play" to King Lear exactly as they prefer acrostics to sonnets. As a fictionist, my natural way is to imagine characters and spin out a story about them, whether I am writing a novel or a play; and I please myself by reflecting that this has been the way of all great masters of fiction. At the same time I am quite aware that a writer with the necessary constructive ingenuity, and the itch for exercising it for its own sake, can entertain audiences or readers very agreeably by carefully constructing and unravelling mysteries and misunderstandings; and that this ingenuity may be associated with sufficient creative imagination to give a considerable show of humanity and some interest of character to the puppets contrived for the purpose of furthering the plot. The line between the authors who place their imagination at the service of their ingenuity and those who place their ingenuity at the service of their imagination may be hard to draw with precise justice (to Edgar Allan Poe, for instance!); but it is clear that if we draw it as an equator, Scribe and the plot constructors will be at the south pole, and Aeschylus and the dramatic poets at the north. Now, Archer's Rhinegold, in the absence of any convincing evidence that I was an Aeschylus, was designed for the southern hemisphere; and Widowers' Houses was built for the north. I told the story, but discarded the plot; and Archer at once perceived that this step made the enterprise entirely my own, since the resultant play, whether good or bad, must on my method be a *growth* out of the stimulated imagination of the actual writer, and not a manufactured article constructed by an artisan according to plans and specifications supplied by an inventor. The collaboration was therefore dropped; and after finishing the second act, so as to avoid leaving a loose end, and noting such beginnings of the third as had already sprouted, I left the work aside for seven years and thought no more of it. Last August, having been rather overworked by the occurrence of a General Election at the busiest part of the journalistic season in London, I could do nothing for a while but potter aimlessly over my old papers, among which I came across the manuscript of the play; and it so tickled me that I there and then sat down and finished it. But for Mr Grein and the Independent Theatre Society it would probably have gone back to its drawer and lain there for another seven years, if not for ever.

Some idea of the discussion which followed the performance may be gathered from the appendices which will be found at the end of this preface. The entire novelty on the stage of the standpoint taken, which is impartially Socialistic, greatly confused the critics, especially those who are in the habit of accepting as Socialism that spirit of sympathy with the poor and indignant protest against suffering and injustice which, in modern literature, culminated in Victor Hugo's Les Misérables, and has lately been forced into the theatre by the pressure of the Socialist propaganda outside. This "stage Socialism" is represented in my play by the good-natured compunction of my hero, who conceives the horrors of the slums as merely the result of atrocious individual delinquency on the part of the slum landlord. In spite of the unanswerable way in which the shallowness and impracticability of this view are exposed at once by a single speech from a practical business man many of my critics were unable to rid themselves of it. They dismissed the man of business as a sophistical villain, and so got hopelessly astray as to the characterization in the piece. My portraiture of Lickcheese, the slum rent collector, an effective but quite common piece of work, pleased better than any of the rest. My technical skill as a playwright sustained many attacks, all based on the assumption that the only admissible stage technique is the technique of plot construction, an assumption which excludes Shakespear and Goethe from the ranks of competent stage workmen, and which therefore appears to me to reduce itself to absurdity, although I am well aware that many of our critics look on Shakespear and Goethe as literary men who were unfortunately disabled from producing good acting plays by their deficiency in the stagecraft of the ordinary farcical comedy writer and melodramatist. It was further objected that my play, being didactic, was therefore not a work of art—a proposition which, if examined, will be found to mean either that the world's acknowledged masterpieces are not works of art, or else exactly nothing at all. Now, I submit that I could not reasonably be expected to defer to

the authority of canons of art which no artist acknowledges,
and in subjection to which no art would be possible, even
if I had not, by my practice in the profession of music
critic during the remarkable development effected both
in that art and in its criticism by Richard Wagner, been
sufficiently trained in critical processes to recognize the
objections I have cited as nothing more than the common
fallacies and ineptitudes into which all critics fall when first
confronted with a progressive movement. I have also prac-
tised picture criticism, and have had to make up my mind
as to the pre-Raphaelite movement and the Impressionist movement, with the result that I have come to suspect dramatic critics of never having had to make up
their minds about anything, owing to the fact that until
the advent of Ibsen the other day there had not for many
years been anything worth calling a movement in dramatic art. I by no means undervalued their like or dislike of my work, which was written as much to please
them as anyone else; but, as an expert, I found their
critical analysis anything but skilful, and their power of
imposing on themselves by phrase-making, boundless.
Even the best of the younger school will occasionally be
satisfied that he has quite accounted for an unexpected
speech by dismissing it as a wanton paradox (without any
consciousness of having insulted the author); or he will
dispose of an incident by pointing out that it is "incon-
sistent"; or, if he wishes to be specially ingenious, he will
say of a character—a red-haired one, for instance—
that it is not a human being at all, but a type of the
red-haired variety of mankind. I make free to criticize
my critics thus because some of them are my personal
friends; others have dealt so handsomely by me that I
cannot very well except them without a ridiculous appearance of returning the compliment; and the rest will be all
the better for being brought to book. Besides, I may
offer my Quintessence of Ibsenism, written and published
before there was any question of finishing or producing
Widowers' Houses, as a substantial proof that my interest
in the art of criticism is not at bottom merely the protest of my own sensitiveness against the very disrespectful
way in which my work has been handled in various
quarters. There must, however, be no mistake as to the
ground upon which I challenge criticism for the play, now
that I submit it in print to the public. It is a propagandist

play—a didactic play—a play with a purpose; but I do not therefore claim any special indulgence for it from people who go to the theatre to be entertained. I offer it as a technically good practicable stage play, one which will, if adequately acted, hold its proper audience and drive its story home to the last word.

But in claiming place for my play among works of art, I must make a melancholy reservation. One or two friendly readers may find it interesting, amusing, even admirable, as far as a mere topical farce can excite admiration; but nobody will find it a beautiful or lovable work. It is saturated with the vulgarity of the life it represents: the people do not speak nobly, live gracefully, or sincerely face their own position: the author is not giving expression in pleasant fancies to the underlying beauty and romance of happy life, but dragging up to the smooth surface of "respectability" a handful of the slime and foulness of its polluted bed, and playing off your laughter at the scandal of the exposure against your shudder at its blackness. I offer it as my own criticism of the author of Widowers' Houses that the disillusion which makes all great dramatic poets tragic has here made him only derisive; and derision is by common consent a baser atmosphere than that of tragedy. I had better have written a beautiful play, like Twelfth Night, or a grand play, like the tragic masterpieces; but, frankly, I was not able to: modern commercialism is a bad art school, and cannot, with all its robberies, murders and prostitutions, move us in the grand manner to pity and terror: it is squalid, futile, blundering, mean, ridiculous, for ever uneasily pretending to be the wide-minded, humane, enterprising thing it is not. It is not my fault, reader, that my art is the expression of my sense of moral and intellectual perversity rather than of my sense of beauty. My life has been passed mostly in big modern towns, where my sense of beauty has been starved whilst my intellect has been gorged with problems like that of the slums in this play, until at last I have come, in a horrible sort of way, to relish them enough to make them the subjects of my essays as an artist. Such art as can come out of these conditions for a man of my endowment I claim to have put into my work; and therefore you will please judge it, not as a pamphlet in dialogue, but as in intention a work of art as much as any comedy of Molière's is a work of art, and as pretending to be a better made play for actual use and long wear on the boards than anything that has yet been turned out by the patent constructive machinery. And I claim that its value in both respects is enhanced by the fact that it deals with a burning social question, and is deliberately intended to induce people to vote on the Progressive side at the next County Council election in London. So, as the clown says in All's Well, "Spare not me." I am no novice in the current critical theories of dramatic art; and what I have done I have done on purpose.

JOHN MILLINGTON SYNGE
(1871-1909)

The Playboy of the Western World[1] (1907)

IN WRITING *The Playboy of the Western World*, as in my other plays, I have used one or two words only that I have not heard among the country people of Ireland, or spoken in my own nursery before I could read the newspapers. A certain number of the phrases I employ I have heard also from herds and fishermen along the coast from Kerry to Mayo, or from beggarwomen and ballad singers near Dublin; and I am glad to acknowledge how much I owe to the folk imagination of these fine people. Anyone who has lived in real intimacy with the Irish peasantry will know that the wildest sayings and ideas in this play are tame indeed, compared with the fancies one may hear in any little hillside cabin in Geesala, or Carraroe, or Dingle Bay. All art is a collaboration; and there is little doubt that in the happy ages of literature, striking and beautiful phrases were as ready to the storyteller's or the playwright's hand, as the rich cloaks and dresses of his time. It is probable that when the Elizabethan dramatist took his inkhorn and sat down to his work he used many phrases that he had just heard, as he sat at dinner, from his mother or his children. In Ireland, those of us who know the people have the same privilege. When I was writing *The Shadow of the Glen*, some years ago, I got more aid than any learning could have given me from a chink in the floor of the old Wicklow house where I was staying, that let me hear what was being said by the servant girls in the kitchen. This matter, I think, is of importance, for in countries where the imagination of the people, and the language they use, is rich and living, it is possible for

[1] *The Complete Works of John M. Synge* (New York: Random House, 1935), pp. 3, 177–78. Copyright 1935 by the Modern Library, Inc. Reprinted by permission of Random House, Inc., and George Allen and Unwin, Ltd., London.

a writer to be rich and copious in his words, and at the
same time to give the reality, which is the root of all
poetry, in a comprehensive and natural form. In the
modern literature of towns, however, richness is found
only in sonnets, or prose poems, or in one or two elab-
rate books that are far away from the profound and
common interests of life. One has, on one side, Mallarmé
and Huysmans producing this literature; and, on the other,
Ibsen and Zola dealing with the reality of life in joyless
and pallid words. On the stage one must have reality,
and one must have joy; and that is why the intellectual
modern drama has failed, and people have grown sick
of the false joy of the musical comedy that has been given
them in place of the rich joy found only in what is superb
and wild in reality. In a good play every speech should be
as fully flavored as a nut or apple, and such speeches
cannot be written by anyone who works among people who
have shut their lips on poetry. In Ireland, for a few
years more, we have a popular imagination that is fiery
and magnificent, and tender; so that those who wish to
write start with a chance that is not given to writers in
places where the springtime of the local life has been
forgotten, and the harvest is a memory only, and the
straw has been turned into bricks.

The Tinker's Wedding

THE DRAMA is made serious—in the French sense of
the word—not by the degree in which it is taken up with
problems that are serious in themselves, but by the
degree in which it gives the nourishment, not easy to
define, on which our imaginations live. We should not
go to the theatre as we go to a chemists', or a dram
shop, but as we go to a dinner, where food we need is
taken with pleasure and excitement. This was nearly always so in Spain and England and France, where the
drama was at its richest—but in these days the playhouse
is too often stocked with the drugs of many seedy problems, or with the absinthe or vermouth of the last musical comedy.

The drama, like the symphony, does not teach or
prove anything. Analysts with their problems, and teachers
with their systems, are soon as old-fashioned as the

pharmacopoeia of Galen—look at Ibsen and the Germans—but the best plays of Ben Jonson and Molière can no more go out of fashion than the blackberries on the hedges.

Of the things which nourish the imagination humor is one of the most needful, and it is dangerous to limit or destroy it. Baudelaire calls laughter the greatest sign of the Satanic element in man; and when a country loses its humor, as some towns in Ireland are doing, there will be morbidity of mind, as Baudelaire's mind was morbid.

In the greater part of Ireland, however, the whole people, from the tinkers to the clergy, have still a life and view of life, that are rich and genial and humorous. I do not think that these country people, who have so much humor themselves, will mind being laughed at without malice, as the people in every country have been laughed at in their comedies.

LUIGI PIRANDELLO
(1867-1936)

Six Characters in Search of an Author[1] (1925)

IT SEEMS like yesterday but is actually many years ago that a nimble little maidservant entered the service of my art. However, she always comes fresh to the job.

She is called Fantasy.

A little puckish and malicious, if she likes to dress in black no one will wish to deny that she is often positively bizarre and no one will wish to believe that she always does everything in the same way and in earnest. She sticks her hand in her pocket, pulls out a cap and bells, sets it on her head, red as a cock's comb, and dashes away. Here today, there tomorrow. And she amuses herself by bringing to my house—since I derive stories and novels and plays from them—the most disgruntled tribe in the world, men, women, children, involved in strange adventures which they can find no way out of; thwarted in their plans; cheated in their hopes; with whom, in short, it is often torture to deal.

Well, this little maidservant of mine, Fantasy, several years ago, had the bad inspiration or ill-omened caprice to bring a family into my house. I wouldn't know where she fished them up or how, but, according to her, I could find in them the subject for a magnificent novel.

I found before me a man about fifty years old, in a dark jacket and light trousers, with a frowning air and ill-natured, mortified eyes; a poor woman in widow's weeds leading by one hand a little girl of four and by the other a boy of rather more than ten; a cheeky and "sexy" girl, also clad in black but with an equivocal and brazen pomp, all atremble with a lively, biting contempt for the

[1] Luigi Pirandello, Preface, *Six Characters in Search of an Author,* translated by Eric Bentley, *Naked Masks* (New York: E. P. Dutton & Co.), pp. 363–75. Copyright 1952 by E. P. Dutton & Co., Inc. Reprinted by permission of E. P. Dutton & Co., Inc.

mortified old man and for a young fellow of twenty who stood on one side closed in on himself as if he despised them all. In short, the six characters who are seen coming on stage at the beginning of the play. Now one of them and now another—often beating down one another—embarked on the sad story of their adventures, each shouting his own reasons, and projecting in my face his disordered passions, more or less as they do in the play to the unhappy Manager.

What author will be able to say how and why a character was born in his fantasy? The mystery of artistic creation is the same as that of birth. A woman who loves may desire to become a mother; but the desire by itself, however intense, cannot suffice. One fine day she will find herself a mother without having any precise intimation when it began. In the same way an artist imbibes very many germs of life and can never say how and why, at a certain moment, one of these vital germs inserts itself into his fantasy, there to become a living creature on a plane of life superior to the changeable existence of every day.

I can only say that, without having made any effort to seek them out, I found before me, alive—you could touch them and even hear them breathe—the six characters now seen on the stage. And they stayed there in my presence, each with his secret torment and all bound together by the one common origin and mutual entanglement of their affairs, while I had them enter the world of art, constructing from their persons, their passions, and their adventures a novel, a drama, or at least a story.

Born alive, they wished to live.

To me it was never enough to present a man or a woman and what is special and characteristic about them simply for the pleasure of presenting them; to narrate a particular affair, lively or sad, simply for the pleasure of narrating it; to describe a landscape simply for the pleasure of describing it.

There are some writers (and not a few) who do feel this pleasure and, satisfied, ask no more. They are, to speak more precisely, historical writers.

But there are others who, beyond such pleasure, feel a more profound spiritual need on whose account they admit only figures, affairs, landscapes which have been soaked, so to speak, in a particular sense of life and acquire from it a universal value. These are, more precisely, philosophical writers.

I have the misfortune to belong to these last.

I hate symbolic art in which the presentation loses all spontaneous movement in order to become a machine, an allegory—a vain and misconceived effort because the very fact of giving an allegorical sense to a presentation clearly shows that we have to do with a fable which by itself has no truth either fantastic or direct; it was made for the demonstration of some moral truth. The spiritual need I speak of cannot be satisfied—or seldom, and that to the end of a superior irony, as for example in Ariosto—by such allegorical symbolism. This latter starts from a concept, and from a concept which creates or tries to create for itself an image. The former on the other hand seeks in the image—which must remain alive and free throughout—a meaning to give it value.

Now, however much I sought, I did not succeed in uncovering this meaning in the six characters. And I concluded therefore that it was no use making them live.

I thought to myself: "I have already afflicted my readers with hundreds and hundreds of stories. Why should I afflict them now by narrating the sad entanglements of these six unfortunates?"

And, thinking thus, I put them away from me. Or rather I did all I could to put them away.

But one doesn't give life to a character for nothing.

Creatures of my spirit, these six were already living a life which was their own and not mine any more, a life which it was not in my power any more to deny them.

Thus it is that while I persisted in desiring to drive them out of my spirit, they, as if completely detached from every narrative support, characters from a novel miraculously emerging from the pages of the book that contained them, went on living on their own, choosing certain moments of the day to reappear before me in the solitude of my study and coming—now one, now the other, now two together—to tempt me, to propose that I present or describe this scene or that, to explain the effects that could be secured with them, the new interest which a certain unusual situation could provide, and so forth.

For a moment I let myself be won over. And this condescension of mine, thus letting myself go for a

while, was enough, because they drew from it a new incre-
ment of life, a greater degree of clarity and addition, consequently a greater degree of persuasive power over me.
And thus as it became gradually harder and harder for
me to go back and free myself from them, it became
easier and easier for them to come back and tempt me.
At a certain point I actually became obsessed with them.
Until, all of a sudden, a way out of the difficulty flashed
upon me.

"Why not," I said to myself, "present this highly strange
fact of an author who refuses to let some of his characters
live though they have been born in his fantasy, and the
fact that these characters, having by now life in their veins,
do not resign themselves to remaining excluded from the
world of art? They are detached from me; live on their
own; have acquired voice and movement; have by themselves—in this struggle for existence that they have had
to wage with me—become dramatic characters, characters that can move and talk on their own initiative;
already see themselves as such; have learned to defend
themselves against me; will even know how to defend
themselves against others. And so let them go where
dramatic characters do go to have life: on a stage. And
let us see what will happen."

That's what I did. And, naturally, the result was what
it had to be: a mixture of tragic and comic, fantastic
and realistic, in a humorous situation that was quite new
and infinitely complex, a drama which is conveyed by
means of the characters, who carry it within them and
suffer it, a drama, breathing, speaking, self-propelled,
which seeks at all costs to find the means of its own
presentation; and the comedy of the vain attempt at an
improvised realization of the drama on stage. First, the
surprise of the poor actors in a theatrical company rehearsing a play by day on a bare stage (no scenery, no
flats). Surprise and incredulity at the sight of the six
characters announcing themselves as such in search of
an author. Then, immediately afterward, through that sudden fainting fit of the Mother veiled in black, their instinctive interest in the drama of which they catch a glimpse
in her and in the other members of the strange family, an
obscure, ambiguous drama, coming about so unexpectedly on a stage that is empty and unprepared to receive
it. And gradually the growth of this interest to the burst-

ing forth of the contrasting passions of Father, of Stepdaughter, of Son, of that poor Mother, passions seeking,
as I said, to overwhelm each other with a tragic, lacer-
ating fury.

And here is the universal meaning at first vainly
sought in the six characters, now that, going on stage
of their own accord, they succeed in finding it within
themselves in the excitement of the desperate struggle
which each wages against the other and all wage against
the Manager and the actors, who do not understand them.

Without wanting to, without knowing it, in the strife of
their bedeviled souls, each of them, defending himself
against the accusations of the others, expresses as his
own living passion and torment the passion and torment
which for so many years have been the pangs of my
spirit: the deceit of mutual understanding irremediably
founded on the empty abstraction of the words, the multiple personality of everyone corresponding to the possibilities of being to be found in each of us, and finally
the inherent tragic conflict between life (which is always
moving and changing) and form (which fixes it, immutable).

Two above all among the six characters, the Father
and the Stepdaughter, speak of that outrageous unalterable fixity of their form in which he and she see
their essential nature expressed permanently and im-
mutably, a nature that for one means punishment and
for the other revenge; and they defend it against the
factitious affectations and unaware volatility of the actors,
and they try to impose it on the vulgar Manager who
would like to change it and adapt it to the so-called exigencies of the theatre.

If the six characters don't all seem to exist on the
same plane, it is not because some are figures of first
rank and others of the second, that is, some are main
characters and others minor ones—the elementary perspective necessary to all scenic or narrative art—nor is
it that any are not completely created—for their purpose. They are all six at the same point of artistic
realization and on the same level of reality, which is
the fantastic level of the whole play. Except that the
Father, the Stepdaughter, and also the Son are realized
as mind; the Mother as nature; the Boy as a presence

watching and performing a gesture and the Baby unaware
of it all. This fact creates among them a perspective of
a new sort. Unconsciously I had had the impression that
some of them needed to be fully realized (artistically
speaking), others less so, and others merely sketched in
as elements in a narrative or presentational sequence:
the most alive, the most completely created, are the Father
and the Stepdaughter who naturally stand out more and
lead the way, dragging themselves along beside the almost dead weight of the others—first, the Son, holding
back; second, the Mother, like a victim resigned to her
fate, between the two children who have hardly any substance beyond their appearance and who need to be
led by the hand.

And actually! actually they had each to appear in that
stage of creation which they had attained in the author's
fantasy at the moment when he wished to drive them away.

If I now think about these things, about having in-
tuited that necessity, having unconsciously found the way
to resolve it by means of a new perspective, and about
the way in which I actually obtained it, they seem like
miracles. The fact is that the play was really conceived
in one of those spontaneous illuminations of the fantasy
when by a miracle all the elements of the mind answer
to each other's call and work in divine accord. No
human brain, working "in the cold," however stirred up it
might be, could ever have succeeded in penetrating far
enough, could ever have been in a position to satisfy all
the exigencies of the play's form. Therefore the reasons
which I will give to clarify the values of the play must not
be thought of as intentions that I conceived beforehand
when I prepared myself for the job and which I now
undertake to defend, but only as discoveries which I have
been able to make afterward in tranquillity.

I wanted to present six characters seeking an author.
Their play does not manage to get presented—precisely
because the author whom they seek is missing. Instead is
presented the comedy of their vain attempt with all that it
contains of tragedy by virtue of the fact that the six
characters have been rejected.

But can one present a character while rejecting him?
Obviously, to present him one needs, on the contrary, to
receive him into one's fantasy before one can express

him. And I have actually accepted and realized the six characters: I have, however, accepted and realized them as rejected: in search of *another* author.

What have I rejected of them? Not themselves, obviously, but their drama, which doubtless is what interests them above all but which did not interest me—for the reasons already indicated.

And what is it, for a character—his drama?

Every creature of fantasy and art, in order to exist, must have his drama, that is, a drama in which he may be a character and for which he *is* a character. This drama is the character's *raison d'être,* his vital function, necessary for his existence.

In these six, then, I have accepted the "being" without the reason for being. I have taken the organism and entrusted to it, not its own proper function, but another more complex function into which its own function entered, if at all, only as a datum. A terrible and desperate situation especially for the two—Father and Stepdaughter—who more than the others crave life and more than the others feel themselves to be characters, that is, absolutely need a drama and therefore their own drama—the only one which they can envisage for themselves yet which meantime they see rejected: an "impossible" situation from which they feel they must escape at whatever cost; it is a matter of life and death. True, I have given them another *raison d'être,* another function: precisely that "impossible" situation, the drama of being in search of an author and rejected. But that this should be a *raison d'être,* that it should have become their real function, that it should be necessary, that it should suffice, they can hardly suppose; for they have a life of their own. If someone were to tell them, they wouldn't believe him. It is not possible to believe that the sole reason for our living should lie in a torment that seems to us unjust and inexplicable.

I cannot imagine, therefore, why the charge was brought against me that the character of the Father was not what it should have been because it stepped out of its quality and position as a character and invaded at times the author's province and took it over. I who understand those who don't quite understand me see that the charge derives from the fact that the character expresses and makes his own a torment of spirit which is recognized as mine.

Which is entirely natural and of absolutely no significance. Aside from the fact that this torment of spirit in the character of the Father derives from causes, and is suffered and lived for reasons that have nothing to do with the drama of my personal experience, a fact which alone removes all substance from the criticism, I want to make it clear that the inherent torment of my spirit is one thing, a torment which I can legitimately—provided that it be organic—reflect in a character, and that the activity of my spirit as revealed in the realized work, the activity that succeeds in forming a drama out of the six characters in search of an author is another thing. If the Father participated in this latter activity, if he competed in forming the drama of the six characters without an author, then and only then would it by all means be justified to say that he was at times the author himself and therefore not the man he should be. But the Father suffers and does not create his existence as a character in search of an author. He suffers it as an inexplicable fatality and as a situation which he tries with all his powers to rebel against, which he tries to remedy; hence it is that he is a character in search of an author and nothing more, even if he expresses as his own the torment of my spirit. If he, so to speak, assumed some of the author's responsibilities, the fatality would be completely explained. He would, that is to say, see himself accepted, if only as a rejected character, accepted in the poet's heart of hearts, and he would no longer have any reason to suffer the despair of not finding someone to construct and affirm his life as a character. I mean that he would quite willingly accept the *raison d'être* which the author gives him and without regrets would forgo his own, throwing over the Manager and the actors to whom in fact he runs as his only recourse.

There is one character, that of the Mother, who on the other hand does not care about being alive (considering being alive as an end in itself). She hasn't the least suspicion that she is *not* alive. It has never occurred to her to ask how and why and in what manner she lives. In short, she is not aware of being a character inasmuch as she is never, even for a moment, detached from her role. She doesn't know she has a role.

This makes her perfectly organic. Indeed, her role of Mother does not of itself, in its natural essence, em-

brace mental activity. And she does not exist as a mind.
She lives in an endless continuum of feeling, and therefore she cannot acquire awareness of her life—that is,
of her existence as a character. But with all this, even she,
in her own way and for her own ends, seeks an author,
and at a certain stage seems happy to have been brought
before the Manager. Because she hopes to take life from
him, perhaps? No: because she hopes the Manager will
have her present a scene with the Son in which she would
put so much of her own life. But it is a scene which does
not exist, which never has and never could take place. So
unaware is she of being a character, that is, of the life
that is possible to her, all fixed and determined, moment
by moment, in every action, every phrase.

She appears on stage with the other characters but
without understanding what the others make her do. Obviously, she imagines that the itch for life with which the
husband and the daughter are afflicted and for which she
herself is to be found on stage is no more than one of the
usual incomprehensible extravagances of this man who is
both tortured and torturer and—horrible, most horrible
—a new equivocal rebellion on the part of that poor
erring girl. The Mother is completely passive. The events
of her own life and the values they assume in her eyes,
her very character, are all things which are "said" by the
others and which she only once contradicts, and that
because the maternal instinct rises up and rebels within
her to make it clear that she didn't at all wish to abandon
either the son or the husband: the Son was taken from
her and the husband forced her to abandon him. She is
only correcting data; she explains and knows nothing.

In short, she is nature. Nature fixed in the figure of a
mother.

This character gave me a satisfaction of a new sort,
not to be ignored. Nearly all my critics, instead of
defining her, after their habit, as "unhuman"—which
seems to be the peculiar and incorrigible characteristic of
all my creatures without exception—had the goodness to
note "with real pleasure" that at last a *very human* figure
had emerged from my fantasy. I explain this praise to
myself in the following way: since my poor Mother is entirely limited to the natural attitude of a Mother with no
possibility of free mental activity, being, that is, little
more than a lump of flesh completely alive in all its

functions—procreation, lactation, caring for and loving its young—without any need therefore of exercising her brain, she realizes in her person the true and complete "human type." That must be how it is, since in a human organism nothing seems more superfluous than the mind.

But the critics have tried to get rid of the Mother with this praise without bothering to penetrate the nucleus of poetic values which the character in the play represents. A very human figure, certainly, because mindless, that is, unaware of being what she is or not caring to explain it to herself. But not knowing that she is a character doesn't prevent her from being one. That is her drama in my play. And the most living expression of it comes spurting out in her cry to the Manager, who wants her to think all these things have happened already and therefore cannot now be a reason for renewed lamentations: "No, it's happening now, it's happening always! My torture is not a pretense, signore! I am alive and present, always, in every moment of my torture: it is renewed, alive, and present always!" This she *feels*, without being conscious of it, and feels it therefore as something inexplicable: but she feels it so terribly that she doesn't think it *can* be something to explain either to herself or to others. She feels it and that is that. She feels it as pain and this pain is immediate; she cries it out. Thus she reflects the growing fixity of life in a form—the same thing, which in another way, tortures the Father and the Stepdaughter. In them, mind. In her, nature. The mind rebels and, as best it may, seeks an advantage; nature, if not aroused by sensory stimuli, weeps.

Conflict between life-in-movement and form is the inexorable condition not only of the mental but also of the physical order. The life which in order to exist has become fixed in our corporeal form little by little kills that form. The tears of a nature thus fixed lament the irreparable, continuous aging of our bodies. Hence the tears of the Mother are passive and perpetual. Revealed in three faces, made significant in three distinct and simultaneous dramas, this inherent conflict finds in the play its most complete expression. More: the Mother declares also the particular value of artistic form—a form which does not delimit or destroy its own life and which life does not consume—in her cry to the Manager. If the Father and Stepdaughter began their scene a hundred thousand times in succession, always, at the appointed moment, at the instant when the life of the work of art must be expressed with that cry, it would always be heard, unaltered and unalterable in its form, not as a mechanical repetition, not as a return determined by external necessities, but, on the contrary, alive every time and as new, suddenly born *thus forever!* embalmed alive in its incorruptible form. Hence, always, as we open the book, we shall find Francesca alive and confessing to Dante her sweet sin, and if we turn to the passage a hundred thousand times in succession, a hundred thousand times in succession Francesca will speak her words, never repeating them mechanically, but saying them as though each time were the first time with such living and sudden passion that Dante every time will turn faint. All that lives, by the fact of living, has a form, and by the same token must die—except the work of art which lives forever in so far as it *is* form.

The birth of a creature of human fantasy, a birth which is a step across the threshold between nothing and eternity, can also happen suddenly, occasioned by some necessity. An imagined drama needs a character who does or says a certain necessary thing; accordingly this character is born and is precisely what he had to be. In this way Madame Pace is born among the six characters and seems a miracle, even a trick, realistically portrayed on the stage. It is no trick. The birth is real. The new character is alive not because she was alive already but because she is now happily born as is required by the fact of her being a character—she is obliged to be as she is. There is a break here, a sudden change in the level of reality of the scene, because a character can be born in this way only in the poet's fancy and not on the boards of a stage. Without anyone's noticing it, I have all of a sudden changed the scene: I have gathered it up again into my own fantasy without removing it from the spectator's eyes. That is, I have shown them, instead of the stage, my own fantasy in the act of creating—my own fantasy in the form of this same stage. The sudden and uncontrollable changing of a visual phenomenon from one level of reality to another is a miracle comparable to those of the saint who sets his own statue in motion: it is neither wood nor stone at such a moment. But the miracle is not arbitrary. The stage—a stage which accepts the fantastic reality of the six characters—is no fixed, immutable datum. Nothing in this play exists as given and preconceived. Everything is in the making, is in motion, is a sudden experiment: even the place in which this unformed life, reaching after its own form, changes and changes again contrives to shift position organically. The level of reality changes. When I had the idea of bringing Madame Pace to birth right there on the stage, I felt I could do it and I did it. Had I noticed that this birth was unhinging and silently, unnoticed, in a second, giving another shape, another reality to my scene, I certainly wouldn't have brought it about. I would have been afraid of the apparent lack of logic. And I would have committed an ill-omened assault on the beauty of my work. The fervor of my mind saved me from doing so. For, despite appearances, with their specious logic, this fantastic birth is sustained by a real necessity in mysterious, organic relation with the whole life of the work.

That someone now tells me it hasn't all the value it could have because its expression is not constructed but chaotic, because it smacks of romanticism, makes me smile.

I understand why this observation was made to me: because in this work of mine the presentation of the drama in which the six characters are involved appears tumultuous and never proceeds in an orderly manner. There is no logical development, no concatenation of the events. Very true. Had I hunted it with a lamp I couldn't have found a more disordered, crazy, arbitrary, complicated, in short, romantic way of presenting "the drama in which the six characters are involved." Very true. But I have not presented that drama. I have presented another—and I won't undertake to say again what!—in which, among the many fine things that everyone, according to his tastes, can find, there is a discreet satire on romantic procedures: in the six characters thus excited to the point where they stifle themselves in the roles which each of them plays in a certain drama while I present them as characters in another play which they don't know and don't suspect the existence of, so that this inflammation of their passions—which belongs to the realm of romantic procedures—is humorously "placed," located in the void. And the drama of the six characters presented not as it would have been organized by my

fantasy had it been accepted but in this way, as a rejected
drama, could not exist in the work except as a "situation,"
with some little development, and could not come out
except in indications, stormily, disorderedly, in violent
foreshortenings, in a chaotic manner: continually inter-
rupted, sidetracked, contradicted (by one of its characters), denied, and (by two others) not even seen.

There is a character indeed—he who denies the drama
which makes him a character, the Son—who draws all his
importance and value from being a character not of the
comedy in the making—which as such hardly appears—
but from the presentation that I made of it. In short,
he is the only one who lives solely as a "a character in
search of an author"—inasmuch as the author he seeks is
not a dramatic author. Even this could not be otherwise.
The character's attitude is an organic product of my
conception, and it is logical that in the situation it should
produce greater confusion and disorder and another
element of romantic contrast.

But I had precisely to *present* this organic and natural
chaos. And to present a chaos is not at all to present
chaotically, that is, romantically. That my presentation is
the reverse of confused, that it is quite simple, clear,
and orderly, is proved by the clarity which the intrigue,
the characters, the fantastic and realistic, dramatic and
comic levels of the work have had for every public in
the world and by the way in which, for those with more
searching vision, the unusual values enclosed within it
come out.

Great is the confusion of tongues among men if criticisms thus made find words for their expression. No less
great than this confusion is the intimate law of order
which, obeyed in all points, makes this work of mine
classical and typical and at its catastrophic close forbids the use of words. Though the audience eventually
understands that one does not create life by artifice and
that the drama of the six characters cannot be presented
without an author to give them value with his spirit, the
Manager remains vulgarly anxious to know how the thing
turned out, and the "ending" is remembered by the Son
in its sequence of actual moments, but without any
sense and therefore not needing a human voice for its
expression. It happens stupidly, uselessly, with the going
off of a mechanical weapon on stage. It breaks up and

disperses the sterile experiment of the characters and the actors, which has apparently been made without the assistance of the poet.

The poet, unknown to them, as if looking on at a distance during the whole period of the experiment, was at the same time busy creating—with it and of it—his own play.

ERNST TOLLER
(1893-1939)

Transfiguration[1]

IT HAS often been said about my plays that they are not
unbiased, not impartial. What does the bourgeois critic
call unbiased, impartial? The body of attitudes and perceptions in the traditional tracks of which he jogs along,
and which in reality signify the spiritual legitimization of
middle-class rule. It is this very form of rule that revolutionary art wants to shake up. What the working people
need is a theatre which is intimately bound up with our
era. Great art has never been timeless. Whether we consider Sophocles, Aristophanes, Dante, Shakespeare, Kleist,
Büchner, Schiller, they all use "topical" problems, and
try to give them an "eternal" interpretation. They were the
mouthpieces of an idea inspired by the era, of a community struggling in the era. Many of their works have met
with the same criticism which nowadays tries to hack to
pieces contemporary writings.

No serious artist will dispute the fact that in art there
are "timeless" elements, expressions of cosmic relationships
in which changes are hardly noticeable.

Even revolutionary dramatic and epic art will awaken
within us the consciousness of that ultimateness which
Angelus Silesius called "Unio Mystica," and which I would
like to call: Silence of the Universe. Fulfilled by the
sensual present, the militant artist will create it by instinctive presentiment.

The lyric poet, who by giving form to his feelings overcomes the private aloneness of man—his relationships,
happy by nature but saddened with knowledge—follows
other laws.

Unfortunately, today we have no dramatic theory with

[1] Ernst Toller, "My Works," translated by Marketa Goetz
in *The Tulane Drama Review*, March 1959, pp. 99–106.
Reprinted by permission of *The Tulane Drama Review* and
Sidney Kaufman.

a contemporary value, such as Lessing created for his period. It is not the abundance of various artistic figures that creates confusion but the lack of clear critical concepts.

The great "pure form" is in theory always the "eternal." But, as a note has to reach a certain high or low pitch in order to be perceived by the human ear, so the poetic work must sound a certain height or depth in order to be perceived by the period. Understand me correctly: today we may be deaf to a great work of art, tomorrow we will hear it. How often we have laid books aside without receiving any particular impression; when we take them up again years later we discover that they really concern us. Let us avoid that mental pharisaism which Trotsky calls "patriotism of the period." If we reject a work of art for ourselves, we must have sufficient sense of distance not to admit the possibility of its relation to other periods, other cultures. No epoch contains the yardstick of all things.

Beauty, too, as a concept has various contents. Any artist at any time strives toward formal beauty; the revolutionary, the socialist within the artist, fights for beauty as reality.

Transfiguration I wrote in the middle of the war. I made copies of the scenes in the military hospital, and handed them out to women during the strike in the beginning of 1918. At that time only one thing mattered to me in my writing: to work for freedom. The play is called Expressionistic. "Reality scenes" and "dream scenes" alternate with each other. Today many people smile at Expressionism; at that time it was a necessary artistic form. It took a stand against that kind of art which was satisfied with lining up impressions side by side, asking no questions about the essence, the responsibility, the idea. The Expressionist wanted to do more than take photographs. Realizing that the artist's environment, as it were, penetrates him and is reflected in the mirror of his soul, he wanted to re-create this environment in its very essence. For it was the intention of Expressionism to influence this environment; it was to be changed, to be given a juster, a brighter face. Reality was to be caught in the bright beam of the idea.

Everything that happened resolved itself into an outer and an inner happening, both being equally important, as equally strong motive forces. The style of Expression-

ism—I only speak about good style—was terse, almost
like a telegram, avoiding minor issues, always penetrating
to the center of things. In the Expressionist drama, man
was no incidental private person. He was a type, applying
to many by leaving out their superficial features. By skin-
ning the human being one hoped to find his soul under
the skin.

The realities of the time were so varied and powerful
that no one could cope with them. One was able to
dominate them only by abstraction, by shedding light on
those patterns that established the reason for things.

The period of Expressionism gave place to the New
Factuality and to that artistic genre which is called
Reportage. I think that the "new objectivity" was a form of
modern Biedermeier style; the artist, working with this
"new objectivity," was not close to people and things but
to their photographs.

Today, when we have gained distance from the individual events, when important matters can be distinguished from unimportant ones, when a thousand details
have been forgotten, we have attained a style which is
saturated with reality, and yet is founded on an idea. Experience and objectivity fuse once again.

Whether Expressionism has brought forth works that
will last will be known in fifty years. One must not, however, forget that it had been born out of a period, and
wanted to go to work on that period. Since Schiller's
Robbers, since *Intrigue and Love,* the theatre has never
been to such an extent the platform of contemporary
events, surrounded by the squabbles and conflicts of public
opinion. Passionate sympathy on one hand, fierce re-
proaches for biased prejudice on the other.

Every author wants to crowd into his first work all he
knows, all he has ever experienced. I did the same. And
thus it is not surprising that the private, the lyrical element
is more prominent than dramatic structure may permit.

Masses and Man

IN *Masses and Man,* the form is purer. It was very
strange: after the play had been performed, one group
said it was counterrevolutionary because it condemns
any form of violence; others said that it was Bolshevistic

because the representative of non-violence is destroyed, and
the masses, in spite of suffering defeat for the time being,
remain victorious in the long run. Only a few recognized
that the battle between individual and masses did not take
place merely on the outside, that everyone is intrinsically
individual and "mass" at the same time. As an individual
he acts in accordance with the moral idea that is considered right. He wants to live by it, even if the world
goes to ruin. As a part of the mass, he is driven by social impulses and situations; he wants to reach the goal,
even if he has to give up the moral idea. Even today
this paradox is insoluble for the politically active man,
and I wanted to demonstrate this very insolubility.

The City Theatre in Nuremberg ventured to stage the
premiere of *Masses and Man.* Soon Prime Minister von
Kahr prohibited all public and even all closed performances
of the drama, and stated the reasons for this uncon-
stitutional measure in the meeting of the Landtag. He
supported his argument, among other reasons, with a
complaint from the Central Society of German Citizens
of Jewish faith, who had "taken offense" against the scene
in the stock market.

The greater my concern with social problems, the more
resolutely I became a socialist, the more clearly I recognized the limit to any possibility of happiness that can be
fought for and attained by individual and social strength
of will. The revolutionary poet of the nineteenth century
believed in the romantic paradise on earth. We know that
socialism, too, will end only the pain which comes from
the insufficiency of social systems; that there remains a
residue of insoluble tragedy, occasioned by the action of
cosmic forces. As long as we are not able to overcome
lightning and earthquakes, fires and hail storms, hunch-
backs and ugly faces, blind eyes and crooked souls,
sterility and death, we ought to become humbler.

We know that beauty does not move us as much as misery. We know that it is our task to give form to this misery
in a work of art, and to separate ourselves from it in
reality. Our social tragedy is a different tragedy from that
of the Greeks, which represented pain and misery as
something unavoidable that man is destined to submit to.
Our tragedy is a different tragedy from that of the Middle
Ages, which represented misery as the way to heavenly
salvation. We do not want any heavenly salvation. We have

realized that two kinds of misery press upon us: the misery
that arises from human life, and the misery that arises from
the injustice of the social system.

The Machine-Wreckers

IN PERIODS of violent social battles, the theatre will
reflect these battles. The proletarian who appears in drama
today is no longer the proletarian of the nineteenth century. The stagnating, hopeless air of *The Lower Depths*,
though deeply moving, is not his air any more. The proletarian of the nineteenth century suffered gloomily under the
burden of his fate, under want, exploitation, excessive
work, little pay. The proletarian of the twentieth century
became a conscious fighter, the defender of an idea. He
does not only criticize, he creates pictures of new realities
that he wants to build. His language, influenced by the
leading article of his party newspaper, is poorer in strong
images, richer in dialectic strength. It could not surprise
anyone, then, that on the stage too he repels those who
attack him in real life.

In *The Machine-Wreckers* I tried to show the rise
of this new proletarian type.

I consciously reject the tendency to worship the proletarian, to carry on an inverted Byzantine cult in his
honor. He is the historic bearer of a great new idea; that
is what matters. It is possible that the central figure in a
poetic work is a bourgeois with a "pure heart," the ideal,
"good" human being. In spite of this, he confutes the system of society in which he lives because of the divergency
between his own personal actions and the actions of the
ruling forces, thus producing an effect upon the audience
that we might call spiritually revolutionizing.

There is only one type of *Tendenz* not permitted to the
artist—the tendency to produce a black-and-white drawing, showing man on one side as devil, on the other as
angel. This concept is more decisive than the mixture of
good and bad qualities. But in spite of the law of strict
impartiality that shapes figures out of their innate necessities, the creative artist is conscious of being precisely the
person who arrives at a collectively valid subjectivity. He
does not balance values and ideas. A hierarchy is arranged
within him that separates superior values from inferior
ones.

One must not confuse political creative writing with propaganda that uses poetic means. The latter serves exclusively for daily purposes, it is both more and less than creative writing. More: because it contains the possibility of inciting the audience, in the strongest, the best hypothetical case, to act immediately. Less: because it never explores the depths which are reached by literature in order to communicate to the audience the sense of a tragicomical basis. In other words: when propaganda demonstrates ten "problems" it presupposes that all ten are soluble, and it has the right to demand the solution of all ten. To express it only with a vague example, in the case of ten problems literature will bring about the solution of nine, and demonstrate the tragic insolubility of the last. Whether this is done in a lofty, a resigned, or a pessimistic way, or with the demand implied by "and yet . . . !" is a question of mental attitude, of artistic temperament, but not of the essence.

Political literature merely elaborates upon the daily editorials of the party, it is occasioned by the demands of the idea.

All the dramas which I wrote in prison suffer from "too much." The artist who is "free" can experience this or that excitement, this or that resentment, this or that thought in some form unconnected with his art. My mouth was closed, and my pen was bound by the strict censorship of the fortress. The only place where I could to a certain extent let off steam was in a work of art. There the censorship was not as strict as with letters. Thus I crowded into my dramas all suppressed thoughts and feelings, even those that did not necessarily belong to the individual work. When my dramas are staged again today, I always shorten them and try to cut sentences which arose from an accidental situation.

Hoppla, Such Is Life!

Hoppla, Such Is Life! is the title of the first work that I wrote "in liberty." Again it dealt with the clash of the man who wants to realize the absolute completely, this very day, with the forces of the era and with his contemporaries who either give up that wish through weakness, treachery, cowardice, or else prepare for a later realization of the wish through force, loyalty, courage. Karl Thomas does not understand either group, he equates their motives and actions, and is destroyed. Having been alienated from true art by the American "happy end," many critics and members of the audience today demand of the dramatist something that is not his task at all: to send them home at the end of the play with those silly little verses for the home which our parents had painted on Chesterfield cushions, plates, picture posters for utility purposes: "Be true and honest," "Look not into others' doings but keep to your own," "Be joyful of heart"—or, as Dursus wrote in the 134th issue of *The Red Flag* in 1930: "Let's get going in the fresh air of nature with the fresh air of the class war!" Officials of the proletarian cult and critics in the entertainment column of capitalistic newspapers, having a bad conscience and craving to saunter through newspaper columns as eternal happy wanderers, became more aggressively revolutionary than those who worked actively for the revolution, called the outcome of this drama which has been repeated and will be repeated many times, not "revolutionary" because it did not send them home with little moral treatises and the cry: "Long live political trend number 73."

Today I am sorry that, influenced by the fashion of the day, I destroyed the architecture of the original work in favor of the architecture of the directing. Its intended form was stronger than the one that was shown on the stage. I alone am responsible for this but I have learned something, and today I prefer a director to get too little out of a work rather than put too much into it. By the way, Piscator in Gasbarra's book *The Political Theatre* has really no reason to complain about me and my style.[2]

2 Or are the sentences which Piscator suggested instead of the ones I had written, "functional, accelerating the dramatic action, intensifying the mental tension," in short, do they provide "the realistic foundation" and "replace the poetic, lyrical element" of the author? I quote from Piscator's manuscript: Scene after the murder of Wilhelm Kilmann. Monologue Karl Thomas.

Thomas: They shoot him because he is a revolutionary, I wanted to shoot him because he wasn't, and now I am firing at his murderers as if I were defending Kilmann's accomplices which would make me in turn his friend, brother and comrade. . . . Nothing but a transfer, a short step, was needed and the world's liberation from national hatred, disgraceful class subjugation, faulty [administration of the law] justice would have been helped to victory. (In a some

While working at it I took into consideration three conclusions, but never the one of "voluntary return to prison" which has been unhesitatingly forced on me in the above-mentioned book. In my first draft, Thomas, who did not understand the world of 1927, runs into the asylum to the psychoanalyst, realizes in his conversation with the physician that there are two types of dangerous madmen: those who are kept in isolated cells, and those who rage against humanity as politicians and military men. At this point he understands the old comrades who carry on the idea in dogged daily work, he wants to leave the asylum but, as he has comprehended, as he has reached the mature human being's sense of reality, the psychiatric official will not let him out any more. Only now, the latter claims, has he become "dangerous to the state," not before when he had been an inconvenient dreamer.

A few more words about a new play *Draw the Fires!* It deals with the battle in the Skagerrak, the German navy revolt, and the lawsuit against Köbis, Reichpietsch, Beckers, Sachse, Weber. I call this play a historical drama. I have changed places of action, shifted the time of events, invented characters, because I think that a dramatist should create that picture of an era out of his experience of it

---

what raised voice.) That this is not the case, Wilhelm—a terrible guilt on my part. Albert Kroll, Mother Meller, Eve, guilty, guilty. You there, down in the orchestra, guilty, guilty, we and they (he wants to continue speaking) . . .
Or: Final scene in prison. Karl Thomas's monologue.
Thomas: . . . I am awake. So widely awake that I can see through you, yet I would not learn anything new . . . Oh, the merry-go-round turns, everything begins at the beginning again. Yes, you dear people, and you my enemies, aren't you noticing that the earth is splitting underneath your feet? Kilmann, dead man, maybe celebrated by your murderers . . . if you lived, comrade, you wouldn't start at the beginning again. Man, undo it, undo it: tactics, treason. Volcanoes, fiery eyes of the earth are opening up, are breaking open before you. You are standing on the edge of the crater. What kind of madness has obsessed you, to keep crouching there and staring into the white heat! Save yourselves! Save yourselves! It rises! The lava shapes itself in a boiling base into a terrible weapon of destruction! It rises incessantly! Its hissing and malicious laughter at your stupidity that does not see the solution: divide et impera. . . .
Not to speak of the scene which was rehearsed one day, having been "inserted into" the play overnight without my even being asked. With a shock I recognized it from the names of the characters.

without photographing each historical detail. Artistic truth may coincide with historical truth, but the two are not necessarily identical in every detail.

The question of the formal strength of the new drama must not be overlooked, but how difficult it is to pass judgments on problematic new isues in our time when aesthetic laws have been shattered, when old values and norms have lost their binding validity. We know that we are not producing classical art. Classicism is the expression of self-contained superior calm. We, however, do not want to be calm, we do not want to build ivory towers into which we retreat; we want to take part in the struggles of our era, and we are not afraid of the rebuke that our life is just as ragged as life on the outside. Our art does not want to be merely an art of compassion, it was born from comradeship in arms. We, too, ask ourselves frequently: can art influence reality? Can the poet from his writing desk exert any influence on the politics of his age? There are authors who answer this question with "no," I answer it with "yes." All art has magical consequences. In what way is the effect of art distinguished from, say, the effect of a speech at a meeting? A speech at a meeting, at best, makes a problem understandable to the listener, it "educates" him. (Did education prevent the World War?)

Art reaches further than reason, it firmly establishes the emotion. It supplies the established emotion with rational legitimacy. I believe, therefore, that the artist should not prove a thesis but create examples. Art belongs among those rare spiritual means of stirring up buried instincts, of training brave attitudes, of deepening spontaneous feeling for humanity, freedom, and beauty.

In our era people use many expressions which no longer correspond to what we perceive and know. It is necessary to dissolve certain ideas, to re-create and name them more honestly from the greater nearness to things and people which we have reached. Also, in the ideological realm of the revolution, of the working classes, we must not admit pharisaical phrases, false coinage, deceitful distortions.

Outward successes have been of little use to me; before every new work I felt that I was at the beginning. And when the creative impulse failed me for several months, I feared it had left me forever. Only the creative artist knows the terrible crisis that occurs at such a time.

When I am working I am possessed by work, but I know that again decisions may be taken in which personal efforts are more important than art.

FEDERICO GARCÍA LORCA
(1899-1936)

Mariana Pineda[1] (1933)

"MARIANA PINEDA" was one of the greatest emotional experiences of my childhood. With children of my own age, we used to join hands and form circles that opened and closed in rhythm; and we would sing in a melancholy tone which I imagined to be tragic:

> *Oh! qué día tan triste en Granada*
> *que a las piedras hacía llorar*
> *al ver que Marianita se muere*
> *en cadalso por no declarar.*
>
> *Marianita, sentada en su cuarto,*
> *no paraba de considerar:*
> *"Si Pedrosa me viera bordando*
> *la bandera de la libertad."*

> (Oh! So sad a day in Granada
> which made the stones weep
> to see Marianita die on the scaffold
> because she would not inform.
>
> Marianita, sitting in her room,
> did not pause to consider:
> "If Pedrosa could only see me
> embroidering the flag of freedom.")

To me, Marianita, the flag of freedom, and Pedrosa assumed legendary and immaterial outlines—like a cloud, a very violent downpour of rain, a fluffy white mist; things which came to us from the Sierra Nevada and wrapped our little town in a cotton-like whiteness and silence.

One day, holding onto my mother's hand, I came to

[1] Marie Laffranque, "Federico García Lorca: Déclarations et Interviews Retrouvés" *Bulletin Hispanique,* July–September, 1956, pp. 325–26, 328–31. From an interview in *La Nación* of Buenos Aires, December 29, 1933, on the occasion of the first performance in Argentina of *Mariana Pineda.* Reprinted by courtesy of Francisco García Lorca. Written in 1923, this play is based on incidents in the life of Mariana Pineda who, in a period of extreme reaction in nineteenth century Spain, was executed for embroidering a revolutionary flag.

Granada. Again the popular ballad rose up before me, also sung by children whose voices were graver and more solemn, even more dramatic than those which had filled the streets of my little home town; and with an anxious heart I asked questions, inquired into and watched out for many things. I came to the conclusion that Mariana Pineda was a woman, a marvel of a woman; and the reason for her existence, the chief motive of her life, was love and freedom.

Nailed to these two crosses of sorrow and happiness —the two immortal illusions created by the gods to give man's life some hopeful meaning—Mariana Pineda appeared before me like some fabulous and most beautiful being, her mysterious eyes following with ineffable tenderness all the movements of the city. Materializing this ideal figure, I imagined the Alhambra to be a moon adorning my heroine's breast; her skirt the surrounding lowland embroidered in a thousand tones of green; the white petticoat the snow of the mountain etched against the blue sky; and the scalloped hem the golden flame of a copper-colored lamp.

To the characters created by the writers of the Golden Age whom I read with liveliest emotion, I added the figure of Mariana Pineda, seeing her with all the inspiration of heroic poetry. At that time Mariana Pineda would have sprung from my mind and hands dressed in the armor of the Great Captain, slaying with her broadsword all those who refused to accept love of liberty as the fundamental essence of life.

Enveloped in high-sounding eleven-syllable lines, in acrostics and royal eight-line stanzas, Mariana Pineda clothed in her sturdy armor rose constantly before my imagination, while my heart softly told me "that was not it"; Mariana lifted two weapons, love and freedom, in her hands—not to conquer but to die on the gallows. They were two fists beating constantly on her own heart.

But I also told myself that to create this legendary being it was absolutely necessary to falsify history; and history is an incontrovertible fact which leaves the imagination no other way out save that of clothing it in the poetry of words, in the emotion of silence and the things surrounding it.

I was aware of what I had to do. I had pledged myself to

offer to Granada—Granada of the singing and crystalline water—the homage of my love and admiration. So I began work on the popular ballad sung in the streets by the pure and solemn voices of the children, and I finished, murmuring between the latticework and gratings in a prayerful tone which drew tears from my eyes:

> *Oh! qué día tan triste en Granada*
> *que a las piedras hacía llorar*

Sticking as closely as possible to the facts of history, I imbued them with emotion, with the sweet poetry that comes from children, little nuns, and the silence of convents; with the robust and virile poetry that accompanies those romantic *caballeros* of love and freedom in the eighteenth century—and above all that admirable woman who, with the one wing of love shattered, is able with the other wing of freedom to conquer space and be crowned with the glory of immortality.

My Mariana Pineda is a woman deeply rooted in Spain. Yet I have intended her to sing the song of her life to love and freedom, in a form that embraces the concept of universality in those two great emotions. So at the end of the play my heroine cries out in a voice that comes from afar:

> *Yo soy la libertad porque el amor lo quiso*
> *Pedro! La libertad por la cual me dejaste.*
> *Yo soy la libertad herida por los hombres*
> *Amor, amor, amor y eternas soledades.*

> (I am freedom because love wanted it so;
> Pedro! the freedom for which you left me.
> I am freedom stricken by men
> Love, love, love and eternal solitudes.)

Although not my first work, it is one of my earliest; and I feel toward it like a young bridegroom. It was written in 1923.

Most of the Madrid critics praised the literary and dramatic merit of *Mariana Pineda* to an extent that surprised me. In general they asserted that it was more than just promising; it was a real achievement by a playwright who brought to the theatre a technique aware of the limitations of historical drama and an abundance of poetry that flowed naturally and continuously, not only from the characters but also from their surroundings. They found in it an emotional power highlighted as much in the tragic phrases of *Mariana Pineda* as in the sweet and sorrowful words of the little nuns when they set out toward the scaffold. This concept of *Mariana Pineda* is the one that satisfies me most, because I sincerely believe that theatre is not and cannot be anything but emotion and poetry —in word, action, gesture.

There are those who say that I am a playwright because of Lola Membrives and that that great artist is an actress because of me. Such a comment may well be true, in a general sense. As the mother in *Blood Wedding,* the shoemaker's wife in *The Shoemaker's Prodigious Wife,* but above all because of the penetrating understanding and emotion—at times compassionate and always exalted— with which Lola Membrives studies and creates my characters, I believe this to be so.

The Shoemaker's Prodigious Wife[2] (1933)

I WROTE *The Shoemaker's Prodigious Wife* in 1926, shortly after finishing *Mariana Pineda*. It did not have its first performance until 1930, at the hands of Margarita Xirgu's company. But the work which I staged at the Teatro Español was a chamber version, in which the farce gained greater intimacy but lost all its rhythmic aspects.

In reality Buenos Aires is seeing its true premiere, together with eighteenth- and nineteenth-century songs and danced with unusual grace by Lola Membrives and her company.

The Shoemaker's Prodigious Wife is a simple farce, in the pure classic manner, describing the spirit of a woman who is like all other women. At the same time—and with tenderness—it is an apologia of the human soul.

Thus, the shoemaker's wife is both a type and an archetype; she is a primal creature and a myth of our pure unsated illusion.

It was the summer of 1926. I was in the city of Granada, surrounded by black fig trees, ears of grain, tiny pools of water; I was possessor of a fund of joy,

[2] From an interview in *La Nación* of Buenos Aires, November 30, 1933, on the occasion of the premiere of *The Shoemaker's Prodigious Wife.*

intimate friend of the roses; and I wanted to set an example in play form of a simple style, revealing in fresh tones the essence of disillusioned fantasies.

The disturbing letters I received from my friends in Paris, struggling beautifully but grimly with abstract art, led me, as a reaction, to create this legend which is almost vulgar in its direct immediacy. Through it I wanted an invisible thread of poetry to flow; from it humor and the comic shout emerge, clearly and unequivocally, from the very outset.

In my *Shoemaker's Wife* I sought to express—within the limits of ordinary farce, and without laying hands on the elements of poetry within my reach—the struggle of reality with fantasy that exists within every human being. (By fantasy I mean everything that is unrealizable.)

The shoemaker's wife fights constantly with ideas and real objects because she lives in her own world, in which every idea and object has a mysterious meaning which she herself does not know. She has only lived and had suitors on the other bank of the river, which she cannot and will not ever be able to reach.

The other characters serve her in their performances without having any more importance than the story and tempo of the play require. The only characters are herself and the crowd of people who encircle her with a girdle of thorns and shrieks of laughter.

The most characteristic thing about the shoemaker's crazy little wife is that her only friend is a small child, tenderness personified and symbol of things in bloom, yet still very far from blossoming forth as a flower. The most characteristic thing about this simple farce is the staging, closely knit and lively, and the musical score which I use to make the stage seem unreal and to erase from the audience's mind any notion that "this is really and truly taking place." I also use the music to raise the poetic level—in the same sense in which our classical dramatists used music.

The language is popular, spoken with a Castilian accent; but it contains Andalusian forms and expressions, enabling me at times—such as when the shoemaker preaches—to produce a slightly caricatural effect in the manner of Cervantes.

Translated by Joseph M. Bernstein

EUGENE O'NEILL
(1888-1953)

The Sea Plays[1] (1919)

. . . To ME *In the Zone* seems the least significant of all the plays. It is too facile in its conventional technique, too full of clever theatrical tricks, and its long run as a successful headliner in vaudeville proves conclusively to my mind that there must be "something rotten in Denmark." At any rate, this play in no way represents the true me or what I desire to express. It is a situation drama lacking in all spiritual import—there is no big feeling for life inspiring it. Given the plot and a moderate ability to characterize, an industrious playwright could have reeled it off. . . .

Whereas, *The Moon of the Caribbees,* for example (my favorite), is distinctly my own. The spirit of the sea —a big thing—is in this latter play the hero. While *In the Zone* might have happened just as well, if less picturesquely, in a boardinghouse of munitions workers. Let me illustrate by a concrete example what I am trying to get at. Smitty in the stuffy, grease-paint atmosphere of *In the Zone* is magnified into a hero who attracts our sentimental sympathy. In *The Moon,* posed against a background of that beauty, sad because it is eternal, which is one of the revealing moods of the sea's truth, his silhouetted gestures of self-pity are reduced to their proper insignificance, his thin whine of weakness is lost in the silence which it was mean enough to disturb, we get the perspective to judge him—and the others—and we find his sentimental posing much more out of harmony with truth, much less in tune with beauty, than the honest vulgarity of his mates. To me *The Moon* works with truth, and *Beyond the Horizon* also, while *In the Zone* substitutes theatrical sentimentalism. I will say nothing of the worth of the method used in the two short plays save

[1] Barrett H. Clark, *Eugene O'Neill: The Man and his Plays* (New York: Dover Publications, 1947), pp. 56, 58–59, 66, 72, 84, 104–06. Copyright 1947 by Barrett H. Clark. Reprinted by courtesy of Mrs. Barrett H. Clark.

that I consider *In the Zone* a conventional construction of the theatre as it is, and *The Moon* an attempt to achieve a higher plane of bigger, finer values. But I hope to have all this out with you when we meet. Perhaps I can explain the nature of my feeling for the impelling, inscrutable forces behind life which it is my ambition to at least faintly shadow at their work in my plays.

Beyond the Horizon (1918)

I THINK the real-life experience from which the idea of *Beyond the Horizon* sprang was this: On the British tramp steamer on which I made a voyage as ordinary seaman, Buenos Aires to New York, there was a Norwegian A.B., and we became quite good friends. The great sorrow and mistake of his life, he used to grumble, was that as a boy he had left the small paternal farm to run away to sea. He had been at sea twenty years, and had never gone home once in that time. . . . Yet he cursed the sea and the life it had led him—affectionately. He loved to hold forth on what a fool he had been to leave the farm. There was the life for you. . . . At exactly the right moment . . . he turned up in my memory. I thought: "What if he had stayed on the farm, with his instincts? What would have happened?" But I realized at once he never would have stayed. . . . It amused him to pretend he craved the farm. He was too harmonious a creature of the God of Things as They Are. . . . And from that point I started to think of a more intellectual, civilized type from the standpoint of the above-mentioned God— a man who would have my Norwegian's inborn craving for the sea's unrest, only in him it would be conscious, too conscious, intellectually diluted into a vague, intangible wanderlust. His powers of resistance, both moral and physical, would also probably be correspondingly watered. He would throw away his instinctive dream and accept the thralldom of the farm for—why, for almost any nice little poetical craving—the romance of sex, say.

The Emperor Jones (1924)

THE IDEA of *The Emperor Jones* came from an old circus man I knew. This man told me a story current in Haiti

concerning the late President Sam. This was to the effect
that Sam had said they'd never get him with a lead
bullet; that he would get himself first with a silver one
. . . . This notion about the silver bullet struck me, and
I made a note of the story. About six months later I got
the idea of the woods, but I couldn't see how it could be
done on the stage, and I passed it up again. A year elapsed.
One day I was reading of the religious feasts in the Congo
and the uses to which the drum is put here: how it starts
at a normal pulse and is slowly intensified until the heartbeat of everyone present corresponds to the frenzied beat
of the drum. There was an idea and an experiment. How
would this sort of thing work on an audience in a theatre?
The effect of the tropical forest on the human imagination
was honestly come by. It was the result of my own experience while prospecting for gold in Spanish Honduras.

The Hairy Ape[2] (1922)

IT WAS on two voyages that I got to know the stokers,
although it did not really begin aboard ship. There is
class distinction even among the groups that make up the
crew of an ocean liner. But in this case, one group does
not regard another as superior to it. Each has a healthy
contempt for the other.

I shouldn't have known the stokers if I hadn't happened
to scrape an acquaintance with one of our own furnace-
room gang at Jimmy the Priest's![3] His name was Driscoll,
and he was a Liverpool Irishman. It seems that years ago
some Irish families settled in Liverpool. Most of them
followed the sea, and they were a hard lot. To sailors all
over the world, a "Liverpool Irishman" is the synonym for
a tough customer. It was through Driscoll that I got to
know other stokers. Driscoll himself came to a strange
end. He committed suicide by jumping overboard in mid-

[2] Mary B. Mullett, "The Extraordinary Story of Eugene
O'Neill," *The American Magazine,* November, 1922, pp. 34,
114–20. By permission of The Crowell-Collier Publishing Company.
[3] "In New York I lived at 'Jimmy the Priest's'; a waterfront
dive, with a back room where you could sleep with your head
on the table if you bought a schooner of beer. 'Jimmy the
Priest's' is the original of the saloon in *Anna Christie*."

ocean . . . it was the *why* of Driscoll's suicide that gave me the germ of the idea for my play *The Hairy Ape*. . . .

Yank is really yourself, and myself. He is *every* human being. But, apparently, very few people seem to get this. They have written, picking out one thing or another in the play, "how true" it is. But no one has said "I am Yank. Yank is my own self."

Yet that was what I meant him to be. His struggle to "belong," to find the thread that will make him a part of the fabric of Life—we are all struggling to do just that. One idea I had in writing the play was to show that the missing thread, literally "the tie that binds," is understanding of one another.

In the scene where the bell rings for the stokers to go on duty, you remember that they all stand up, come to attention, then go out in a lockstep file. Some people think even that is an actual custom aboard ship! But it is only symbolic of the regimentation of men who are the slaves of machinery. In a larger sense, it applies to all of us, because we all are more or less the slaves of convention, or of discipline, or of a rigid formula of some sort.

The whole play is expressionistic. The coal shoveling in the furnace room, for instance. Stokers do not really shovel coal that way. But it is done in the play in order to contribute to the rhythm. For rhythm is a powerful factor in making anything expressive. People do not know how sensitive they are to rhythm. You can actually produce and control emotions by that means alone.

In *Beyond the Horizon,* there are three acts of two scenes each. One scene is out of doors, showing the horizon, suggesting the man's desire and dream. The other is indoors, the horizon gone, suggesting what has come between him and his dream. In that way I tried to get rhythm, the alternation of longing and loss.

Probably very few people who saw the play knew that this was definitely planned to produce the effect. But I am sure they all unconsciously got the effect. It is often easier to express an idea through such means than through words or mere copies of real actions. Sometimes I try to do it in the one way, sometimes in the other. If there was *only* one way . . . I should be following the mechanistic creed, which is the very thing I condemn.

The Hairy Ape (1924)

The Hairy Ape was propaganda in the sense that it was a symbol of man, who has lost his old harmony with nature, the harmony which he used to have as an animal and has not yet acquired in a spiritual way. Thus, not being able to find it on earth nor in heaven, he's in the middle, trying to make peace, taking the "woist punches from bot' of 'em." This idea was expressed in Yank's speech. The public saw just the stoker, not the symbol, and the symbol makes the play either important or just another play. Yank can't go forward, and so he tried to go back. This is what his shaking hands with the gorilla meant. But he can't go back to "belonging" either. The gorilla kills him. The subject here is the same ancient one that always was and always will be the one subject for drama, and that is man and his struggle with his own fate. The struggle used to be with the gods, but is now with himself, his own past, his attempt "to belong."

The Great God Brown (1926)

I REALIZE that when a playwright takes to explaining he thereby automatically places himself "in the dock." But where an open-faced avowal by the play itself of the abstract theme underlying it is made impossible by the very nature of that hidden theme, then perhaps it is justifiable for the author to confess the mystical pattern which manifests itself as an overtone in *The Great God Brown,* dimly behind and beyond the words and actions of the characters.

I had hoped the names chosen for my people would give a strong hint of this. (An old scene, admitted—Shakespeare and multitudes since.) Dion Anthony—Dionysus and St. Anthony—the creative pagan acceptance of life, fighting eternal war with the masochistic, life-denying spirit of Christianity as represented by St. Anthony—the whole struggle resulting in this modern day in mutual exhaustion—creative joy in life for life's sake frustrated, rendered abortive, distorted by morality from Pan into Satan, into a Mephistopheles mocking himself in order to feel alive; Christianity, once heroic in martyrs for its intense faith, now pleading weakly for intense belief in anything, even Godhead itself. (In the play it is Cybele, the pagan Earth Mother, who makes the assertion with authority: "Our Father, Who Art!" to the dying Brown, as it is she who tries to inspire Dion Anthony with her certainty in life for its own sake.)

Margaret is my image of the modern direct descendant of the Marguerite of *Faust*—the eternal girl-woman with a virtuous simplicity of instinct, properly oblivious to everything but the means to her end of maintaining the race.

Cybel is an incarnation of Cybele, the Earth Mother doomed to segregation as a pariah in a world of unnatural laws but patronized by her segregators who are thus themselves the first victims of their laws.

Brown is the visionless demigod of our new materialistic myth—a Success—building his life of exterior things, inwardly empty and resourceless, an uncreative creature of superficial preordained social grooves, a by-product forced aside into slack waters by the deep main current of life desire.

Dion's mask of Pan which he puts on as a boy is not only a defense against the world for the supersensitive painter-poet underneath it but also an integral part of his character as the artist. The world is not only blind to the man beneath it but it also sneers at and condemns the Pan mask it sees. After that Dion's inner self retrogresses along the line of Christian resignation until it partakes of the nature of the Saint while at the same time the outer Pan is slowly transformed by his struggle with reality into Mephistopheles. It is as Mephistopheles he falls stricken at Brown's feet after having condemned Brown to destruction by willing him his mask, but, this mask falling off as he dies, it is the Saint who kisses Brown's feet in abject contrition and pleads as a little boy to a big brother to tell him a prayer.

Brown has always envied the creative life force in Dion —what he himself lacks. When he steals Dion's mask of Mephistopheles he thinks he is gaining the power to live creatively while in reality he is only stealing that creative power made self-destructive by complete frustration. This devil of mocking doubt makes short work of him. It enters him, rending him apart, torturing and transfiguring him until he is even forced to wear a mask of his Success, William A. Brown, before the world, as well as Dion's

mask toward wife and children. Thus Billy Brown becomes
not himself to anyone. And thus he partakes of Dion's
anguish—more poignantly, for Dion had the Mother, Cybele—and in the end out of this anguish his soul is born,
a tortured Christian soul such as the dying Dion's, begging
for belief, and at the last finding it on the lips of Cybel.

And now for an explanation regarding this explanation.
It was far from my idea in writing *Brown* that this background pattern of conflicting tides in the soul of Man
should ever overshadow and thus throw out of proportion
the living drama of the recognizable human beings, Dion,
Brown, Margaret, and Cybel. I meant it always to be
mystically within and behind them, giving them a significance beyond themselves, forcing itself through them to
expression in mysterious words, symbols, actions they do
not themselves comprehend. And that is as clearly as I
wish an audience to comprehend it. It is Mystery—the
mystery any one man or woman can feel but not understand as the meaning of any event—or accident—in any
life on earth. And it is this mystery I want to realize
in the theatre. The solution, if there ever be any, will
probably have to be produced in a test tube and turn out
to be discouragingly undramatic.

JEAN COCTEAU
(b. 1891)

Les Mariés de la Tour Eiffel[1] (1922)

EVERY WORK of a poetic nature includes what Gide, in his preface to *Paludes,* rightly calls God's share. This share, which escapes the poet himself, has surprises in store for him. A phrase or gesture which had value for him only in the sense that mass is valuable to a painter, contains a secret meaning which everyone subsequently interprets in his own way. The true symbol is never foreseen. It emerges by itself, provided the bizarre and unreal do not enter into the picture.

In a fairy-like spot fairies do not appear. They move about in it invisibly. They can only appear to mortals on prosaic terra firma.

Simple minds see fairies more easily than others, because they do not fight against the miracle with set minds. I may say that the chief electrician, with his fits and starts, has often clarified the play for me.

I have read, in André Antoine's memoirs, about the scandal caused by the presence on stage of real hunks of

---

[1] Jean Cocteau, Preface, *Les Mariés de la Tour Eiffel* (Paris: Éditions de la Nouvelle Française, 1924). Reprinted by courtesy of Jean Cocteau. *Les Mariés de la Tour Eiffel* was first performed in 1921 in Paris by the Swedish Ballet Company of Mr. Rolf de Maré, with music by Germaine Tailleferre, Georges Auric, Arthur Honegger, Darius Milhaud, and Francis Poulenc, costumes and masks by Jean Victor-Hugo, and choreography by Jean Cocteau and Jean Borlin. The scene is the first platform of the Eiffel Tower. The bellows of a camera the size of a man form a corridor which extends into the wings. The front of the camera opens and shuts like a door to let the characters in and out. Downstage, on either side, are two phonographs. Each one contains an actor. The phonographs deliver all the lines of the characters and the scenes are enacted in mime and dance as they are described. The "ridiculous action" concerns the visit of a wedding party to the Eiffel Tower.

meat and a water fountain. Now we are in a period in which the theatregoing public, convinced by Antoine, is angry if the stage is not set with real-life objects, or if the audience is not confronted with plots as long and as complicated as those from which the theatre should divert it.

Les Mariés de la Tour Eiffel, because of its frankness, is more disappointing than an esoteric play. Mystery inspires a kind of fear in the audience. In this play I renounce mystery. I light up everything; I underline everything. Sunday boredom, human cattle, ready-made expressions, dissociations of ideas in flesh and blood, fierceness of childhood, poetry and miracle of everyday life: that is my play, which the young musicians who accompany it have understood so well.

A phrase by the photographer might serve as my frontispiece: "Since these mysteries are beyond me, let us pretend to be the organizers of them." This is our phrase, par excellence. The conceited man always finds a last refuge in responsibility. Thus, for example, he prolongs a war after the phenomenon which decides the outcome of the war has come to an end.

In *Les Mariés* God's share is great. Human phonographs, stage right and stage left, like the ancient Greek chorus, like the gossipy old man and woman, comment—without the least bit of "literature"—on the ridiculous action that takes place in dance and mime in the middle of the stage. I say "ridiculous" because, instead of trying to remain on this side of the ridiculous in life, instead of trying to moderate and rearrange it, as we rearrange an adventure in which we played an unfavorable part when we subsequently narrate it, I on the contrary emphasize it, I carry it further along, and I try to depict things *more truthfully than truth.*

The poet must bring objects and feelings from behind their veils and their mists; he must show them suddenly, so nakedly and so swiftly that it hurts man to recognize them. Then they impress him with their youth, as if they had never become official old men.

This is the case with commonplaces, old, powerful, and universally accepted in the same way as masterpieces, but whose beauty and originality, by dint of usage, no longer surprise us.

In my play I rehabilitate the commonplace. I have

sought to place it and present it from such an angle that
it regains its youthfulness.

A generation of obscurity, of insipid reality, cannot be
rejected by a mere shrug of the shoulder. I know that my
text appears to be too simple, too *legibly written*, like a
school alphabet. But, I ask you, aren't we in school?
Aren't we deciphering the first signs?

The new music finds itself in a similar situation. It is
creating, with any material it can lay hands on, a new
clarity, frankness, and good humor. The naïve person is
mistaken. He thinks he is listening to a café orchestra.
His ear is committing the same mistake as an eye which
makes no distinction between a loud-colored material and
that same material copied by Ingres.

Every live work offers its own sideshow—seen only
by those who do not enter the main tent. But the surface
of a new work shocks, intrigues, and annoys the spectator
too much for him to enter it. He is turned away from
the soul by the face, by the novel expression which dis-
tracts him like the grimace of a clown at the door. This
is the phenomenon which fools even those critics who
are least slaves of routine. They do not realize that they
are watching a work which they must follow as closely
as they do a hit play of the boulevards. They think they
are at some annual county fair. A conscientious critic,
writing about a "hit," would never say, "The duchess
kisses the maître d'hôtel" instead of "The maître d'hôtel
hands the duchess a letter"; yet, writing about *Les Mariés,*
he doesn't hesitate to get the lady bicycle rider or the
collector out of the giant-size camera—which is just as
absurd. Not organized, deliberate, good absurdity; just
simply absurd. He doesn't know the difference yet. Only
one critic, M. Bidou, subtler and more aware of contemporary trends, explained to the readers of the *Journal des
Débats* that my play was a *construction of the mind.*

The action of my play is imaged while the text is not.
Thus I try to substitute a "theatre poetry" for "poetry in
the theatre." Poetry in the theatre is a delicate lace fabric,
impossible to see from afar. Theatre poetry should be a
coarser lace; a lace made of ropes, a boat on the ocean.
Les Mariés may have the terrible look of a drop of

poetry under the microscope. The scenes fit together like the words of a poem.

The secret of the theatre, which needs quick success, is to set a trap, thanks to which a part of the audience has a good time at the door so that the other part can take seats on the inside. Shakespeare, Molière, Charlie Chaplin do this.

After the hisses, the tumult, and the ovations of the opening night on which the Swedish company presented my play at the Théâtre des Champs-Élysées, I would have thought that I had failed, if the sophisticated people had not given way to the real audience. This audience always listens to me.

After *Les Mariés,* a woman in the audience criticized me because the actors did not get sufficiently across the foot-lights. Since this complaint astounded me (masks and megaphones get across the footlights better than real faces and voices), the lady confessed she was so fond of the Maurice Denis ceiling which decorates the theatre that she bought the seats highest up—which prevented her from getting a good look at the stage.

I cite this confession as an example of some of the comments made by a small circle—lacking brains and a heart—which the newspapers call the elite.

Furthermore, our senses are so unused to reacting to-gether that the critics, and even my publishers, thought that *Les Mariés de la Tour Eiffel* constituted two or three pages of text. This lack of perspective must also be at-tributed to the lack of development of ideas—a develop-ment which the ear has been accustomed to hear since the thesis play and symbolism. Jarry's *Ubu Roi* and Apollinaire's *Les Mamelles de Tirésias* are both symbolist and thesis plays.

The diction of Pierre Bertin and Marcel Herrand, my human phonographs, is partially responsible for this error. It is a diction as black as ink, as big and clear as the capital letters on an advertisement. Here, O surprise! the actors try to serve the text instead of exploiting it. Another poetic novelty to which audiences are not accustomed.

Now what about the criticism of clowning often made

of me in our era so enamored of the falsely sublime and —let us admit—still in love with Wagner?

If cold meant night and warm meant light, lukewarm would mean semidarkness. Ghosts love the semidarkness. Audiences love the lukewarm. Now apart from the fact that the spirit of clowning requires lighting that is unfavorable to ghosts (here I call ghosts what audiences call poetry), apart from the fact that Molière is more of a poet in *Pourceaugnac* and *Le Bourgeois Gentilhomme* than in his verse plays, the clowning spirit is the only one that permits certain liberties.

The public goes to the theatre to relax. It is clever to amuse it, to show it the puppets and sweets in the same way one does to reluctant children so as to give them a dose of medicine. Once the medicine is taken, we pass on to other activities.

With persons like Serge Diaghilev and Rolf de Maré we are witnessing, little by little, the rise of a type of theatre in France which is not, strictly speaking, ballet, and which is not at home either at the Opéra, the Opéra-Comique, or in any of our boulevard theatres. With them, the future is taking shape on the periphery. Our friend Lugné-Poë notes this in one of his articles and is frightened by it. This new type of theatre, more in tune with the modern spirit, is still an unknown world, rich in discoveries.

The venture of the Swedish troupe has just opened wide the door to explorers. The young people can pursue their efforts in which fantasy, dance, acrobatics, pantomime, drama, satire, orchestra, and the spoken word combined reappear in a novel form. The Swedish company will present, without any large outlay of money, what professional performers consider to be workshop farces. Yet this type of theatre is just as much the plastic expression of poetry.

Besides, in Paris good and bad humor join to form the most living atmosphere in the world. Serge Diaghilev told me one day that this could not be found in any other capital in the world.

Hisses and plaudits. Insulting press notices. A few "shocker" articles. Three years later the hissers applaud and no longer remember having hissed. That is the history of *Parade,* and of all works which change the rules of the game.

A theatre play should be written, stage-set, costumed, accompanied by music, played, and danced by one human being alone. Such a complete athlete does not exist. It is therefore necessary to substitute for the individual what most resembles the individual: an intimate group.

There are many cliques, but few of these groups. I have had the good luck to form one with several young musicians, poets, and painters. *Les Mariés de la Tour Eiffel,* in its over-all effect, is the image of a poetic state of mind to which I have already contributed much—and I am proud of it.

Thanks to Jean Victor-Hugo, my characters, instead of being, as so often happens in the theatre, too small and too real to support the weight of the lighting and stage scenery, are built, adjusted, padded, repainted, and brought by artifice to assume epic features and scope. I find in Jean Victor-Hugo a kind of atavism of monstrous reality. Thanks to Irene Lagut, our *Les Mariés* evokes forget-me-nots and the silken paper of compliments.

Georges Auric's overture, "The 14th of July," with marching soldiers whose band bursts forth at a corner of the street and then dies down, evokes also the powerful charm of the sidewalk, of popular holidays, of platforms made of red bunting resembling the guillotine, around which stenographers, sailors, and clerks dance to the rhythm of drums and cornets. These flourishes, muted, accompany the pantomime just as at the circus the orchestra repeats a theme during the acrobats' number.

The same atmosphere pervades Milhaud's "Wedding March," Germaine Tailleferre's "Quadrille" and "Waltz," Poulenc's "The Lady Bather of Trouville" and "The General's Speech." Arthur Honegger has a good time parodying what our music critics call "Music" with a capital "M." It is superfluous to add that all fell into the trap. No sooner are the opening themes of the march heard, all the long ears are on the alert. No one realized that the march was beautiful as a piece of sarcasm, composed with taste and an extraordinary sense of timing. None of the critics, all of whom agreed in praising this piece, recognized the waltz from *Faust* which served as the bass.

How shall I thank Rolf de Maré and Borlin? The former by his perceptivity and breadth, the latter by his modesty, have enabled me to achieve a formula I had attempted in *Parade* and *Le Boeuf sur le Toit*.

Translated by Joseph M. Bernstein

SEAN O'CASEY
(b. 1884)

Cock-A-Doodle-Dandy[1] (1958)

THE FIRST thing I try to do is to make a play live: live as a part of life, and live in its own right as a work of drama. Every character, every life, however minor, to have something to say, comic or serious, and to say it well. Not an easy thing to do. These are the commonest things around us. We see them everywhere we go; see what they do, hear what they say; often laugh, sometimes wonder. But there are other parts, phases of life, and these, to my mind, should be prominent in the play.

Above all, there is the imagination of man and that of the playwright; the comic, the serious, and the poetical imagination; and, to my mind, these too should flash from any play worthy of an appearance on the stage; the comic imagination as in *The Frogs:* the sad imagination as in *A Dream Play.* Blake thought imagination to be the soul; Shaw thought it to be the Holy Ghost, and perhaps they weren't far out; for it is the most beautiful part of life whether it be on its knees in prayer or gallivanting about with a girl.

To me what is called naturalism, or even realism, isn't enough. They usually show life at its meanest and commonest, as if life never had time for a dance, a laugh, or a song. I always thought that life had a lot of time for these things, for each was a part of life itself; and so I broke away from realism into the chant of the second act of the *The Silver Tassie.* But one scene in as a chant or a work of musical action and dialogue was not enough, so I set about trying to do this in an entire play, and brought forth *Cock-a-Doodle-Dandy.* It is my favorite play; I think it is my best play—a personal opinion; the

[1] Sean O'Casey: "O'Casey's Credo," the New York *Times,* November 9, 1958, Drama Section. Reprinted by permission of the author.

minds of others, linked with time, must decide whether
I'm wrong or right.

The play is symbolical in more ways than one. The
action manifests itself in Ireland, the mouths that speak
are Irish mouths; but the spirit is to be found in action
everywhere: the fight made by many to drive the joy of
life from the hearts of men; the fight against this fight to
vindicate the right of the joy of life to live courageously
in the hearts of men. It isn't the clergy alone who boo
and bluster against this joy of life in living, in dance,
song, and story (many clerics, even bishops, are fair, broad-
minded, and help the arts; like the Catholic Bishop of
Ferns and Leighlin, who is the worthy patron of the
Wexford Opera Festival); who interfere in the free flow
of thought from man to man. Playwrights and poets have
had, are having, a share in squeezing the mind of man
into visions of woe and lamentations. Not only is there
none who doeth good; no, not one, with them; but also
they seem determined to deny the right of man to a laugh.
They labor hard to get us all down.

Joyce said that "God may be a cry in the street," and
O'Casey says now that He may be a laugh or a song in
the street, too. Political fellas, too, in the United States,
in the Soviet Union, in England and especially, in Ireland
—everywhere in fact—political fellas run out and shout
down any new effort made to give a more modern slant
or a newer sign to any kind of artistic thought or imagination; menacing any unfamiliar thing appearing in picture,
song, poem, or play. They are fools, but they are menacing
fools, and should be fought everywhere they shake a
fist, be they priest, peasant, prime minister, or proletarian.
To discuss and argue about these things is fine and, if
the discussion be sincere, can but lead to a wider knowledge of all things; but when hateful ignorance rushes out
and tries to down the artist with a bawl, it is high time
to cry a halt!

The Cock, of course, is the joyful, active spirit of life
as it weaves a way through the Irish scene (for, like
Joyce, it is only through an Irish scene that my imagination can weave a way, within the Irish shadows or out in
the Irish sunshine, if it is to have a full, or at least a
fair, chance to play).

In spite of the fanciful nature of the play, almost all
the incidents are factual—the priest that struck the blow;

the rough fellows manhandling the young, gay girl; the bitter opposition to any sign of the strange ways of a man with a maid; the old, menacing fool, full of false piety, going round inflicting fear of evil things on all who listen to him; and, above all, through the piety, through the fear, the never-ending quest for money. In spite, too, of the fantasy and the fear, there is courage, reason, and laughter in the play, and I hope that with its shape and form, and all that is within them, those who see it may have a gay and a thoughtful time.

So, to end this explanation, I leave the play in the hands of actors, director, designer, and in yours, dear playgoers, turning my last words into a question from the poet Yeats:

**Lift up the head
And clap the wings,
Red Cock, and crow!**

T. S. ELIOT
(b. 1888)

Murder in the Cathedral[1] (1950)

. . . I AM GOING to venture to make some observations
based on my own experience, which will lead me to comment on my intentions, failures, and partial successes, in
my own plays. I do this in the belief that any explorer
or experimenter in new territory may, by putting on record
a kind of journal of his explorations, say something of
use to those who follow him into the same regions and
who will perhaps go further.

The first thing of any importance that I discovered
was that a writer who has worked for years, and achieved
some success, in writing other kinds of verse, has to approach the writing of a verse play in a different frame of
mind from that to which he has been accustomed in his
previous work. In writing other verse, I think that one is
writing, so to speak, in terms of one's own voice: the
way it sounds when you read it to yourself is the test.
For it is yourself speaking. The question of communication, of what the reader will get from it, is not paramount:
if your poem is right to you, you can only hope that the
readers will eventually come to accept it. The poem can
wait a little while; the approval of a few sympathetic and
judicious critics is enough to begin with; and it is for
future readers to meet the poet more than halfway. But
in the theatre, the problem of communication presents
itself immediately. You are deliberately writing verse for
other voices, not for your own, and you do not know
whose voices they will be. You are aiming to write lines
which will have an immediate effect upon an unknown
and unprepared audience, to be interpreted to that audience by unknown actors rehearsed by an unknown pro-

[1] T. S. Eliot, *Poetry and Drama,* The First Theodore Spencer
Memorial Lecture, November 12, 1950 (Cambridge, Mass.:
Harvard University Press, c. 1951), pp. 23–44. Reprinted by
permission of the President and Fellows of Harvard University.

ducer. And the unknown audience cannot be expected to show any indulgence toward the poet. The poet cannot afford to write his play merely for his admirers, those who know his non-dramatic work and are prepared to receive favorably anything he puts his name to. He must write with an audience in view which knows nothing and cares nothing about any previous success he may have had before he ventured into the theatre. Hence one finds out that many of the things one likes to do, and knows how to do, are out of place; and that every line must be judged by a new law, that of dramatic relevance.

When I wrote *Murder in the Cathedral* I had the advantage for a beginner of an occasion which called for a subject generally admitted to be suitable for verse. Verse plays, it has been generally held, should either take their subject matter from some mythology, or else should be about some remote historical period, far enough away from the present for the characters not to need to be recognizable as human beings, and therefore for them to be licensed to talk in verse. Picturesque period costume renders verse much more acceptable. Furthermore, my play was to be produced for a rather special kind of audience—an audience of those serious people who go to "festivals" and expect to have to put up with poetry—though perhaps on this occasion some of them were not quite prepared for what they got. And finally it was a religious play, and people who go deliberately to a religious play at a religious festival expect to be patiently bored and to satisfy themselves with the feeling that they have done something meritorious. So the path was made easy.

It was only when I put my mind to thinking what sort of a play I wanted to do next, that I realized that in *Murder in the Cathedral* I had not solved any general problem; that from my point of view the play was a dead end. For one thing, the problem of language which that play had presented to me was a special problem. Fortunately, I did not have to write in the idiom of the twelfth century, because that idiom, even if I knew Norman French and Anglo-Saxon, would have been unintelligible. But the vocabulary and style could not be exactly those of modern conversation—as in some modern French plays using the plot and personages of Greek drama—because I had to take my audience back to an historical event; and they could not afford to be archaic, first because archaism would only have suggested the wrong period, and second because I wanted to bring home to the audience the contemporary relevance of the situation. The style therefore had to be *neutral*, committed neither to the present nor to the past. As for the versification, I was only aware at this stage that the essential was to avoid any echo of Shakespeare, for I was persuaded that the primary failure of nineteenth-century poets when they wrote for the theatre (and most of the greatest English poets had tried their hand at drama) was not in their theatrical technique, but in their dramatic language; and that this was due largely to their limitation to a strict blank verse which, after extensive use for non-dramatic poetry, had lost the flexibility which blank verse must have if it is to give the effect of conversation. The rhythm of regular blank verse had become too remote from the movement of modern speech. Therefore what I kept in mind was the versification of *Everyman*, hoping that anything unusual in the sound of it would be on the whole advantageous. An avoidance of too much iambic, some use of alliteration, and occasional unexpected rhyme, helped to distinguish the versification from that of the nineteenth century.

The versification of the dialogue in *Murder in the Cathedral* has therefore, in my opinion, only a *negative* merit: it succeeded in avoiding what had to be avoided, but it arrived at no positive novelty; in short, in so far as it solved the problem of speech in verse for writing today, it solved it for this play only, and provided me with no clue to the verse I should use in another kind of play. Here, then, were two problems left unsolved: that of the idiom and that of the metric (it is really one and the same problem) for general use in any play I might want to write in the future. I next became aware of my reasons for depending, in that play, so heavily upon the assistance of the chorus. There were two reasons for this, which in the circumstances justified it. The first was that the essential action of the play—both the historical facts and the matter which I invented—was somewhat limited. A man comes home, foreseeing that he will be killed, and he is killed. I did not want to increase the number of characters, I did not want to write a chronicle of twelfth-century politics, nor did I want to tamper unscrupulously with the meager records as Tennyson did (in introducing Fair Rosamund, and in suggesting that Becket had been crossed in love in early youth). I wanted to concentrate on death and martyrdom. The introduction of a chorus of excited and sometimes hysterical women, reflecting in their emotion the significance of the action, helped wonderfully. The second reason was this: that a poet writing for the first time for the stage is much more at home in choral verse than in dramatic dialogue. This, I felt sure, was something I could do, and perhaps the dramatic weaknesses would be somewhat covered up by the cries of the women. The use of a chorus strengthened the power and concealed the defects of my theatrical technique. For this reason I decided that next time I would try to integrate the chorus more closely into the play.

I wanted to find out, also, whether I could learn to dispense altogether with the use of prose. I have already given the justification of this aim. The two prose passages in *Murder in the Cathedral* could not have been written in verse. Certainly, with the kind of dialogue verse which I used in that play, the audience would have been uncomfortably aware that it was verse they were hearing. A sermon cast in verse is too unusual an experience for even the most regular churchgoer: nobody could have responded to it as a sermon at all. And in the speeches of the knights, who are quite aware that they are addressing an audience of people living eight hundred years after they themselves are dead, the use of platform prose is intended of course to have a special effect: to shock the audience out of their complacency. But this is a kind of trick: that is, a device tolerable only in one play and of no use for any other. I may, for aught I know, have been slightly under the influence of *Saint Joan*.

I do not wish to give you the impression that I would rule out of dramatic poetry these three things: historical or mythological subject matter, the chorus, and traditional blank verse. I do not wish to lay down any law that the only suitable characters and situations are those of modern life, or that a verse play should consist of dialogue only, or that a wholly new versification is necessary. I am only tracing out the route of exploration of one writer, and that one myself. If the poetic drama is

to reconquer its place, it must, in my opinion, enter into
overt competition with prose drama. As I have said, people are prepared to put up with verse from the personages dressed in the fashion of some distant age; they
should be made to hear it from people dressed like ourselves, living in houses and apartments like ours, and
using telephones and motorcars and radio sets. Audiences are prepared to accept poetry recited by a chorus,
for that is a kind of poetry recital, which it does them
credit to enjoy. And audiences (those who go to a verse
play because it is in verse) expect poetry to be in rhythms
which have lost touch with colloquial speech. What we
have to do is to bring poetry into the world in which the
audience lives and to which it returns when it leaves the
theatre; not to transport the audience into some imaginary world totally unlike their own, an unreal world in
which poetry can be spoken. What I should hope might
be achieved, by a generation of dramatists having the
benefit of our experience, is that the audience should
find, at the moment of awareness that it is hearing
poetry, that it is saying to itself: "I could talk in poetry
too!" Then we should not be transported into an artificial
world; on the contrary, our own sordid, dreary, daily
world would be suddenly illuminated and transfigured.

The Family Reunion

I WAS determined, therefore, in my next play to take a
theme of contemporary life, with characters of our own
time living in our own world. *The Family Reunion* was the
result. Here my first concern was the problem of versification, to find a rhythm close to contemporary speech, in
which the stresses could be made to come wherever we
should naturally put them, in uttering the particular
phrase on the particular occasion. What I worked out
is substantially what I have continued to employ: a line
of varying length and varying number of syllables, with
a caesura and three stresses. The caesura and the stresses
may come at different places, almost anywhere in the
line; the stresses may be close together or well separated
by light syllables, the only rule being that there must
be one stress on one side of the caesura and two on
the other. In retrospect, I soon saw that I had given

my attention to versification, at the expense of plot and character. I had, indeed, made some progress in dispensing with the chorus; but the device of using four of the minor personages, representing the Family, sometimes as individual character parts and sometimes collectively as chorus, does not seem to me very satisfactory. For one thing, the immediate transition from individual, characterized part to membership of a chorus is asking too much of the actors: it is a very difficult transition to accomplish. For another thing, it seemed to me another trick, one which, even if successful, could not have been applicable in another play. Furthermore, I had in two passages used the device of a lyrical duet further isolated from the rest of the dialogue by being written in shorter lines with only two stresses. These passages are in a sense "beyond character," the speakers have to be presented as falling into a kind of trancelike state in order to speak them. But they are so remote from the necessity of the action that they are hardly more than passages of poetry which might be spoken by anybody; they are too much like operatic arias. The member of the audience, if he enjoys this sort of thing, is putting up with a suspension of the action in order to enjoy a poetic fantasia: these passages are really less related to the action than are the choruses in *Murder in the Cathedral*. I observed that when Shakespeare, in one of his mature plays, introduces what might seem a purely poetic line or passage, it never interrupts the action, or is out of character, but, on the contrary, in some mysterious way supports both action and character. When Macbeth speaks his so often quoted words beginning

Tomorrow and tomorrow and tomorrow

or when Othello, confronted at night with his angry father-in-law and friends, utters the beautiful line

*Keep up your bright swords, for the dew will
rust them*

we do not feel that Shakespeare has thought of lines which are beautiful poetry and wishes to fit them in somehow, or that he has for the moment come to the end of his dramatic inspiration and has turned to poetry to fill up with. The lines are surprising, and yet they fit in with the character; or else we are compelled to adjust our conception of the character in such a way that the lines will be appropriate to it. The lines spoken by Macbeth reveal the weariness of the weak man who had been forced by his wife to realize his own halfhearted desires and her ambitions, and who, with her death, is left without the motive to continue. The line of Othello expresses irony, dignity, and fearlessness; and incidentally reminds us of the time of night in which the scene takes place. Only poetry could do this; but it is *dramatic* poetry: that is, it does not interrupt but intensifies the dramatic situation.

It was not only because of the introduction of passages which called too much attention to themselves as poetry, and could not be dramatically justified, that I found *The Family Reunion* defective: there were two weaknesses which came to strike me as more serious still. The first was that I had taken far too much of the strictly limited time allowed to a dramatist in presenting a situation, and not left myself enough time, or provided myself with enough material, for developing it in action. I had written what was, on the whole, a good first act; except that for a first act it was much too long. When the curtain rises again, the audience is expecting, as it has a right to expect, that something is going to happen. Instead, it finds itself treated to a further exploration of the background: in other words, to what ought to have been given much earlier if at all. The beginning of the second act presents much the most difficult problem to producer and cast: for the audience's attention is beginning to wander. And then, after what must seem to the audience an interminable time of preparation, the conclusion comes so abruptly that we are, after all, unready for it. This was an elementary fault in mechanics. But the deepest flaw of all was in a failure of adjustment between the Greek story and the modern situation. I should either have stuck closer to Aeschylus or else taken a great deal more liberty with his myth. One evidence of this is the appearance of those ill-fated figures, the Furies. They must, in future, be omitted from the cast, and be understood to be visible only to certain of my characters, and not to the audience. We tried every possible manner of presenting them. We put them on the stage, and they looked like uninvited guests who had strayed in from a fancy-dress ball. We concealed them behind gauze, and they suggested a

still out of a Walt Disney film. We made them dimmer, and
they looked like shrubbery just outside the window. I have
seen other expedients tried: I have seen them signaling
from across the garden, or swarming onto the stage
like a football team, and they are never right. They never
succeed in being either Greek goddesses or modern spooks.
But their failure is merely a symptom of the failure to adjust the ancient with the modern. A more serious evidence
is that we are left in a divided frame of mind, not knowing
whether to consider the play the tragedy of the mother or
the salvation of the son. The two situations are not reconciled. I find a confirmation of this in the fact that my sym-
pathies now have come to be all with the mother, who
seems to me, except perhaps for the chauffeur, the only
complete human being in the play; and my hero now strikes
me as an insufferable prig.

The Cocktail Party

WELL, I had made some progress in learning how to
write the first act of a play, and I had—the one thing
of which I felt sure—made a good deal of progress in
finding a form of versification and an idiom which would
serve all my purposes, without recourse to prose, and
be capable of unbroken transition between the most intense speech and the most relaxed dialogue. You will
understand, after my making these criticisms of *The
Family Reunion*, some of the errors that I endeavored to
avoid in designing *The Cocktail Party*. To begin with, no
chorus, and no ghosts. I was still inclined to go to a Greek
dramatist for my theme, but I was determined to take
this merely as a point of departure, and to conceal the
origins so well that nobody would identify them until I
pointed them out myself. In this at least I have been successful; for no one of my acquaintance (and no dramatic
critics) recognized the source of my story in the *Alcestis*
of Euripides. In fact, I have had to go into detailed explanation to convince them—I mean, of course, those
who were familiar with the plot of that play—of the
genuineness of the inspiration. But those who were at first
disturbed by the eccentric behavior of my unknown guest,
and his apparently intemperate habits and tendency to
burst into song, have found some consolation after I have

called their attention to the behavior of Heracles in Euripides' play. In the second place, I laid down for myself the ascetic rule to avoid poetry which could not stand the test of strict dramatic utility: with such success, indeed, that it is perhaps an open question whether there is any poetry in the play at all. And finally, I tried to keep in mind that in a play, from time to time, something should happen; that the audience should be kept in constant expectation that something is going to happen; and that, when it does happen, it should be different, but not too different, from what the audience has been led to expect.

I have not yet got to the end of my investigation of the weaknesses of this play, but I hope and expect to find more than those of which I am yet aware. I say "hope" because while one can never repeat a success, and therefore must always try to find something different, even if less popular, to do, the desire to write something which will be free of the defects of one's last work is a very powerful and useful incentive. I am aware that the last act of my play only just escapes, if indeed it does escape, the accusation of being not a last act but an epilogue; and I am determined to do something different, if I can, in this respect. I also believe that while the self-education of a poet trying to write for the theatre seems to require a long period of disciplining his poetry, and putting it, so to speak, on a very thin diet in order to adapt it to the needs of the drama, there may be a later stage, when (and if) the understanding of theatrical technique has become second nature, at which he can dare to make more liberal use of poetry and take greater liberties with ordinary colloquial speech. I base that belief on the evolution of Shakespeare, and on some study of the language in his late plays. But to give reason for this belief involves an examination and defense of Shakespeare's late plays as plays; and this obviously is the subject for a separate essay.

In devoting so much time to an examination of my own plays, I have, I believe, been animated by a better motive than egotism. It seems to me that if we are to have a poetic drama, it is more likely to come from poets learning how to write plays, than from skillful prose dramatists learning to write poetry. That some poets can learn how to write plays, and write good ones, may be only a hope, but I believe a not unreasonable hope; but that a man who has started by writing successful prose plays should then learn how to write good poetry seems to me extremely unlikely. And, under present-day conditions, and until the verse play is recognized by the larger public as a possible source of entertainment, the poet is likely to get his first opportunity to work for the stage only after making some sort of reputation for himself as the author of other kinds of verse. I have therefore wished to put on record, for what it may be worth to others, some account of the difficulties I have encountered, and the weaknesses I have had to try to overcome, and the mistakes into which I have fallen.

I should not like to close, however, without attempting to set before myself, and, if I can, before you, though only in dim outline, the ideal toward which it seems to me that poetic drama should strive. It is an unattainable ideal: and that is why it interests me, for it provides an incentive toward further experiment and exploration, beyond any goal which there is prospect of attaining. It is a function of all art to give us some perception of an order in life, by imposing an order upon it. The painter works by selection, combination, and emphasis among the elements of the visible world; the musicians, in the world of sound. It seems to me that beyond the namable, classifiable emotions and motives of our conscious life when directed toward action—the part of life which prose drama is wholly adequate to express—there is a fringe of indefinite extent, of feeling which we can only detect, so to speak, out of the corner of the eye and can never completely focus; of feeling of which we are only aware in a kind of temporary detachment from action. There are great prose dramatists—such as Ibsen and Chekhov— who have at times done things of which I would not otherwise have supposed prose to be capable, but who seem to me, in spite of their success, to have been hampered in expression by writing in prose. This peculiar range of sensibility can be expressed by dramatic poetry, at its moments of greatest intensity. At such moments, we touch the border of those feelings which only music can express. We can never emulate music, because to arrive at the condition of music would be the annihilation of poetry, and especially of dramatic poetry. Nevertheless, I have before my eyes a kind of mirage of the perfec

tion of verse drama, which would be a design of human
action and of words, such as to present at once the
two aspects of dramatic and of musical order. It seems
to me that Shakespeare achieved this at least in certain
scenes—even rather early, for there is the balcony scene
of *Romeo and Juliet*—and that this was what he was striving toward in his late plays. To go as far in this direction
as it is possible to go, without losing that contact with the
ordinary everyday world with which drama must come to
terms, seems to me the proper aim of dramatic poetry.
For it is ultimately the function of art, in imposing a
credible order upon ordinary reality, and thereby elicit-
ing some perception of an order *in* reality, to bring us to
a condition of serenity, stillness, and reconciliation; and
then leave us, as Virgil left Dante, to proceed toward
a region where that guide can avail us no further.

ARTHUR MILLER
(b. 1915)

Death of a Salesman[1] (1958)

. . . THE FIRST IMAGE that occurred to me which was to
result in *Death of a Salesman* was of an enormous face the
height of the proscenium arch which would appear and
then open up, and we would see the inside of a man's
head. In fact, *The Inside of His Head* was the first title. It
was conceived half in laughter, for the inside of his head
was a mass of contradictions. The image was in direct
opposition to the method of *All My Sons*—a method one
might call linear or eventual in that one fact or incident
creates the necessity for the next. The *Salesman* image
was from the beginning absorbed with the concept that
nothing in life comes "next" but that everything exists
together and at the same time within us; that there is no
past to be "brought forward" in a human being, but that
he is his past at every moment and that the present is
merely that which his past is capable of noticing and
smelling and reacting to.

I wished to create a form which, in itself as a form,
would literally be the process of Willy Loman's way of
mind. But to say "wished" is not accurate. Any dramatic
form is an artifice, a way of transforming a subjective
feeling into something that can be comprehended through
public symbols. Its efficiency as a form is to be judged—
at least by the writer—by how much of the original vision
and feeling is lost or distorted by this transformation. I
wished to speak of the salesman most precisely as I felt
about him, to give no part of that feeling away for the sake
of any effect or any dramatic necessity. What was wanted
now was not a mounting line of tension, nor a gradually
narrowing cone of intensifying suspense, but a bloc, a single

[1] Arthur Miller, Introduction, *Collected Plays* (New York:
the Viking Press, 1958), pp. 23–38. Copyright 1957 by Arthur
Miller. Reprinted by permission of the Viking Press, Inc.

chord presented as such at the outset, within which all
the strains and melodies would already be contained. The
strategy, as with *All My Sons*, was to appear entirely
unstrategic but with a difference. This time, if I could, I
would have told the whole story and set forth all the
characters in one unbroken speech or even one sentence
or a single flash of light. As I look at the play now its
form seems the form of a confession, for that is how it is
told, now speaking of what happened yesterday, then suddenly following some connection to a time twenty years
ago, then leaping even further back and then returning to
the present and even speculating about the future.

Where in *All My Sons* it had seemed necessary to
prove the connections between the present and the past,
between events and moral consequences, between the mani-
fest and the hidden, in this play all was assumed as proven
to begin with. All I was doing was bringing things to mind.
The assumption, also, was that everyone knew Willy
Loman. I can realize this only now, it is true, but it is
equally apparent to me that I took it somehow for
granted then. There was still the attitude of the unveiler,
but no bringing together of hitherto unrelated things;
only pre-existing images, events, confrontations, moods,
and pieces of knowledge. So there was a kind of confidence underlying this play which the form itself expresses,
even a naïveté, a self-disarming quality that was in part
born of my belief in the audience as being essentially the
same as myself. If I had wanted, then, to put the audience
reaction into words, it would not have been "What happens next and why?" so much as "Oh, God, of course!"

In one sense a play is a species of jurisprudence, and
some part of it must take the advocate's role, something
else must act in defense, and the entirety must engage
the Law. Against my will, *All My Sons* states, and even
proclaims, that it is a form and that a writer wrote it and
organized it. In *Death of a Salesman* the original impulse
was to make that same proclamation in an immeasurably
more violent, abrupt, and openly conscious way. Willy
Loman does not merely suggest or hint that he is at the
end of his strength and of his justifications, he is hardly
on the stage for five minutes when he says so; he does
not gradually imply a deadly conflict with his son, an
implication dropped into the midst of serenity and surface calm, he is avowedly grappling with that conflict at

the outset. The ultimate matter with which the play will close is announced at the outset and is the matter of its every moment from the first. There is enough revealed in the first scene of *Death of a Salesman* to fill another kind of play which, in service to another dramatic form, would hold back and only gradually release it. I wanted to proclaim that an artist had made this play, but the nature of the proclamation was to be entirely "inartistic" and avowedly unstrategic; it was to hold back nothing, at any moment, which life would have revealed, even at the cost of suspense and climax. It was to forgo the usual preparations for scenes and to permit—and even seek— whatever in each character contradicted his position in the advocate-defense scheme of its jurisprudence. The play was begun with only one firm piece of knowledge and this was that Loman was to destroy himself. How it would wander before it got to that point I did not know and resolved not to care. I was convinced only that if I could make him remember enough he would kill himself, and the structure of the play was determined by what was needed to draw up his memories like a mass of tangled roots without end or beginning.

As I have said, the structure of events and the nature of its form are also the direct reflection of Willy Loman's way of thinking at this moment of his life. He was the kind of man you see muttering to himself on a subway, decently dressed, on his way home or to the office, perfectly integrated with his surroundings excepting that unlike other people he can no longer restrain the power of his experience from disrupting the superficial sociality of his behavior. Consequently he is working on two logics which often collide. For instance, if he meets his son Happy while in the midst of some memory in which Happy disappointed him, he is instantly furious at Happy, despite the fact that Happy at this particular moment deeply desires to be of use to him. He is literally at that terrible moment when the voice of the past is no longer distant but quite as loud as the voice of the present. In dramatic terms the form, therefore, *is* this process, instead of being a once-removed summation or indication of it.

The way of telling the tale, in this sense, is as mad as Willy and as abrupt and as suddenly lyrical. And it is difficult not to add that the subsequent imitations of the form had to collapse for this particular reason. It is not possible, in my opinion, to graft it onto a character whose psychology it does not reflect, and I have not used it since because it would be false to a more integrated—or less disintegrating—personality to pretend that the past and the present are so openly and vocally intertwined in his mind. The ability of people to down their past is normal, and without it we could have no comprehensible communication among men. In the hands of writers who see it as an easy way to elicit anterior information in a play it becomes merely a flashback. There are no flashbacks in this play but only a mobile concurrency of past and present, and this, again, because in his desperation to justify his life Willy Loman has destroyed the boundaries between now and then, just as anyone would do who, on picking up his telephone, discovered that this perfectly harmless act had somehow set off an explosion in his basement. The previously assumed and believed-in results of ordinary and accepted actions, and their abrupt and unforeseen—but apparently logical—effects, form the basic collision in this play, and, I suppose, its ultimate irony.

It may be in place to remark, in this connection, that while the play was sometimes called cinematographic in its structure, it failed as a motion picture. I believe that the basic reason—aside from the gross insensitivity permeating its film production—was that the dramatic tension of Willy's memories was destroyed by transferring him, literally, to the locales he had only imagined in the play. There is an inevitable horror in the spectacle of a man losing consciousness of his immediate surroundings to the point where he engages in conversations with unseen persons. The horror is lost—and drama becomes narrative—when the context actually becomes his imagined world. And the drama evaporates because psychological truth has been amended, a truth which depends not only on what images we recall but in what connections and contexts we recall them. The setting on the stage was never shifted, despite the many changes in locale, for the precise reason that, quite simply, the mere fact that a man forgets where he is does not mean that he has really moved. Indeed, his terror springs from his never-lost awareness of time and place. It did not need this play to teach me that the screen is time-bound and earth-bound compared to the stage, if only because its preponderant emphasis is on the visual image, which, however rapidly it may be changed before our eyes, still displaces its predecessor, while scene-changing with words is instantaneous; and because of the flexibility of language, especially of English, a preceding image can be kept alive through the image that succeeds it. The movie's tendency is always to wipe out what has gone before, and it is thus in constant danger of transforming the dramatic into narrative. There is no swifter method of telling a "story" but neither is there a more difficult medium in which to keep a pattern of relationships constantly in being. Even in those sequences which retained the real backgrounds for Willy's imaginary confrontations the tension between now and then was lost. I suspect this loss was due to the necessity of shooting the actors close up—effectively eliminating awareness of their surroundings. The basic failure of the picture was a formal one. It did not solve, nor really attempt to find, a resolution for the problem of keeping the past constantly alive, and that friction, collision, and tension between past and present was the heart of the play's particular construction.

A great deal has been said and written about what *Death of a Salesman* is supposed to signify, both psychologically and from the socio-political viewpoints. For instance, in one periodical of the far Right it was called a "time bomb expertly placed under the edifice of Americanism," while the *Daily Worker* reviewer thought it entirely decadent. In Catholic Spain it ran longer than any modern play and it has been refused production in Russia but not, from time to time, in certain satellite countries, depending on the direction and velocity of the wind. The Spanish press, thoroughly controlled by Catholic orthodoxy, regarded the play as commendable proof of the spirit's death where there is no God. In America, even as it was being cannonaded as a piece of Communist propaganda, two of the largest manufacturing corporations in the country invited me to address their sales organizations in conventions assembled, while the road company was here and there picketed by the Catholic War Veterans and the American Legion. It made only a fair impression in London, but in the area of the Norwegian Arctic Circle fishermen whose only contact with civilization was the radio and the occasional visit of the government boat insisted on seeing it night after night—the same few people—believing it to be some kind of religious rite. One organization of salesmen raised me up nearly to patron-sainthood, and another, a national sales managers' group, complained that the difficulty of recruiting salesmen was directly traceable to the play. When the movie was made, the producing company got so frightened it produced a sort of trailer to be shown before the picture, a documentary short film which demonstrated how exceptional Willy Loman was; how necessary selling is to the economy; how secure the salesman's life really is; how idiotic, in short, was the feature film they had just spent more than a million dollars to produce. Fright does odd things to people.

On the psychological front the play spawned a small hill of doctoral theses explaining its Freudian symbolism, and there were innumerable letters asking if I was aware that the fountain pen which Biff steals is a phallic symbol. Some, on the other hand, felt it was merely a fountain pen and dismissed the whole play. I received visits from men over sixty from as far away as California who had come across the country to have me write the stories of their lives, because the story of Willy Loman was exactly like theirs. The letters from women made it clear that the central character of the play was Linda; sons saw the entire action revolving around Biff or Happy, and fathers wanted advice, in effect, on how to avoid parricide. Probably the most succinct reaction to the play was voiced by a man who, on leaving the theatre, said, "I always said that New England territory was no damned good." This, at least, was a fact.

That I have and had not the slightest interest in the selling profession is probably unbelievable to most people, and I very early gave up trying even to say so. And when asked what Willy was selling, what was in his bags, I could only reply, "Himself." I was trying neither to condemn a profession nor particularly to improve it, and, I will admit, I was little better than ignorant of Freud's teachings when I wrote it. There was no attempt to bring down the American edifice nor to raise it higher, to show up family relations or to cure the ills afflicting that inevitable in-stitution. The truth, at least of my aim—which is all I can speak of authoritatively—is much simpler and more complex.

The play grew from simple images. From a little frame house on a street of little frame houses, which had once been loud with the noise of growing boys, and then was empty and silent and finally occupied by strangers. Strangers who could not know with what conquistadorial joy Willy and his boys had once reshingled the roof. Now it was quiet in the house, and the wrong people in the beds.

It grew from images of futility—the cavernous Sunday afternoons polishing the car. Where is that car now? And the chamois cloths carefully washed and put up to dry, where are the chamois cloths?

And the endless, convoluted discussions, wonderments, arguments, belittlements, encouragements, fiery resolutions, abdications, returns, partings, voyages out and voyages back, tremendous opportunities, and small, squeaking denouements—and all in the kitchen now occupied by strangers who cannot hear what the walls are saying.

The image of aging and so many of your friends already gone and strangers in the seats of the mighty who do not know you or your triumphs or your incredible value.

The image of the son's hard, public eye upon you, no longer swept by your myth, no longer rousable from his separateness, no longer knowing you have lived for him and have wept for him.

The image of ferocity when love has turned to something else and yet is there, is somewhere in the room if one could only find it.

The image of people turning into strangers who only evaluate one another.

Above all, perhaps, the image of a need greater than hunger or sex or thirst, a need to leave a thumbprint somewhere on the world. A need for immortality, and by admitting it, the knowing that one has carefully inscribed one's name on a cake of ice on a hot July day.

I sought the relatedness of all things by isolating their unrelatedness, a man superbly alone with his sense of not having touched, and finally knowing in his last extremity that the love which had always been in the room unlocated was now found.

The image of a suicide so mixed in motive as to be unfathomable and yet demanding statement. Revenge was in it and a power of love, a victory in that it would bequeath a fortune to the living and a flight from emptiness. With it an image of peace at the final curtain, the peace that is between wars, the peace leaving the issues aboveground and viable yet.

And always, throughout, the image of private man in a world full of strangers, a world that is not home nor even an open battleground but only galaxies of high promise over a fear of falling.

And the image of a man making something with his hands being a rock to touch and return to. "He was always so wonderful with his hands," says his wife over his grave, and I laughed when the line came, laughed with the artist-devil's laugh, for it had all come together in this line, she having been made by him though he did not know it or believe in it or receive it into himself. Only rank, height of power, the sense of having won he believed was real—the galaxy thrust up into the sky by projectors on the rooftops of the city he believed were real stars.

It came from structural images. The play's eye was to revolve from within Willy's head, sweeping endlessly in all directions like a light on the sea, and nothing that formed in the distant mist was to be left uninvestigated. It was thought of as having the density of the novel form in its interchange of viewpoints, so that while all roads led to Willy the other characters were to feel it was their play, a story about them and not him.

There were two undulating lines in mind, one above the other, the past webbed to the present moving on together in him and sometimes openly joined and once, finally, colliding in the showdown which defined him in his eyes at least— and so to sleep.

Above all, in the structural sense, I aimed to make a play with the veritable countenance of life. To make one the many, as in life, so that "society" is a power and a mystery of custom and inside the man and surrounding him, as the fish is in the sea and the sea inside the fish, his birthplace and burial ground, promise and threat. To speak commonsensically of social facts which every businessman knows and talks about but which are too prosaic to mention or are usually fancied up on the stage as philosophical problems. When a man gets old you fire him, you have to, he can't do the work. To speak and even to celebrate the common sense of businessmen, who love the personality that wins the day but know that you've got to have the right goods at the right price, handsome and well spoken as you are. (To some, these were scandalous and infamous arraignments of society when uttered in the context of art. But not to the businessmen themselves; they knew it was all true and I cherished their clear-eyed talk.)

The image of a play without transitional scenes was there in the beginning. There was too much to say to waste precious stage time with feints and preparations, in themselves agonizing "structural" bridges for a writer to work out since they are not why he is writing. There was a resolution, as in *All My Sons,* not to waste motion or moments, but in this case to shear through everything up to the meat of a scene; a resolution not to write an unmeant word for the sake of the form but to make the form give and stretch and contract for the sake of the thing to be said. To cling to the process of Willy's mind as the form the story would take.

The play was always heroic to me, and in later years the academy's charge that Willy lacked the "stature" for the tragic hero seemed incredible to me. I had not understood that these matters are measured by Greco-Elizabethan paragraphs which hold no mention of insurance payments, front porches, refrigerator fan belts, steering knuckles, Chevrolets, and visions seen not through the portals of Delphi but in the blue flame of the hot-water heater. How could "Tragedy" make people weep, of all things?

I set out not to "write a tragedy" in this play, but to show the truth as I saw it. However, some of the attacks upon it as a pseudo-tragedy contain ideas so misleading, and in some cases so laughable, that it might be in place here to deal with a few of them.

Aristotle having spoken of a fall from the heights, it goes without saying that someone of the common mold cannot be a fit tragic hero. It is now many centuries since Aristotle lived. There is no more reason for falling down in a faint before his *Poetics* than before Euclid's geometry, which has been amended numerous times by men with new insights; nor, for that matter, would I choose to have my illnesses diagnosed by Hippocrates rather than the most ordinary graduate of an American medical school, despite the Greek's genius. Things do change, and even a genius is limited by his time and the nature of his society.

I would deny, on grounds of simple logic, this one of Aristotle's contentions if only because he lived in a slave society. When a vast number of people are divested of alternatives, as slaves are, it is rather inevitable that one will not be able to imagine drama, let alone tragedy, as being possible for any but the higher ranks of society. There is a legitimate question of stature here, but none of rank, which is so often confused with it. So long as the hero may be said to have had alternatives of a magnitude to have materially changed the course of his life, it seems to me that in this respect at least, he cannot be debarred from the heroic role.

The question of rank is significant to me only as it reflects the question of the social application of the hero's career. There is no doubt that if a character is shown on the stage who goes through the most ordinary actions, and is suddenly revealed to be the President of the United States, his actions immediately assume a much greater magnitude, and pose the possibilities of much greater meaning, than if he is the corner grocer. But at the same time, his stature as a hero is not so utterly dependent upon his rank that the corner grocer cannot outdistance him as a tragic figure—providing, of course, that the grocer's career engages the issues of, for instance, the survival of the race, the relationships of man to God —the questions, in short, whose answers define humanity and the right way to live so that the world is a home, instead of a battleground or a fog in which disembodied spirits pass each other in an endless twilight.

In this respect *Death of a Salesman* is a slippery play to categorize because nobody in it stops to make a speech objectively stating the great issues which I believe it embodies. If it were a worse play, less closely articulating its meanings with its actions, I think it would have more quickly satisfied a certain kind of criticism. But it was meant to be less a play than a fact; it refused admission to its author's opinions and opened itself to a revelation of process and the operations of an ethic, of social laws of action no less powerful in their effects upon individuals than any tribal law administered by gods with names. I need not claim that this play is a genuine solid gold tragedy for my opinions on tragedy to be held valid. My purpose here is simply to point out a historical fact which must be taken into account in any consideration of tragedy, and it is the sharp alteration in the meaning of rank in society between the present time and the distant past. More important to me is the fact that this particular kind of argument obscures much more relevant considerations.

One of these is the question of intensity. It matters not at all whether a modern play concerns itself with a grocer or a president if the intensity of the hero's commitment to his course is less than the maximum possible. It matters not at all whether the hero falls from a great height or a small one, whether he is highly conscious or only dimly aware of what is happening, whether his pride brings the fall or an unseen pattern written behind clouds; if the intensity, the human passion to surpass his given bounds, the fanatic insistence upon his self-conceived role —if these are not present there can only be an outline of tragedy but no living thing. I believe, for myself, that the lasting appeal of tragedy is due to our need to face the fact of death in order to strengthen ourselves for life, and that over and above this function of the tragic viewpoint there are and will be a great number of formal variations which no single definition will ever embrace.

Another issue worth considering is the so-called tragic victory, a question closely related to the consciousness of the hero. One makes nonsense of this if a "victory" means that the hero makes us feel some certain joy when, for instance, he sacrifices himself for a "cause," and unhappy and morose because he dies without one. To begin at the bottom, a man's death is and ought to be an essentially terrifying thing and ought to make nobody happy. But in a great variety of ways even death, the ultimate negative, can be, and appear to be, an assertion of bravery, and can serve to separate the death of man from the death of animals; and I think it is this distinction which underlies any conception of a victory in death. For a society of faith, the nature of the death can prove the existence of the spirit, and posit its immortality. For a secular society it is perhaps more difficult for such a victory to document itself and to make itself felt, but, conversely, the need to offer greater proofs of the humanity of man can make that victory more real. It goes without saying that in a society where there is basic disagreement as to the right way to live, there can hardly be agreement as to the right way to die, and both life and death must be heavily weighted with meaningless futility.

It was not out of any deference to a tragic definition that Willy Loman is filled with a joy, however brokenhearted, as he approaches his end, but simply that my sense of his character dictated his joy, and even what I felt was an exultation. In terms of his character, he has achieved a very powerful piece of knowledge, which is that he is loved by his son and has been embraced by him and forgiven. In this he is given his existence, so to speak— his fatherhood, for which he has always striven and which until now he could not achieve. That he is unable to take this victory thoroughly to his heart, that it closes the circle for him and propels him to his death, is the wage of his sin, which was to have committed himself so completely to the counterfeits of dignity and the false coinage embodied in his idea of success that he can prove his existence only by bestowing "power" on his posterity, a power deriving from the sale of his last asset, himself, for the price of his insurance policy.

I must confess here to a miscalculation, however. I did not realize while writing the play that so many people in the world do not see as clearly or would not admit, as I thought they must, how futile most lives are; so there could be no hope of consoling the audience for the death of this man. I did not realize either how few would be impressed by the fact that this man is actually a very brave spirit who cannot settle for half but must pursue his dream of himself to the end. Finally, I thought it must be clear, even obvious, that this was no dumb brute heading mindlessly to his catastrophe.

I have no need to be Willy's advocate before the jury which decides who is and who is not a tragic hero. I am merely noting that the lingering ponderousness of so many ancient definitions has blinded students and critics to the facts before them, and not only in regard to this play. Had Willy been unaware of his separation from values that endure he would have died contentedly while polishing his car, probably on a Sunday afternoon with the ball game coming over the radio. But he was agonized by his awareness of being in a false position, so constantly haunted by the hollowness of all he had placed his faith in, so aware, in short, that he must somehow be filled in his spirit or fly apart, that he staked his very life on the ultimate assertion. That he had not the intellectual fluency to verbalize his situation is not the same thing as saying that he lacked awareness, even an overly intensified consciousness that the life he had made was without form and inner meaning.

To be sure, had he been able to know that he was as much the victim of his beliefs as their defeated exemplar, had he known how much of guilt he ought to bear and how much to shed from his soul, he would be more conscious. But it seems to me that there is of necessity a severe limitation of self-awareness in any character, even the most knowing, which serves to define him as a character, and more, that this very limit serves to complete the tragedy and, indeed, to make it at all possible. Complete consciousness is possible only in a play about forces, like *Prometheus,* but not in a play about people. I think that the point is whether there is a sufficient awareness in the hero's career to make the audience supply the rest. Had Oedipus, for instance, been more conscious and more aware of the forces at work upon him he must surely have said that he was not really to blame for having cohabited with his mother since neither he nor anyone else knew she was his mother. He must surely decide to divorce her, provide for their children, firmly resolve to investigate the family background of his next wife, and thus deprive us of a very fine play and the name for a famous neurosis. But he is conscious only up to a point, the point at which guilt begins. Now he is inconsolable and must tear out his eyes. What is tragic about this? Why is it not even ridiculous? How can we respect a man who goes to such extremities over something he could in no way help or prevent? The answer, I think, is not that we respect the man, but that we respect the Law he has so completely broken, wittingly or not, for it is that Law which, we believe, defines us as men. The confusion of some critics viewing *Death of a Salesman* in this regard is that they do not see that Willy Loman has broken a law without whose protection life is insupportable if not incomprehensible to him and to many others; it is the law which says that a failure in society and in business has no right to live. Unlike the law against incest, the law of success is not administered by statute or church, but it is very nearly as powerful in its grip upon men. The confusion increases because, while it is a law, it is by no means a wholly agreeable one even as it is slavishly obeyed, for to fail is no longer to belong to society, in his estimate. Therefore, the path is opened for those who wish to call Willy merely a foolish man even as they themselves are living in obedience to the same law that killed him. Equally, the fact that Willy's law—the belief, in other words, which administers guilt to him—is not a civilizing statute whose destruction menaces us all; it is, rather, a deeply believed and deeply suspect "good" which, when questioned as to its value, as it is in this play, serves more to raise our anxieties than to reassure us of the existence of an unseen but humane metaphysical system in the world. My attempt in the play was to counter this anxiety with an opposing system which, so to speak, is in a race for Willy's faith, and it is the system of love which is the opposite of the law of success. It is embodied in Biff Loman, but by the time Willy can perceive his love it can serve only as an ironic comment upon the life he sacrificed for power and for success and its tokens.

A play cannot be equated with a political philosophy, at least not in the way a smaller number, by simple multiplication, can be assimilated into a larger. I do not believe that any work of art can help but be diminished by its adherence at any cost to a political program, including its author's, and not for any other reason than that there is no political program—any more than there is a theory of tragedy—which can encompass the complexities of real life. Doubtless an author's politics must be one element, and even an important one, in the germination of his art, but if it is art he has created it must by definition bend itself to his observation rather than to his opinions or even his hopes. If I have shown a preference for plays which seek causation not only in psychology but in society, I may also believe in the autonomy of art, and I believe this because my experience with *All My Sons* and *Death of a Salesman* forces the belief upon me. If the earlier play was Marxist, it was a Marxism of a strange hue. Joe Keller is arraigned by his son for a willfully unethical use of his economic position; and this, as the Russians said when they removed the play from their stages, bespeaks an assumption that the norm of capitalist behavior is ethical or at least can be, an assumption no Marxist can hold. Nor does Chris propose to liquidate the business built in part on soldiers' blood; he will run it himself, but cleanly.

The most decent man in *Death of a Salesman* is a capitalist (Charley) whose aims are not different from

Willy Loman's. The great difference between them is that Charley is not a fanatic. Equally, however, he has learned how to live without that frenzy, that ecstasy of spirit which Willy chases to his end. And even as Willy's sons are unhappy men, Charley's boy, Bernard, works hard, attends to his studies, and attains a worthwhile objective. These people are all of the same class, the same background, the same neighborhood. What theory lies behind this double view? None whatever. It is simply that I knew and know that I feel better when my work is reflecting a balance of the truth as it exists. A muffled debate arose with the success of *Death of a Salesman* in which attempts were made to justify or dismiss the play as a Left-Wing piece, or as a Right-Wing manifestation of decadence. The presumption underlying both views is that a work of art is the sum of its author's political outlook, real or alleged, and more, that its political implications are valid elements in its aesthetic evaluation. I do not believe this, either for my own or other writers' works.

The most radical play I ever saw was not *Waiting for Lefty* but *The Madwoman of Chaillot*. I know nothing of Giraudoux's political alignment, and it is of no moment to me; I am able to read this play, which is the most open indictment of private exploitation of the earth I know about. By the evidence of his plays, Shaw, the socialist, was in love not with the working class, whose characters he could only caricature, but with the middle of the economic aristocracy, those men who, in his estimate, lived without social and economic illusions. There is a strain of mystic fatalism in Ibsen so powerful as to throw all his scientific tenets into doubt, and a good measure besides of contempt—in this radical—for the men who are usually called the public. The list is long and the contradictions are embarrassing until one concedes a perfectly simple proposition. It is merely that a writer of any worth creates out of his total perception, the vaster part of which is subjective and not within his intellectual control. For myself, it has never been possible to generate the energy to write and complete a play if I know in advance everything it signifies and all it will contain. The very impulse to write, I think, springs from an inner chaos crying for order, for meaning, and that meaning must be discovered in the process of writing or the work lies dead as it is finished. To speak, therefore, of a play as though it were the objective work of a propagandist is an almost biological kind of nonsense, provided, of course, that it is a play, which is to say a work of art.

TENNESSEE WILLIAMS
(b. 1914)

Camino Real[1] (1953)

FOREWORD

It is amazing and frightening how completely one's whole being becomes absorbed in the making of a play. It is almost as if you were frantically constructing another world while the world that you live in dissolves beneath your feet, and that your survival depends on completing this construction at least one second before the old habitation collapses.

More than any other work that I have done, this play has seemed to me like the construction of another world, a separate existence. Of course, it is nothing more nor less than my conception of the time and world that I live in, and its people are mostly archetypes of certain basic attitudes and qualities with those mutations that would occur if they had continued along the road to this hypothetical terminal point in it.

A convention of the play is existence outside of time in a place of no specific locality. If you regard it that way, I suppose it becomes an elaborate allegory, but in New Haven we opened directly across the street from a movie theatre that was showing *Peter Pan* in Technicolor and it did not seem altogether inappropriate to me. Fairy tales nearly always have some simple moral lesson of good and evil, but that is not the secret of their fascination any more, I hope, than the philosophical import that might be distilled from the fantasies of *Camino Real* is the principal element of its appeal.

To me the appeal of this work is its unusual degree of

[1] Tennessee Williams, Foreword and Afterword, *Camino Real* (New York: New Directions, 1953), pp. viii–xiii. Copyright 1953 by the New York *Times*. Reprinted by permission of New Directions. Written prior to the Broadway premiere of *Camino Real* and published in the New York *Times* on Sunday, March 15, 1953.

freedom. When it began to get under way I felt a new sensation of release, as if I could "ride out" like a tenor sax taking the breaks in a Dixeland combo or a piano in a bop session. You may call it self-indulgence, but I was not doing it merely for myself. I could not have felt a purely private thrill of release unless I had hope of sharing this experience with lots and lots of audiences to come.

My desire was to give these audiences my own sense of something wild and unrestricted that ran like water in the mountains, or clouds changing shape in a gale, or the continually dissolving and transforming images of a dream. This sort of freedom is not chaos nor anarchy. On the contrary, it is the result of painstaking design, and in this work I have given more conscious attention to form and construction than I have in any work before. Freedom is not achieved simply by working freely.

Elia Kazan was attracted to this work mainly, I believe, for the same reason—its freedom and mobility of form. I know that we have kept saying the word "flight" to each other as if the play were merely an abstraction of the impulse to fly, and most of the work out of town, his in staging, mine in cutting and revising, has been with this impulse in mind: the achievement of a continual flow. Speech after speech and bit after bit that were nice in themselves have been remorselessly blasted out of the script and its staging wherever they seemed to obstruct or divert this flow.

There have been plenty of indications already that this play will exasperate and confuse a certain number of people which we hope is not so large as the number it is likely to please. At each performance a number of people have stamped out of the auditorium, with little regard for those whom they have had to crawl over, almost as if the building had caught on fire, and there have been sibilant noises on the way out and demands for money back if the cashier was foolish enough to remain in his box.

I am at a loss to explain this phenomenon, and if I am being facetious about one thing, I am being quite serious about another when I say that I had never for one minute supposed that the play would seem obscure and confusing to anyone who was willing to meet it even less than halfway. It was a costly production, and for this reason I had to read it aloud, together with a few of the actors on one occasion, before large groups of prospective backers, before the funds to produce it were in the till. It was only then that I came up against the disconcerting surprise that some people would think that the play needed clarification.

My attitude is intransigent. I still don't agree that it needs any explanation. Some poet has said that a poem should not mean but be. Of course, a play is not a poem, not even a poetic play has quite the same license as a poem. But to go to *Camino Real* with the inflexible demands of a logician is unfair to both parties.

In Philadelphia a young man from a literary periodical saw the play and then cross-examined me about all its dreamlike images. He had made a list of them while he watched the play, and afterward at my hotel he brought out the list and asked me to explain the meaning of each one. I can't deny that I use a lot of those things called symbols but, being a self-defensive creature, I say that symbols are nothing but the natural speech of drama.

We all have in our conscious and unconscious minds a great vocabulary of images, and I think all human communication is based on these images as are our dreams; and a symbol in a play has only one legitimate purpose which is to say a thing more directly and simply and beautifully than it could be said in words.

I hate writing that is a parade of images for the sake of images; I hate it so much that I close a book in disgust when it keeps on saying one thing is like another; I even get disgusted with poems that make nothing but comparisons between one thing and another. But I repeat that symbols, when used respectfully, are the purest language of plays. Sometimes it would take page after tedious page of exposition to put across an idea that can be said with an object or a gesture on the lighted stage.

To take one case in point: the battered portmanteau of Jacques Casanova is hurled from the balcony of a luxury hotel when his remittance check fails to come through. While the portmanteau is still in the air, he shouts, "Careful, I have—" —and when it has crashed to the street he continues—"fragile—mementoes. . . ." I suppose that is a symbol, at least it is an object used to express as directly and vividly as possible certain things which could be said in pages of dull talk.

As for those patrons who departed before the final scene, I offer myself this tentative bit of solace: that these theatregoers may be a little domesticated in their theatrical tastes. A cage represents security as well as confinement to a bird that has grown used to being in it; and when a theatrical work kicks over the traces with such apparent insouciance, security seems challenged and, instead of participating in its sense of freedom, one out of a certain number of playgoers will rush back out to the more accustomed implausibility of the street he lives on.

To modify this effect of complaisance I would like to admit to you quite frankly that I can't say with any personal conviction that I have written a good play, I only know that I have felt a release in this work which I wanted you to feel with me.

AFTERWORD

Once in a while someone will say to me that he would rather wait for a play to come out as a book than see a live performance of it, where he would be distracted from its true values, if it has any, by so much that is mere spectacle and sensation and consequently must be meretricious and vulgar. There are plays meant for reading. I have read them. I have read the works of "thinking playwrights" as distinguished from us who are permitted only to feel, and probably read them earlier and appreciated them as much as those who invoke their names nowadays like the incantation of Aristophanes' frogs. But the incontinent blaze of a live theatre, a theatre meant for seeing and for feeling, has never been and never will be extinguished by a bucket brigade of critics, new or old, bearing vessels that range from cut-glass punch bowl to Haviland teacup. And in my dissident opinion, a play in a book is only the shadow of a play and not even a clear shadow of it. Those who did not like Camino Real on the stage will not be likely to form a higher opinion of it in print, for of all the works I have written, this one was meant most for the vulgarity of performance. The printed script of a play is hardly more than an architect's blueprint of a house not yet built or built and destroyed.

The color, the grace and levitation, the structural pattern in motion, the quick interplay of live beings, suspended like fitful lightning in a cloud, these things are the play, not words on paper, nor thoughts and ideas of an author, those shabby things snatched off basement counters at Gimbel's.

My own creed as a playwright is fairly close to that expressed by the painter in Shaw's play *The Doctor's Dilemma:* "I believe in Michelangelo, Velasquez and Rembrandt; in the might of design, the mystery of color, the redemption of all things by beauty everlasting and the message of art that has made these hands blessed. Amen."

How much art his hands were blessed with or how much mine are, I don't know, but that art is a blessing is certain and that it contains its message is also certain, and I feel, as the painter did, that the message lies in those abstract beauties of form and color and line, to which I would add light and motion.

In these following pages are only the formula by which a play could exist.

Dynamic is a word in disrepute at the moment, and so, I suppose, is the word *organic,* but those terms still define the dramatic values that I value most and which I value more as they are more deprecated by the ones self-appointed to save what they have never known.

EUGENE IONESCO
(b. 1912)

The Bald Soprano[1]

THE "SOCIETY" I have tried to depict in *The Bald Soprano* is a society which is perfect, I mean where all social problems have been resolved. Unfortunately this has no effect upon life as it is lived. The play deals with a world where economic worries are a thing of the past, a universe without mystery, in which everything runs smoothly, for one section of humanity at least. I have no doubt that this is the world of tomorrow. In America, Russia, China, Africa, and so on, the march of science and industrialization must finally arrive at stability and social contentment.

In *The Bald Soprano,* which is a completely unserious play where I was most concerned with solving purely theatrical problems, some people have seen a satire on bourgeois society, a criticism of life in England, and heaven knows what. In actual fact, if it is criticism of anything, it must be of all societies, of language, of clichés—a parody of human behavior, and therefore a parody of the theatre too. I am thinking both of the commercial theatre and the theatre of Brecht. In fact, I believe that it is precisely when we see the last of economic problems and class warfare (if I may avail myself of one of the most crashing clichés of our age) that we shall also see that this solves nothing, indeed that our problems are only beginning. We can no longer avoid asking ourselves what we are doing here on earth, and how, having no deep sense of our destiny, we can endure the crushing weight of the material world.

This is the *eternal problem* if ever there was one; for living means alienation. Other problems, even those of the Brechtian theatre, only confuse the real issue of

[1] "The World of Eugene Ionesco," the New York *Times,* June 1, 1958. Reprinted by courtesy of Eugene Ionesco.

alienation—that being Brecht's theme. When there is no more incentive to be wicked, and everyone is good, what shall we do with our goodness, or our non-wickedness, our non-greed, our ultimate neutrality? The people in *The Bald Soprano* have no hunger, no conscious desires; they are bored stiff. But people who are unconsciously alienated don't even know they are bored. They feel it vaguely, hence the final explosion—which is quite useless, as the characters and situations are both static and interchangeable, and everything ends where it started.

In my plays I have treated this comically, for the human drama is as absurd as it is painful. The second part of *The New Tenant* is perhaps less comic—or perhaps not, depending on the director. It all comes to the same thing, anyway: comic and tragic are merely two aspects of the same situation, and I have now reached the stage when I find it hard to distinguish one from the other.

The non-metaphysical world of today has destroyed all mystery; and the so-called "scientific" theatre of the period, the theatre of politics and propaganda, anti-poetic and academic, has flattened mankind out, alienating the unfathomable third dimension which makes a whole man. The theatre of ideologies and theses, proposing political solutions and presuming to save humanity, actually saves no one. I have no wish to save humanity—to wish to save it is to kill it—and there are no solutions. To realize that is the only healthy solution.

Some people have compared Brecht to Shakespeare, which seems to me pure madness. At this very moment, in France, there are several authors much more important than Brecht—I mean Ghelderode, Beckett, Jean Genet, Vauthier, and even the Sartre of *No Exit*—because they question the whole state of man, and offer us clear proofs that man is more than merely a social animal; the great authors are tragic, and all great drama is unbearable; when Richard II is killed in his cell, I see the death of all kings on earth, I witness the agonizing desecration and downfall of all values and civilizations. It is beyond our control, and therefore it is true. I am myself a dying king.

There are no alternatives; if man is not tragic, he is ridiculous and painful, "comic" in fact, and by revealing his absurdity one can achieve a sort of tragedy. In fact I think that man must either be unhappy (meta-physically unhappy) or stupid.

The Chairs

I HAVE often chosen to write plays about nothing, rather than about secondary problems (social, political, sexual, etc.). There is no action in *The Bald Soprano,* simply theatrical machinery functioning, as it were, in a void. It shows a hollow automatism being taken to pieces and put together in the wrong order, as well as automatic men speaking and behaving automatically; and to this extent it illustrates "comically" the emptiness of a world without metaphysics and a humanity without problems.

In *The Chairs* I have tried to deal more directly with the themes that obsess me; with emptiness, with frustration, with this world, at once fleeting and crushing, with despair and death. The characters I have used are not fully conscious of their spiritual rootlessness, but they feel it instinctively and emotionally. They feel "lost" in the world, something is missing which they cannot, to their grief, supply.

By "directly" I mean according to the rules of tragic construction (or comic and tragic at the same time)—but using what I might call pure theatre, which progresses not through a predetermined subject and plot, but through an increasingly intense and revealing series of emotional states.

Thus I have tried to give the play a classical form. I believe that the aim of the avant-garde should be to rediscover—not invent—in their purest state, the permanent forms and forgotten ideals of the theatre. We must cut through the clichés and break free of a hidebound "traditionalism"; we must rediscover the one true and living tradition. I make no claim to have succeeded in this. But others will succeed, and show that all truth and all reality is classical and eternal.

APPENDIX

From Friedrich Hebbel's *Journals*[1]

1836

The devil take what nowadays passes for beautiful language! This language in drama is the counterpart of "How beautifully put!" in conversation. Chintz, chintz, and more chintz! It may glitter but it gives no heat.

1838

"Form is the expression of necessity," I say in a critical piece.

Best definition: Content presents the task; form, the solution.

1839

Whether the idea masters the poet or the poet the idea —everything depends on this.

Every great man falls by his own sword. Only no one knows it.

Form is the highest content.

Bad playwrights with good heads give us their scheme instead of characters and their system instead of passions.

[1] Reprinted by courtesy of Eric Bentley. No playwright has said better things about the drama than Hebbel, yet very little of what he said on this subject has been done into English. As the present book does not have room for the major essays ("One Word about the Drama," "My Word about the Drama," Preface to *Mary Magdalene*, etc.), it has been thought appropriate to quote from the *Journals*, where, oddly enough, the dramatist expressed himself most pithily. (Translator's note.) Copyright 1960 by Eric Bentley.

There are dramas without ideas in which people take a walk and meet with bad luck on the way.

Most writers of historical tragedy don't give us historical characters but parodies of them.

1840

In Shakespeare we find, amid the great wealth, the most miserly economy. In general a sign of the highest genius.

All life is a battle of the individual with the universe.

1841

Dramatic deeds are not the ones that go straight ahead like bullets.

Drama shouldn't present new stories but new relationships.

1844

In the drama, what we shall see as bad we must also be able to see as good.

The problematic is the life breath of poetry. . . .

1845

A genuine drama is comparable to one of those big buildings which have almost as many rooms and corridors below ground as above ground. People in general are aware only of the latter; the master builder of the former as well.

1847

To present the necessary in the form of the accidental: that is the whole secret of dramatic style.

Ballet: I see people in a ballet as deaf-mutes who've gone crazy.

1848

All dramatic art has to do with impropriety and incomprehension, for what is more improper and uncomprehending than passion?

1850

Ultimately, play-acting is only living at speed, at unimaginable speed! Hence, when a critic writes about an actor, he is criticizing the life process of a human being.

1851

By shortening a play, you can lengthen it.

In drama no character should ever utter a thought; from the thought in a play come the speeches of *all* the characters.

1853

The worst plays often start out like the best ones. The battle that's most ignominiously lost starts out with thunder and lightning just like the one that will be most gloriously won.

1854

Let the What in drama be known and throw no shadows; but not the How.

We know that a man must die; we don't know what fever he will die of.

1857

The bad conscience of mankind invented tragedy.

1859

The final destiny of a play is always: to be read. Why shouldn't it begin the way it's going to end anyhow?

Ideas are to drama what counterpoint is to music: nothing in themselves but the *sine qua non* for everything.

1861

Every genuine comic figure must resemble the hunchback who's in love with himself.

Monologues: pure respirations of the soul.

1862

"Tragic," literally translated: goatish, goatlike, a meaning which especially French writers of tragedy often still give to the word.

Opera is the most decisive break with banal illusion: and yet it works.

1865

The Schiller-Calderon-Racine kind of drama stands to the Shakespearean as vocal to instrumental music.

All material is dead; all life stems from form.

Ideas. You can't have a play without ideas, any more than a living man without air. But does it follow that, because there's earth, fire, air, and water in a man, he is nothing but a receptacle for these four elements?

In modern French plays, morality is the orange in the dead pig's mouth.

That the religious origin of the drama is no accident.

Translated by Eric Bentley

BIBLIOGRAPHY

A Selected Bibliography of Playwrights on Playwriting.

"American Playwrights Self-Appraised," compiled by Henry Hewes, *Saturday Review of Literature*, September 3, 1955, pp.18–19.

Anderson, Maxwell. "The Basis of Artistic Creation in Literature," in *The Bases of Artistic Creation*. New Brunswick, N.J.: Rutgers University Press, 1942, pp. 3–18.

————. *The Essence of Tragedy and other Footnotes and Papers*. Washington, D.C.: Anderson House, 1939.

Anouilh, Jean. "Jean Anouilh et l'artifice," *Les Nouvelles Littéraires*, March 27, 1937, p. 10.

Archer, William. *Playmaking*. Boston: Small, Maynard, 1923.

The Art of Playwriting: Lectures delivered at the University of Pennsylvania by Jesse Lynch Williams, Langdon Mitchell, Lord Dunsany, Gilbert Emery, Rachel Crothers. Philadelphia: University of Pennsylvania Press, 1928.

Auden, W. H. "Notes on the Comic," *Thought* (Fordham University Quarterly), 1952, pp. 57–71.

Becque, Henri. *Souvenirs d'un auteur dramatique*. Paris: Bibliothèque Artistique et Littéraire, 1895.

Bennett, Arnold. "Writing Plays," *The English Review*, July 1913, pp. 556–568.

Bourdet, Édouard. "Play Endings," *Theatre Arts*, February 1930, pp. 121–27.

————. "Playwriting as a Profession," *Theatre Arts Monthly*, February 1931, pp. 125–133; April 1931, pp. 292–300.

Brecht, Bertolt. "Chinese Acting," translated by Eric Bentley, *Furioso* (Carleton College, Northfield, Minnesota), Autumn 1949, pp. 68–77.

————. "German Drama: Pre-Hitler," *The Left Review*, July 1936, pp. 504–08.

————. "A Model for Epic Theatre," translated by Eric Bentley, *Sewanee Review*, July-September 1949, pp. 425–436.

————. "Notes for *The Threepenny Opera*," translated by Eric Bentley, *From the Modern Repertoire*, Series One. University of Denver Press, 1949, pp. 391–400.

————. "On Unrhymed Lyrics in Irregular Rhythms," translated by Beatrice Gottlieb, *Tulane Drama Review*, November 1957, pp. 33–38.

————. *Schriften zum Theater; über eine nicht-Aristotelische Dramatik*. Berlin: Suhrkamp Verlag, 1957.

————. *Theaterarbeit: 6 Aufführungen des Berliner Ensembles*. VVVDresdner Verlag, 1951.

————. "Über experimentelles Theater," *Theater der Zeit*, April 1959.

Bridie, James. *See* "The Play of Ideas."
"Can the Craft of Playwriting be Learned?" *World Theatre,*
    Vol. I, No. 3, Paris, 1951, pp. 15–35.
Capek, Karel. *How a Play is Produced.* London: G. Bles, 1928.
──────. "The Making of a Play," in *How They Do It,* trans-
    lated by M. and R. Weatherall. London: George Allen
    and Unwin, 1945.
Chekhov, Anton. *Letters on the Short Story, the Drama and
    other Literary Topics,* selected and edited by Louis S.
    Friedland. New York: Minton, Balch & Co., 1924.
──────. *The Life and Letters of Anton Chekhov,* translated
    and edited by S.S. Koteliansky and Philip Tomlinson.
    London: Cassell & Co., 1925.
──────. *The Personal Papers,* with an introduction by Matthew
    Josephson. New York: Lear Publishers, 1948.
Claudel, Paul. *Positions et propositions,* 2 vols. Paris:
    Gallimard, 1934.
──────. "Modern Drama and Music," *Yale Review,* Autumn
    1930, pp. 94–106.
Cocteau, Jean. *Call to Order,* translated by Rollo H. Myers.
    New York: Henry Holt, 1927.
──────. *On the Film,* translated by Vera Traill. London: Denis
    Dobson, Ltd., 1954.
──────. Two Prefaces, *Intimate Relations,* translated by
    Charles Frank, *From the Modern Repertoire,* Series
    Three, edited by Eric Bentley. Bloomington: Indiana
    University Press, 1956, pp. 525–26.
Connelly, Marc. "The Old Theatre and the New Challenge,"
    in *The Arts in Renewal.* Philadelphia: University of
    Pennsylvania Press, 1951, pp. 141–156.
"Dokumente zur Dramaturgie des zeitgenössischen Theaters,"
    Drama zwischen Shaw und Brecht, by Siegfried Melch-
    inger. Bremen: Carl Schünemann Verlag, 1957.
"Dramatic Theory: A Bibliography," compiled by Richard
    B. Vowles. The New York Public Library, 1956.
"The Dramatist's Problems," *World Theatre,* Vol. IV, No. 4,
    Autumn 1955.
Dunsany, Edward John Plunkett. *The Donnellan Lectures,*
    1943. London: W. Heinemann Ltd., 1945.
Eliot, T.S. *Poetry and Drama:* The First Theodore Spencer
    Memorial Lecture, November 21, 1950. Cambridge:
    Harvard University Press, 1951.
──────. *Selected Essays,* 1917–1932. New York: Harcourt
    Brace, 1932.
Ervine, St. John. *How to Write a Play.* New York: Mac-
    millan, 1928.
"Études de psychologie sur les auteurs dramatiques," by Alfred
    Binet and J. Passy, *L'Année Psychologique* (Paris), Vol.
    1, 1894, pp. 60–173. (Interviews with Victorien Sardou,
    Alphonse Daudet, Alexandre Dumas *fils,* Édouard Paill-
    eron, Henry Meilhac, François Coppée, François de
    Curel, Edmond de Goncourt.)
*European Theories of the Drama, with a Supplement on the
    American Drama,* edited by Barrett H. Clark. New York:
    Crown Publishers, 1947.

Evreinoff, Nicolas. *The Theatre in Life,* edited and translated by Alexander I. Nazaroff. New York: Brentano's, 1927.

Fry, Christopher. "Poetry in the Theatre," *Saturday Review,* March 21, 1953, pp. 18–19, 33.

Galsworthy, John. *The Inn of Tranquility: Studies and Essays.* New York: Charles Scribner's Sons, 1919.

García Lorca, Federico. "Declaraciones de García Lorca sobre el teatro," *Anales Organo de la Universidad Central,* Nos. 335–36, January-June, 1953, pp. 316–323 (Quito, Ecuador).

———. Entrevistas, *Obras Completas.* Madrid: Aguilar, 1955, pp. 1608–41.

———. Marie Laffranque: "Federico García Lorca. Encore trois textes oubliés," *Bulletin Hispanique,* January-March, 1957, pp. 62–71 (Quito, Ecuador).

Geddes, Virgil. *Beyond Tragedy: Footnotes on the Drama.* Seattle: University of Washington Chapbooks, No. 42, 1930.

Ghelderode. Michel de. *Les Entretiens d'Ostende.* Paris, L'Arche, 1956.

———. "The Ostend Interviews," translated by George Hauger, *Tulane Drama Review,* March 1959, pp. 3–23.

Gibson, William. *The Seesaw Log: A Chronicle of the Stage Production,* with the text of *Two for the Seesaw.* New York: Knopf, 1959.

Giraudoux, Jean. *Littérature.* Paris: Éditions Bernard Grasset, 1941.

———. *Visitations.* Neuchâtel: Ides et Calendes, 1947.

Gorky, Maxim. "Observations on the Theatre," *English Review,* April 1924, pp. 494–98.

———. *Reminiscences of Tolstoy, Chekhov, and Andreyev.* New York: The Viking Press, 1959.

Granville-Barker, Harley. *On Dramatic Method.* New York: A Dramabook, Hill and Wang, 1956.

———. *On Poetry in Drama.* London: Sidgwick, 1937.

Green, Paul. *Drama and the Weather.* New York: Samuel French, 1958.

———. *Dramatic Heritage.* New York: Samuel French, 1953.

Hebbel, Christian Friedrich. Foreword, *Maria Magdalene.* Hamburg, 1844.

Hellman, Lillian. Introduction, *Four Plays.* New York: The Modern Library, 1942.

Howard, Sidney. Preface, *Lucky Sam McCarver.* New York: Charles Scribner's Sons, 1926.

Ibsen, Henrik. *Letters,* translated by John Nilsen Laurvik and Mary Morison. New York: Duffield and Co., 1908.

———. *Nachgelassene Schriften,* 4 vols. Berlin: J. Fischer Verlag, 1909.

———. Preface, *Cataline,* in *Early Plays.* New York: The American Scandinavian Foundation, 1921.

———. *Speeches and New Letters,* translated by Arne Kildal. Boston: Richard G. Badger, 1910.

———. *The Works of Henrik Ibsen, Vol. XII: From Ibsen's*

Workshop, translated by A.G. Chater. New York: Charles Scribner's Sons, 1912.

Inge, William. Foreword, *Four Plays.* New York: Random House, 1958.

Ionesco, Eugene. "Discovering the Theatre," translated by Leonard C. Pronko, *Tulane Drama Review,* September 1959, pp. 3–18.

————. "Essays," translated by L.C. Pronko, *Theatre Arts,* June 1958, pp. 16–18.

————. "The Playwright's role: A Reply to Kenneth Tynan," *The Observer,* June 29, 1958, p. 14.

————. "Eugene Ionesco Opens Fire," *World Theatre,* Vol. VIII, No. 3, Autumn 1959, pp. 171–202.

James, Henry. *The Scenic Art,* edited, with an Introduction and Notes, by Allan Wade. New York: A Dramabook, Hill and Wang, 1957.

Jones, Henry Arthur. "Henry Arthur Jones, Dramatist Self-revealed; a Conversation on the Art of Writing Plays with Archibald Henderson," *Nation and the Athenaeum* (London), December 5, and December 12, 1925.

Kaiser, Georg. "Man in the Tunnel," translated by Eric Bentley, *The New Leader,* August 9, 1947.

————. "Vision und Figur," *Das Junge Deutschland,* No. 10, 1918, pp. 314–15.

Kanin, Garson. "The Bomb and the Parker 51," *Theatre Arts,* October 1948, p. 43.

Kornfeld, Paul. "Der Beseelte und der Psychologische Mensch," *Das Junge Deutschland,* No. 1, 1918, pp. 1–13.

Lawson, John Howard. Preface, *Processional.* New York: Thomas Seltzer, 1925.

————. *Theory and Technique of Playwriting and Screen-writing.* New York: Putnam, 1949.

Lindsay, Howard. "Notes on Playwriting," *Theatre Arts,* May 1943, pp. 291–98.

McCullers, Carson. "The Vision Shared," *Theatre Arts,* April 1950, pp. 28–30.

MacLeish, Archibald. "A Stage for Poetry," *Essay Annual, 1936.* New York: Scott, Foresman & Co. 1936, pp. 169–175.

————. "The Staging of a Play: The Notebooks and Letters behind Elia Kazan's Staging of *J.B.,*" *Esquire,* May 1959, pp. 144–158.

Maeterlinck, Maurice. Preface, *Théâtre,* Vol. 1. Brussels, 1901. (Extracts in English translated by Barrett H. Clark appear in *European Theories of the Drama.*)

————. *The Treasure of the Humble,* translated by Alfred Sutro. New York: Dodd, Mead, 1916.

Maugham, W. Somerset. *The Summing Up.* New York: Doubleday Doran, 1938.

Miller, Arthur. Introduction, *Collected Plays.* New York: The Viking Press, 1958, pp. 3–55.

————. "The Family in Modern Drama," *Atlantic Monthly,* April 1956, pp. 35–41.

————. "The Shadows of the Gods," *Harper's Magazine,* August 1958, pp. 35–43.

————. "Tragedy and the Common Man," *Theatre Arts,* March 1951, pp. 48–50.

Montherlant, Henry de. *Notes sur mon théâtre.* Paris: L'Arche, 1950.

Niggli, Josephina. *Pointers on Playwriting.* Boston: The Writer, 1945.

O'Casey, Sean. *The Flying Wasp.* London: Macmillan, 1937.

————. *The Green Crow.* New York: George Braziller, 1956.

————. *See* "The Play of Ideas."

O'Neill, Eugene. Letters, in *Eugene O'Neill: The Man and his Plays,* by Barrett H. Clark. New York: Dover, 1947.

————. "Working Notes and Extracts from a Fragmentary Work Diary, *Mourning Becomes Electra,*" in *European Theories of the Drama,* edited by Barrett H. Clark. New York: Crown, 1947. pp. 530–36.

Papers on Playmaking, edited by Brander Matthews. New York: A Dramabook, Hill and Wang, 1957.

Pirandello, Luigi. Premise, *Naked Masks,* edited by Eric Bentley. New York: Dutton, 1958, pp. 209–210.

"The Play of Ideas," *The New Statesman and Nation,* March 4, 1950 (Terence Rattigan); March 11, 1950 (James Bridie); April 1, 1950 (Peter Ustinov); April 8, 1950 (Sean O'Casey); May 9, 1950 (Bernard Shaw).

Priestley, J.B. *The Art of the Dramatist.* London: Heinemann, 1957.

Raphaelson, Samson. *The Human Nature of Playwriting.* New York: Macmillan, 1949.

Rattigan, Terence. "The Characters Make the Play," *Theatre Arts,* April 1947, pp. 45–46.

————. *See* "The Play of Ideas."

Rice, Elmer. Introduction, *Two Plays.* New York: Coward McCann, 1935, pp. v–xviii.

————. *The Living Theatre.* New York: Harper, 1959.

Saroyan, William. "Confessions of a Playwright," *World Review,* April 1949, pp. 9–13; May 1949, pp. 33–35.

————. Preface, *Don't Go Away Mad and Two Other Plays.* New York: Harcourt Brace, 1949, pp. 3–10.

————. "Coming Reality: Preface to *The Time of Your Life,*" Theatre Arts, December 1939, pp. 870–75.

Sartre, Jean Paul. "The Theatre: An Interview," *Evergreen Review,* No. 11, 1960.

Schnitzler, Arthur. "Work and Echo: A Collection of Animadversions on the Artist, The Theory of Abstract Art and Dramatic Art," *Vanity Fair,* November 1928, p. 78.

"Seventeen (British) Playwrights Self-Appraised," *Saturday Review of Literature,* May 7, 1955, pp. 48–49.

Shaw, Bernard. *Dramatic Opinions and Essays.* New York: Brentano's, 1910.

————. *See* "The Play of Ideas."

————. *Plays and Players; Essays on the Theatre,* selected with an introduction by A.C. Ward. New York: Oxford University Press, 1952.

————. Preface to *Three Plays by Brieux.* New York: Brentano's 1911, pp. vii–liv; xxii–xxvii.

————. *Prefaces*. London: Constable, 1934.

————. *The Quintessence of Ibsenism*. New York: A Dramabook, Hill and Wang, 1958.

————. "Self-Revealed: George Bernard Shaw," an interview by Archibald Henderson, *The Fortnightly Review*, April 1, 1926, pp. 433–442; May 1, 1926, pp. 610–618.

————. *Shaw on the Theatre*, edited by E. J. West. New York: Hill and Wang, 1958.

————. *Table Talk of G.B.S.: Conversations on Things in General between George Bernard Shaw and Archibald Henderson*. New York: Harper, 1925.

Sternheim, Carl. "Two Statements," in *The Modern Theatre*, No. 6, edited by Eric Bentley. New York: Doubleday Anchor Books, 1959.

Strindberg, August. "Begreppet intim teater," *Öppna brev till intima teatern*. Stockholm: Bonniers, 1921.

Toller, Ernst. *Quer Durch: Reisebilder und reden*. Berlin: Gustav Kiepenheuer Verlag, 1930.

Ustinov, Peter. *See* "The Play of Ideas."

Van Druten, John. *Playwright at Work*. New York: Harper, 1953.

Wilder, Thornton. *"Our Town* — from Stage to Screen; a Correspondence between Thornton Wilder and Sol Lesser," *Theatre Arts*, November 1940, pp. 815–824.

————. Preface, *Three Plays*. New York: Harper, 1957, pp. vii–xiv.

Williams, Tennessee. "The History of a Play (with Parenthesis)" in *Battle of Angels, Pharos*, Nos. 1 and 2, Spring 1945.

————. "Person-to-Person," *Cat on a Hot Tin Roof*, New York: New Directions, 1955, pp. vi–x.

————. Production Notes, *The Glass Menagerie*. New York: New Directions, 1949, pp. ix–xii.

————. "The Timeless World of a Play," *The Rose Tattoo*. New York: New Directions, 1950, pp. vi–xi.

Yeats, William B. *The Cutting of an Agate*. New York: Macmillan, 1912.

————. *Essays*. New York: Macmillan, 1924.

————. Notes, *Four Plays for Dancers*. New York: Macmillan, 1926.

————. *Ideas of Good and Evil*. London: A.H. Bullen, 1913.

————. *Plays and Controversies*. London: Macmillan, 1923.

Zola, Émile. *The Experimental Novel*. New York: Cassell, 1894.

————. *Nos auteurs dramatiques*. Paris: Charpentier, 1881.

————. Preface to *Thérèse Raquin*, translated by K. Boutall, in *From the Modern Repertoire*, Series 3, edited by Eric Bentley. Bloomington: Indiana University Press, 1956.

INDEX